INTIMATE LETTERS

INTIMATE
LETTERS

Edited by
ROBIN HAMILTON
AND NICOLAS SOAMES

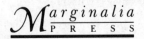

First published in 1994 by
Marginalia Press,
an imprint of
Ippon Books Ltd
55 Long Lane,
London N3 2HY

ISBN: 1-874572-35-6

Special thanks go to Patrick and Jaroslava Lambert for the sensitive translation of selected letters from the famous correspondence between Leoš Janáček and Kamila Stösslová, which gives this book its title.

Thanks: Laura Paton (for the original idea), Jan Fielden and Adam Green (for painstaking production work) and Heather Godwin (for editing).
Designed by Fiona Seddon.

Output and Reprographics by Ads, St Albans, Hertfordshire
Printed by Redwood Books, Trowbridge, Wiltshire

CONTENTS

INTRODUCTION

Of all the trophies of erotic passion, the love letter is the most potent. Other items have provided the currency of love, such lovers' bait as brooches, rings, mirrors, handkerchiefs, ribbons, girdles, gloves, garters, stockings, miniature portraits or lockets for a snippet of hair.

But a *billet-doux* has none of the fetishistic allure or jewelled brilliance of other love-trinkets. Instead, it carries the intimate seal of the lover's own heart. It is a lover's declaration that does not just disperse on the warm night air of some romantic evening, but is set down irrevocably on the page. It becomes a secret and holy relic, not to be pawed over by the uninitiated – let alone be published.

The publication of letters, according to Dr Arbuthnot in the eighteenth century, "adds a new terror to death". Dr Arbuthnot was joined in his disquiet by Charles Dickens, who took steps to remove that terror as far as he could. When asked to allow the publication of some letters he had received in the past, he replied: "I considered the correspondence was with me and not with the general public, and because I could not answer for its privacy being respected when I should be dead, destroyed it". Fortunately, not everyone has taken such drastic measures to secure their posthumous privacy.

Of course, the idea of reading other people's personal mail is one we naturally shrink from. We have only to imagine what it would be like to find our own most intimate correspondence published in this book to know that it isn't on. We should feel mortified. We'd want the earth to open up and swallow us. On precisely the same grounds, however, we may quite reasonably deny privacy to the dead, because of course, they are literally mortified, and the earth has swallowed them up anyway. This was Dr Johnson's attitude, when Boswell asked him if he minded his letters being published after his death: "Nay sir, when I am dead, you may do as you will".

However, it is one thing to publish someone's correspondence and include amongst it their intimate letters. It is another thing entirely to skim off the intimate letters from the mass of correspondence produced by scores of individuals and serve up this rich fare between the covers of a single volume. Yet it has to be admitted that this kind of anthology has been offered to the public more than once before.

J.T.Merydew, the editor of 'Love Letters of Famous Men and Women' had a lip-smacking confidence in the robust appetites of his Victorian readership: "That the majority of love letters were written without the most distant idea of being offered to the world, is naturally and of course a rich inducement to everybody to read them". The same confidence in this deplorable aspect of human nature lay behind the compilation, some fifty years later, of 'Love letters of Great Men and Women', in which D. Charles extended the range of this publishing genre by including translations from other European languages. More recent publications have, however, assumed a more rose-tinted – or rather, perhaps, 'blue-rinsed' – interest in the romantic effusions of lovers long ago.

There is often a conventional disclaimer made at the start of anthologies such as these that a 'personal selection' has been made – as is quite appropriate when the choice of extracts has been made by someone rather eminent. However, in this book we have done our best not to be personal at all. We have tried to put together a collection that is both representative and entertaining. If it entertains, we shall be content. But if it were to be judged truly representative, we should be very surprised indeed. There is such a vast quantity of material to choose from that there will inevitably be gaps and even what will seem to some people to be glaring and eccentric lacunae in our selection. What this means, of course, is that anthologists have little need to overlap in the examples they light upon. There is just one letter which seems to be everybody's favourite – by Richard Steele – and it would seem churlish to leave it out on these grounds alone.

It might be thought that to introduce a book – and recommend its contents – by saying that it has been done before, is self-defeating. In fact, there is no subject that calls for anthologising more urgently than intimate letters. In the days of lengthy courtship and no telephones the leisured classes wrote to each other at length and often. This tender correspondence would then be edited to remove any touches of indiscretion and published in a couple of stout volumes. The resultant mass of endearments all from the same pen is rarely enthralling and usually indigestible. To trawl the bleak wastes of this material in search of some occasional moment of warm-blooded self-disclosure or realisation cannot, in all conscience, be asked of the general reader. Take, for example, the love letters of Otto von Bismarck. A brief glance at a few of them was enough for this editor to surmise that a closer examination of them would reveal some gripping details about the administration of German waterways in the mid-nineteenth century, but nothing beyond the conventional in the way of amative cordiality. However, it may well be that some interesting things have been overlooked in this case as in many others. We can only leave them to be discovered by someone else.

The fact is that the love letter is really a kind of literary form of its own, and it is only in an anthology such as this that one can appreciate its possibilities. But the curious thing about the love letter is that it is a kind of minor esoteric art form which is yet practised by almost everyone at some time in their life. In love, people experience some of the most intense emotions of their lives. It is a crisis, the pressure of which can sometimes be enough to turn them into poets – without the literary skills, perhaps, but with all the focus of the poet. The heightened emotion necessarily raises the pressure on the language to perform beyond its normal prosaic functions, and the result is – as with poetry – either mind-numbingly banale or exquisite.

At the same time no-one wants to submit their efforts in this particular form to public judgement, so these millions of often painstakingly crafted compositions – put together with as much care, sometimes, as a sonnet – are left to blush unseen in locked cabinets or under loose floorboards. Poetry is a public art, in which passion can put on the robes of universality, and in which the good poet is able to suggest the individual lineaments beneath the robe. But it will be evident from this anthology that the love letter is also a form which can carry either the stilted expression of conventional modes of feeling or – just from time to time – the sound of an individual and original voice.

The lyric form of the love letter seems to be characteristic of the Renaissance period, which we have entitled, slightly anachronistically, the Age of Chivalry. From a political point of view the armed knight on horseback had had his day, but the ideals of chivalry and courtly love continued to influence the way lovers expressed themselves well into the seventeenth century. Outstanding examples of the lyric form are those of Pietro Bembo and Lucrezia Borgia, Henry VIII, Michelangelo, Henri II and above all, perhaps, the 'Cavalier' poet, Sir John Suckling. A revival of this self-consciously artful letter around the turn of the present century is represented in this book by Duff Cooper's letters to Lady Diana Manners, and of course by Oscar Wilde. Indeed, central to Wilde's defence during his trial for sodomy was the idea that the love letter to Bosie which was read out in court, was in fact a 'prose sonnet'. Wilde had even taken the trouble, when he had discovered that the letter had been purloined, to have it translated and published as such in France.

All these lyrical letters are performances, graceful and courtly at one end, rather decadent and mannered – but still gem-like – at the other. With the Age of Gallantry the letter as performance becomes a more cynical exercise – under the pen, for example, of the second Earl of Chesterfield – and in a late outgrowth, from Pushkin. During this period there were even letters written that were not so much cynical exercises in gallantry, as simply exercises. The ex-mistress of George II, Mrs Howard, for example, found herself being 'courted' in this rather pointless way by the old Earl of Peterborough in a series of extravagantly clever letters. She understood well enough that nothing serious was meant by them and so the curt rebuff was hardly appropriate. But feeling at a literary disadvantage, she called in the playwright John Gay to provide her side of the correspondence. Such heartless stuff continued to appear well into the Regency period – the arbiter of Regency menswear, Beau Brummell, being a prime exponent of it. The total lack of real feeling in this material has been allowed to rule this kind of letter out of court as far as this collection is concerned.

However, there is a sort of love letter which is not meant to be taken on a literal level, but which still contains a kernel of very real feeling, and examples of these have been included. Such are the schoolgirl fantasies of passion addressed to Frances Apsley from Princess/Queen Mary and Princess Anne. These become particularly engaging when mundane reality begins to break into their vision of true love. When she is pregnant by her husband, William of Orange, Anne writes disarmingly to her fantasy husband: "tho I have played the whore a little I love you of all the world". Charles Dodgson's otherwise rather shocking missives to little girls fall into this category.

The Romantic Age was supposed to replace cynical gallantry with the expression of genuine feeling, but Robert Burns shows how the romantic conventions can be manipulated by a really skilful operator. With James Boswell, on the other hand, we find a would-be gallant trying self-consciously to negotiate these same conventions in their infancy – with ludicrous incompetence. He betrays his lack of confidence by adding at the end of one letter: "P.S. Read this letter with care. It contains very, very romantic sentiments." George, Prince of Wales, later George IV, demonstrates how a sincerely romantic lover can fall over his own feet by trying too hard. It is only when he forgets the sort of things he is supposed to say and writes directly from the heart that he pulls off a genuine romantic letter.

At the opposite end of the scale from the love letter performance are the little notes that Richard Steele scribbled off to his wife, often when he was working late at the office. But the very best letter writers, like Byron and Flaubert, are able to be both natural and intense. There is no sense of strain. Everything is within their reach. This means that they always have that crucial element of self-awareness. With smaller talents there tends to be a sense of forged emotion, of ready-made expression, and an inability to see beyond those emotions.

Such is the significance that we accord to love letters that they are, on occasion, forged, or invented. We have included a letter from Byron which may well be a forgery, but as the supposed forger was his lover, Lady Caroline Lamb, it may be said to have a natural place amongst his correspondence with her. As for what is sometimes held to be the most succinct amorous correspondence on record, we have left it out because it seems that there is no evidence to substantiate it. The Prince de Joinville is supposed to have sent a note to the actress, Rachel Felix, which read "Where? When? How much?" And not to be out done, she is supposed to have replied, "This evening. Your place. Free". It's a pleasing conceit – very French – and the author, Arsène Houssaye is to be congratulated for dreaming it up, but it cannot be allowed to mingle with the genuine article. Even more regretfully we have to turn down the celebrated letters of Frederick Chopin to Delphina Potocka, which are obsessively concerned with the loss of creative energy by the expenditure of 'precious' bodily fluids. "Who knows how many polonaises have been forever engulfed in your little D flat major?" is the whimsical complaint of this unlikely version of Chopin. Again, there is no evidence whatsoever for the authenticity of these letters.

We have tried to emphasise the beauty of a well written love letter, but really, the whole point of letters is their authenticity. Some 250 years ago, Jonathan Swift observed: "Nothing is so capable of giving a true account of History as Letters are; which describe actions while they are alive and breathing, whereas all other relations are of actions past and dead." What we are concerned with here is the record of the actions of the human heart, and it is important that this record be a true one. It is therefore unfortunate that this record has so often been tampered with. It seems that female correspondents are usually the guilty party in this respect, in taking scissors to any compromising passages and indelicate phraseology that might allow future generations to doubt the pure and lofty ideal of love they espoused. We can only lament that many of the finest love letters will have been destroyed over the centuries through jealousy or misdirected vigilance for the reputation of a loved one.

Partly to restore the balance, we have made a point of taking full advantage of the freedom of expression that characterises the correspondence of the modern age. Oscar Wilde and Benjamin Britten speak for the love that has rarely dared to speak its name in past ages, while 'Boston marriages' find a voice at last in the letters of Vita Sackville West and Violet Trefusis. As for the sexually explicit passion of Joyce, Grainger, Henry Miller and Anais Nin, this is altogether a fresh field of lyrical expression peculiar to the twentieth century.

All these letters must come with a few words of caution, however. For a start, even with the most desperate romantics we should bear in mind that people tend to write letters when they are disconsolate rather than when they are feeling on top of the world. And they tend to exaggerate – they adjust the balance of their emotional expression to bring out certain interesting features. Furthermore, letters are the ideal medium – compared, say, with the telephone – for the communication of insincerity. But even when the sincerity is not at issue, the communication achieved in a love letter has to be understood in a very special sense. The mutual incomprehension of the sexes and the complex social rituals of courtship do not make for what we generally think of as clear human communication.

Love letters are not like the correspondence of friends, upon which Dr Johnson writes the following panegyric in a letter to his dear friend Mrs Thrale. "In a man's letters...his soul lies naked, his letters are only the mirror of his breast, whatever passes within him is shown undisguised in its natural process...This is the pleasure of corresponding with a friend, where doubt and distrust have no place, and everything is said as it is thought...These are the letters by which souls are united, and by which minds naturally in unison move each other as they are moved themselves". This ideal of a union of naked souls is, of course, exactly the sort of idealisation of their passion to which ardent lovers aspire and which they are anxious to communicate in their letters. From the evidence of those letters, however, communion of souls without doubt or distrust is by no means a universal, or even common feature of the tender passion.

The force and beauty of some of the best love letters lies, in fact, in the poignant realisation of the impossibility of full communion with the desired but unknowable other. And no culture is focussed so intently on the conundrum, the mystery, the ideal of love as is European culture. Sexual love is a universal phenomenon, but it is only in the modern West that mundane erotic passion has been raised to the status of an ideal. Instead of just having feelings – of delight, jealousy, craving – we are concerned to refine and work with these feelings to make them mean something.

In the past, other cultures have looked upon the western obsession with romance, with the relations between the sexes, as something indecent. Many of them still do. It seems to them extraordinary that most of our imaginative literature is about love and marriage. But there is no doubt that the Western sensibility has been tenderised, made more generous and sympathetic, by its attempts to bring grace and purity to its own erotic yearnings. In Plato's 'Symposium', the character of Aristophanes puts forward the view that we are only a split half of what we once were, and that we are forever seeking our other, lost half. But Socrates points out that the object of love is not one particular object, not one person, but absolute beauty which is there as the essential reality of all things. The Western love tradition is, we may say, an attempt to bridge these two ideas, and the love letters in this book are the living witnesses of this endeavour.

ANCIENT
ATTACHMENTS

A god is Eros, my children . . . . he possesses greater power than Zeus himself. He rules the elements, he rules the stars, he rules his fellow deities . . . .

All flowers are the work of Eros; all these plants are his handiwork; it is through him that rivers flow and breezes blow.

Longus: Daphnis and Chloe

A t the time when the following letters were being written a change was taking place in the way the citizens of ancient Rome saw themselves. Up to this period military and civic virtues were paramount and women found themselves to be little more than pieces of property. Free men would take advantage of slave girls and indeed, it was considered safer from an emotional point of view to take advantage of slave boys. To pleasure a woman was a sign of weakness, and the whole idea of sexual courtesy did not enter their heads. However, with the transition from Republic to Empire women were to become more emancipated than at any time before the present century.

There was a new ideal of conjugal piety pressed forward – by Pliny, amongst others. A wife was now seen as a companion for life, and the marital bond was given equal status with friendship – and sometimes made into an even higher ideal. However, it always remained a rational ideal. By submitting to passion, one became a slave – passion was regarded as a destructive force, a disease. The love for one's wife was supposed to be a tranquil one because it was all-important to be in command, whether of others or oneself.

Most correspondence of the Roman period which we know about, including those of Cicero and Pliny included below, were published and circulated from earliest times. But the other two letters in this section, addressed to an obscure administrator, survive as original documents on papyrus.

MARCUS TULLIUS CICERO
106–43 BC

Cicero, a brilliant lawyer and orator, minor versifier and man of lettters, played an active part in a tumultuous period of Roman history dominated – as far as those who get their ancient history from Shakespeare are concerned – by Julius Caesar, Pompey the Great, Mark Antony, Brutus and Cassius. Whether his enormous influence on Western literature is deserved may be arguable – one of Kingsley Amis' characters neatly sums up one side of the case: 'For a man so long and thoroughly dead it was remarkable how much boredom, and how precise an image of nasty silliness, Cicero could generate' (Take a Girl Like You). Another side of him is found in his letters to his wife, Terentia, dating from a period of exile in 59-8 B. C.

CICERO TO TERENTIA

I do not write to you as often as I might, because, not withstanding I am afflicted at all times, I am quite overcome with sorrow whilst I am writing to you, or reading any letters that I receive from you. If these evils are not to be removed, I must desire to see you, my dearest life, as soon as possible, and to die in your embraces; since neither the gods, whom you always religiously worshipped, nor the men, whose good I always promoted, have rewarded us according to our deserts. What a distressed wretch am I! Should I ask a weak woman, oppressed with cares and sickness, to come and live with me; or shall I not ask her? Can I live without you? But I find I must. If there be any hopes of my return, help it forward, and promote it as much as you are able. But if all that is over, as I fear it is, find out some way or other of coming to me. This you may be sure of, that I shall not look upon myself as quite undone whilst you are with me. But what will become of Tulliola? You must look to that; I must confess I am entirely at a loss about her. Whatever happens, we must take care of the reputation and marriage of that dear unfortunate girl. As for Cicero, he shall live in my bosom, and in my arms. I cannot write any further, my sorrows will not let me. Support yourself, my dear Terentia, as well as you are able. We have lived and flourished together amidst the greatest honours. It is not our crimes, but our virtues, that have brought us to distress; take more than ordinary care of your health; I am more afflicted with your sorrows than my own. Farewell, my Terentia, thou dearest, faithfullest, and best of wives!

Cicero and Terentia were divorced in 46 B.C., after which Cicero married his young and rich ward, Publilia, though this union was even less successful as, after only a few months, they too were divorced. He was assassinated on the orders of Mark Antony, Octavius and Lepidus. It is said that he gazed steadfastly at his assassins as they hacked off his head.

PLINY THE YOUNGER
61-113 A.D.

Born near Lake Como, Pliny was a Roman imperial lawyer and bureaucrat who managed to survive and prosper during Domitian's reign of terror and went on to forge a warm working relationship, legendary amongst bureaucrats, with the Emperor Trajan. His third wife was Calpurnia, orphaned grand-daughter of Calpurnius Fabatus of Comum. They had no children but he evidently adored her. His letters are fussy, anxious and doting.

PLINY TO CALPURNIA

I never was so much offended at business, as when it hindered me from going with you into the country, or following you thither: for I more particularly wish to be with you at present, that I might be sensible of the progress you make in the recovery of your strength and health; as also of the entertainment and diversions you can meet with in your retirement. Believe me, it is an anxious state of mind to live in ignorance of what happens to those whom we passionately love. I am not only in pain for your absence, but also for your indisposition. I am afraid of everything, envisage everything, and as it is the nature of man in fear, I envisage those things most, which I am most afraid of. Let me therefore earnestly desire you to favour me, under these my apprehensions, with one letter every day, or, if possible, with two; for I shall be a little at ease while I am reading your letters, and grow anxious again as soon as I have read them.

PLINY TO CALPURNIA

You tell me, that you are very much afflicted at my absence, and that you have no satisfaction in any thing but my writings, which you often lay by you upon my pillow. You oblige me very much in wishing to see me and making me your comforter in my absence. In return, I must let you know, I am no less pleased with the letters which you write to me, and read them over a thousand times with new pleasure. If your letters are capable of giving me so much pleasure, what would your conversation do? Let me beg of you to write to me often; though at the same time I must confess, your letters give me anguish whilst they give me pleasure.

PLINY TO CALPURNIA

It is impossible to conceive how much I languish for you in your absence; the tender love I bear you is the chief cause of this my uneasiness; which is still the more insupportable, because absence is wholly a new thing to us. I lie awake most part of the night in thinking of you, and several times a day go as naturally to your apartment as if you were there to receive me; but when I miss you, I come away dejected, out of humour, and like a man that had suffered a repulse. There is but one part of the day in which I am relieved from this anxiety, and that is when I am engaged in public affairs.

You may guess at the uneasy condition of one who has no rest but in business, no consolation but in trouble.

APOLLONIOS

Apollonios son of Ptolomeius was a *strategos*, a salaried official in charge of an area within Roman Egypt, and like most of these *strategos* he was a Greek. His sister-wife (in Egypt there was no taboo against marrying close relations) writes to him at the time of the Jewish revolt in 117:

I'm deeply distressed about you because of the time's rumours and you went away from me suddenly, and I find no pleasure in food or drink, but constantly night and day without sleep I have one anxiety only: that for your well-

5

being. Nothing but the care taken by my father bestirs me. And on the first day of the New Year, I declare by your well-being, I'd have gone foodless to bed if my father hadn't come in and forced me to eat. I beg you then to take care of yourself and not expose yourself to danger alone without a guard. Just as the *strategos* here puts his burden on his officials, do the same yourself.

> There was another woman, in all likelihood a favourite slave, who was also passionately concerned for his welfare.

Taus to Apollonios her Lord, very many greetings. Before all else I salute you, Master, and always pray for your health. I was not a little distressed, Lord, to hear you'd been ill, but thanks be to all the gods because they keep you safe and sound. I beg you, Lord, if it seems good to you, to send for me, else I die because I don't behold you daily. Would that I could fly and come to you and make obeisance to you. For I'm torn by anxiety when I don't see you. So be kind and send for me. Goodbye Lord. All is well with us.

THE AGE OF CHIVALRY

Tristan: "Friend, I must fly, and perhaps shall never see you more. My death is near, and far from you my death will come of desire".

Yseult: "O friend, fold your arms round me close and strain me so that our hearts may break and our souls go free at last. Take me to that happy place of which you told me long ago. The fields whence none return, but where great poets sing their songs forever."

The Saracens were astonished at the Crusaders' lack of honour or jealousy in sexual matters. The Crusaders in their turn were revolted by the Moorish idea that a self-respecting man should grovel abjectly at the feet of his beloved. Little did the European knights know it, but their assumption that the love between a man and a woman meant a genial, salty grapple in the shadows was about to disappear for good.

Out of the East appeared an idea that had never been contemplated in Europe before: that sexual love could be taken to an almost impossible pitch of refinement. As the Moors practised it the ideal lay beyond any kind of sexual connection altogether. Their ideal was union of souls in chastity and a delight in the torments of love. For them, erotic passion was a springboard towards the contemplation of pure love and beauty.

Sadly, medieval European society was not quite up to this. The Europeans took this on, but they mixed it with the study of Ovid's *Ars Amatoria*. Ovid also counselled his male readers to submit to the whims of women, but with a definite carnal goal in view. 'True love' had arrived.

At this time it was necessarily adulterous, as marriage was a mundane, practical affair – and indeed, adultery retained its idealistic flavour, amongst the nobility at least, well into the sixteenth century. The letters to Lucrezia Borgia and Diane de Poitiers represent adulterous worship of this kind. It may even be said that the love Heloise offers to Abelard is of this pure, extra-marital kind: it is pure because it is without guarantees or worldly advantages.

Love was established as the most civilising force in society. It made one a better person. It was also a force of liberation for women – though only for those of a certain class, as yet. Love seemed to open the hearts and minds of individuals to the beauty of the world. Indeed, a religious tone entered into the way people expressed their love.

This was regarded as subversively blasphemous and it was a long time before passion was accepted as a normal part of married life.

ABELARD   HELOISE
1079–1142   1101–1164

He was an eminent French philosopher, she a brilliant student. Aggressive ambition had left Abelard without an equal in his field when, aged 38, he met the seventeen year old Heloise. Before long she became pregnant and gave birth to a boy. So far it is a humdrum tale of academic folk.

However, we are in the year 1117. The Renaissance is no more than a twinkle in the eye of a few individuals like Abelard, and the Dark Ages are coming to get him in the shape of Heloise's uncle Fulbert. The lovers marry – secretly, for the sake of Abelard's academic career. Abelard spirits Heloise away from Fulbert's house to the convent of Argenteuil, where he makes the terrible mistake of disguising her as one of the nuns.

Her uncle naturally concludes that Abelard is getting her out of his hair, in the neat fashion of the age, by making her take the veil. Fulbert takes what has to be admitted is an equally neat revenge. His men break into Abelard's lodgings and castrate him. Abelard becomes a monk, and for Heloise, her disguise becomes the real thing. She is not yet twenty years old, with no vocation for the contemplative life. Abelard's sexual martyrdom has been brief, if brutal – but hers is just beginning. Twelve or so years go by. In 1132, Abelard's autobiography *Story of his Misfortunes* comes out and the first letter from Heloise, now Abbess, is her response to it.

In it we get a glimpse of the brief flowering of sensuous beauty in two lives that both before and after were devoted to a rigorous examination of the Good and the True. Her philosophy of love will seem astonishingly advanced for her time, and, to some, shocking even today. Abelard's reply is equally shocking. The reader should bear in mind that the following short extracts do not represent the general tone of the whole series of letters, which is theological and becomes more impersonal as the correspondence progresses.

HELOISE TO ABELARD

To her master, or rather her father, husband, or rather brother; his hand-maid, or rather his daughter, wife, or rather sister; to Abelard, Heloise.

. . . . You know, beloved, as the whole world knows, how much I have lost in you, how at one wretched stroke of fortune that supreme act of flagrant treachery robbed me of my very self in robbing me of you; and how my sorrow for my loss is nothing compared with what I feel for the manner in which I lost you. Surely the greater the cause for grief the greater the need for the help of consolation; and this no one can bring but you; you are the sole cause of my sorrow, and you alone can grant me the grace of consolation. You alone have the power to make me sad, to bring me happiness or comfort; you alone have so great a debt to repay me, particularly now when I have carried out all your orders so implicitly that when I was powerless to oppose you in anything, I found strength at your command to destroy myself. I did more, strange to say – my love rose to such heights of madness that it robbed itself of what it most desired beyond hope of recovery, when immediately at your bidding I changed my clothing along with my mind, in order to prove you the sole possessor of my body and my will alike. God knows I never sought anything in you except yourself; I wanted simply you, nothing of yours. I looked for no marriage-bond, no marriage portions, and it was not my own pleasures and wishes I sought to gratify, as you well know, but yours. The name of wife may seem more sacred or more binding, but sweeter for me will always be the word mistress, or, if you will permit me, that of concubine or whore....

What king or philospher could match your fame? What district, town or village did not long to see you? When you appeared in public, who did not hurry to catch a glimpse of you, or crane his neck and strain his eyes to follow your departure? Every wife, every young girl desired you in absence and was on fire in your presence; queens and great ladies envied me my joys and my bed.

You had besides, I admit, two special gifts whereby to win at once the heart of any woman – your gifts for composing verse and song, in which we know other philosophers have rarely been successful. This was for you no more than a diversion, a recreation from the labours of your philosophic work, but you left many love-songs and verses which won wide popularity for the charm of their words and tunes and kept your name continually on everyone's lips.

The beauty of the airs ensured that even the unlettered did not forget you; more than anything this made women sigh for love of you. And as most of these songs told of our love, they soon made me widely known and roused the envy of many women against me. For your manhood was adorned by every grace of mind and body, and among the women who envied me then, could there be one now who does not feel compelled by my misfortune to sympathize with my loss of such joys? Who is there who was once my enemy, whether man or woman, who is not moved now by the compassion which is my due? Wholly guilty though I am, I am also, as you know, wholly innocent. It is not the deed but the intention of the doer which makes the crime, and justice should weigh not what was done but the spirit in which it is done.

HELOISE TO ABELARD

To her only one after Christ, she who is his alone in Christ.
. . . . Of all wretched women I am the most wretched, and amongst the unhappy I am unhappiest. The higher I was exalted when you preferred me to all other women, the greater my suffering over my own fall and yours, when I was flung down; for the higher the ascent, the heavier the fall . . . .
In my case, the pleasures of lovers which we shared have been too sweet – they can never displease me, and can scarcely be banished from my thoughts. Wherever I turn they are always there before my eyes, bringing with them awakened longings and fantasies which will not even let me sleep. Even during the celebration of the Mass, when our prayers should be purer, lewd visions of those pleasures take such a hold upon my unhappy soul that my thoughts are on their wantonness instead of on prayers. I should be groaning over the sins I have committed, but I can only sigh for what I have lost. Everything we did and also the times and places are stamped on my heart along with your image, so that I live through it all again with you. Even in sleep I know no respite. Sometimes my thoughts are betrayed in a movement of my body, or they break out in an unguarded word. In my utter wretchedness, that cry from a suffering soul could well be mine: 'Miserable creature that I am, who is there to rescue me out of the body doomed to this death?' Would that in truth I could go on: 'The grave of God through Jesus Christ our Lord.' This grave, my dearest, came upon you unsought – a single wound of the body by freeing you from

these torments has healed many wounds in your soul. Where God may seem to you an adversary he has in fact proved himself kind: like an honest doctor who does not shrink from giving pain if it will bring about a cure. But for me, youth and passion and experience of pleasures which were so delightful intensify the torments of the flesh and longings of desire, and the assault is the more over-whelming as the nature they attack is the weaker.

Men call me chaste; they do not know the hypocrite I am. They consider purity of the flesh a virtue, though virtue belongs not to the body but to the soul. I can win praise in the eyes of men but deserve none before God, who searches our hearts and minds and sees in our darkness.

ABELARD TO HELOISE

To the bride of Christ, Christ's servant.

. . . . it may relieve the bitterness of your grief if I prove that this came upon us justly, as well as to our advantage, and that God's punishment was more properly directed against us when we were married than when we were living in sin. After our marriage, when you were living in the cloister with the nuns at Argenteuil and I came one day to visit you privately, you know what my uncontrollable desire did with you there, actually in a corner of the refec-tory, since we had nowhere else to go. I repeat, you know how shamelessly we behaved on that occasion in so hallowed a place, dedicated to the most holy Virgin. Even if our other shameful behaviour was ended, this alone would deserve far heavier punishment. Need I recall our previous fornication and the wanton impurities which preceded our marriage, or my supreme act of betrayal, when I deceived your uncle about you so disgracefully, at a time when I was continuously living with him in his own house? Who would not judge me justly betrayed by the man whom I had first shamelessly betrayed?

. . . . You know the depths of shame to which my unbridled lust had con-signed our bodies, until no reverence for decency or for God even during the days of Our Lord's Passion, or of the greater sacraments could keep me from wallowing in this mire. Even when you were unwilling, resisted to the utmost of your power and tried to dissuade me, as yours was the weaker nature I often forced you to consent with threats and blows. So intense were the fires of lust which bound me to you that I set those wretched, obscene pleasures, which we blush even to name, above God as above myself; nor would it seem that divine mercy could have taken action except by forbiding me these pleasures altogether, without future hope. And so it was wholly just and merciful, although by means of the supreme treachery of your uncle, for me to be reduced in that part of my body which was the seat of lust and sole reason for those desires, so that I could increase in many ways; in order that this member should justly be punished for all its wrongdoing in us, expiate in suffering the sins committed for its amusement, and cut me off from the slough of filth in which I had been wholly immersed in mind as in body. Only thus could I become more fit to approach the holy altars, now that no contagion of carnal impurity would ever again call me from them. How mercifully did he want me to suffer so much only in that member, the privation of which would also further the salvation of my soul without defiling my body nor preventing any performance of my duties! Indeed, it would make me readier to perform whatever can be honourably done by setting me wholly free from the heavy yoke of carnal desire.

Come too, my inseparable companion, and join me in thanksgiving, you who were made my partner both in guilt and in grace. For the Lord is not unmindful also of your own salvation, indeed, he has you much in mind, for by a kind of holy presage of his name he marked you out to be especially his when he named you Heloise, after his own name, Elohim. In his mercy, I say, he intended to provide for two people in one, the two whom the devil sought to destroy in one; since a short while before this happening he had bound us together by the indissoluble bond of the marriage sacrament. At the time I desired to keep you whom I loved beyond measure for myself alone, but he was already planning to use this opportunity for our joint conversion to himself. Had you not been previously joined to me in wedlock, you might easily have clung to the world when I withdrew from it, either at the suggestion of your relatives or in enjoyment of carnal delights.

It was he who truly loved you, not I. My love, which brought us both to sin, should be called lust, not love. I took my fill of my wretched pleasures in you, and this was the sum total of my love. You say I suffered for you, and perhaps that is true, but it was really through you, and even this, unwillingly; not for love of you but under compulsion, and to bring you not salvation but sorrow. But he suffered truly for your salvation, on your behalf of his own free will, and by his suffering he cures all sickness and removes all suffering. To him, I beseech you, not to me, should be directed all your devotion, all your compassion, all your remorse. Weep for the injustice of the great cruelty inflicted on him, not for the just and righteous payment demanded of me, or rather, as I said, the supreme grace granted us both.

Abelard continued to be an outstanding and belligerent teacher, and was persecuted accordingly, being twice condemed as a heretic before his death in 1142. His love for Heloise, and hers for him, evidently developed onto ever higher levels, and his final statement, his Confession of Faith, is addressed to her. It begins, 'Heloise my sister, once dear to me in the world, now dearest to me in Christ…'

She died at the same age as he did, in 1164. Their tomb is in Père Lachaise Cemetery, Paris.

LADY JOAN PELHAM

The earliest surviving love-letter in English, dated 25 July 1399, is from Lady Joan Pelham, informing her husband, Sir John Pelham, that their castle, Pevensey, is under siege from Richard II's men. Pelham was probably with Henry of Derby at the time, making a landing at Ravenspur in a bid to depose the King. On Henry's coronation as Henry IV Pelham was appointed one of the first knights of the Bath. Lady Pelham's letter displays admirable sang-froid. She mentions that half the home counties are literally up in arms against her as if she were announcing that the washing machine had broken down.

My Dear Lord, – I recommend me to your high lordship, with heart and body and all my poor might. And with all this I thank you as my dear Lord, dearest and best beloved of all earthly lords. I say for me, and thank you, my dear Lord, with all this that I said before of your comfortable letter that you sent me from Pontefract, that came to me on Mary Magdalen's day: for by my troth I was never so glad as when I heard by your letter that ye were strong enough with the Grace of God for to keep you from the malice of your enemies. And, dear Lord, if it like to your high Lordship that as soon as ye might that I might hear of your gracious speed, which God Almighty continue and increase. And, my dear Lord, if it like you to know my fare, I am here laid by in a manner of a siege with the County of Sussex, Surrey, and a great parcel of Kent, so that I may out nor no victuals get me, but with much hard. Wherefore, my dear, if it like you by the advice of your wise counsel for to set remedy of the salvation of your castle and withstand the malice of the shires aforesaid. And also that ye be fully informed of the great malice-workers in these shires which have so despitefully wrought to you, and to your castle, to your men and to your tenants; for this country have they wasted for a great while.

Farewell, my dear Lord, the Holy Trinity keep you from your enemies, and soon send me good tidings of you. Written at Pevensey, in the castle, on St. Jacob's day last past, by your own poor J. Pelham

To my true Lord.

THOMAS BETSON
DIED 1486

Thomas Betson, wool-merchant, has long been a favourite amongst historians of fifteenth century English society on account of the glimpses one gets of this singularly good-natured and honest young man in the Stonor Papers, the correspondence of an Oxfordshire family. His affectionate love-letter to the thirteen-year old step-daughter of William Stonor, Katherine Riche, is dated 1 June 1476, two years before their marriage and inscribed: 'To my faithful and heartily beloved cousin Katherine Riche at Stonor, this letter be delivered in haste.' It might seem from the letter that the girl is a bit anorexic but she is probably just a slow developer.

Mine own heartily beloved Cousin Katherine, I recommend me unto you with all the inwardness of my heart. And now lately ye shall understand that I received a token from you, the which was and is to me right heartily welcome, and with glad will I received it; and over that I had a letter from Holake, your gentle squire, by the which I understand right well that ye be in good health of body, and merry at heart. And I pray God heartily in his pleasure to continue the same: for it is to me very great comfort that he so be, so help me Jesu. And if ye would be a good eater of your meat alway, that ye might wax and grow fast to be a woman ye should make me the gladdest man of the world, by my troth; for when I remember your favour and your sad loving dealing to me wards, for sooth ye make me even very glad and joyous in my heart; and on the tother side again, when I remember your young youth, and see well that ye be none eater of your meat, the which should help you greatly in waxing, for sooth then ye make me very heavy again. And therefore I pray you, mine own sweet Cousin, even as you love me, to be merry and eat your meat like a woman. And if ye will so do for my love, look what ye will desire of me, whatsoever it be, and by my troth, I promise you by the help of our Lord to perform it to my power. I can no more say now, but on my coming home I will tell you much more between you and me and God before . . . .

I pray you greet well my horse and pray him to give you four of his years to help you withal; and I will at my coming home give him four of my years and four horse loaves till amends. Tell him that I prayed him so. And Cousin Katherine, I thank you for him, and my wife shall thank you for him hereafter; for ye do great cost upon him, as is told me. Mine own sweet Cousin, it was told me but late that ye were at Calais* to seek me, but could not see me nor find me; forsooth ye might have comen to my counter, and there ye should both find me and see me, and not have faulted of me; but ye sought me in a wrong Calais, and that ye should well know if ye were here and saw this Calais, as would God ye were and some of them with you that were with you at your gentle Calais. I pray you, gently Cousin, commend me to the clock, and pray him to amend his unthrifty manners; for he strikes ever in undue time, and he will be ever afore, and that is a shrewd condition. Tell him without he amend his condition that he will cause strangers to avoid and come no more there. I trust to you that he shall amend against mine coming, the which shall be shortly, with all hands and feet, with God's grace. My very faithful Cousin, I trust to you that though all I have remembered my right worshipful mistress your mother afore in this letter, that ye will of your gentleness recommend me to her mistresship as many times as it shall please you: and ye may say, if it please you, that in Whitsun week next I intend to the mart ward. And I trust you will pray for me; for I shall pray for you and, so it may be, none so well. And Almightly Jesu make you a good woman and send you many good years and long to live in health and virtue to his pleasure. At great Calais, on this side on the sea, the first day of June, when every man was gone to his dinner, and the clock smote nine, and all your household cried after me

*an inn

16

and bade me 'Come down, come down to dinner at once!' – and what answer I gave them, ye know it of old.

By your faithful Cousin and lover Thomas Betson. I send you this ring for a token.

MARGERY BREWS

A number of letters survive from the fifteenth century in English, of which the best-known group is the Paston letters, concerning an upwardly mobile Norfolk family. In a tough old world, with the wars of the Roses in full swing, romance was fairly low in most people's priorities. Marriage was a different matter, however. Marriage was business. During the 1470s, John Paston was entering into complex negotiations over a number of possible unions as well as doing his bit in the wars, receiving an arrow wound in the battle of Barnet. By 1476 he was lowering his sights, asking his brother, Sir John, to find him 'an old thrifty draught-wife from London' but he got lucky in 1477 and fell in love with Margery Brews of Topcroft. The two letters that follow were penned for her by the family chaplain. Negotiations were protracted, and broke down more than once, but all the financial details were ironed out by the summer, and they were married forthwith. By 1485 John was Sheriff of Norwich, and two years later was knighted after helping to put down the rebellion of Lambert Simnel. Margery's letters are heart-rending attempts to assert the primacy of poetry and romance and, indeed, sheer human feelings, over commercial considerations.

MARGERY BREWS TO JOHN PASTON

Right worshipful and well-beloved Valentine, I commend myself to you with all my heart, wishing to hear that all is well with you: I beseech Almighty God to keep you well according to his pleasure and your heart's desire. If you would like to know how I am, I am not well in body or heart, nor shall be until I hear from you.

For no creature knows what pain I endure
On pain of death, I dare not reveal it.

My lady my mother has put the matter very diligently to my father, but she can get no more than you know of, which God knows, I am very sorry about.

But if you love me, as I hope indeed that you do, you will not leave me because of it; if you did not have half the estates you have, I would not forsake you, even if I had to work as hard as any woman alive.

And if you command me to keep me true wherever I go
Indeed I will do all I can to love you, and nothing more.
And if my friends say I do wrong, they shall not stop me from doing it.
My heart bids me to love you for ever
Truly, over anything on earth.
However angry they are, I hope it will be better in future.

No more for now, but the Holy Trinity have you in keeping. Please do not let any creature on earth see this note, but only you. And this letter was written at Topcroft with a very sad heart.

By your own M.B.

MARGERY BREWS TO JOHN PASTON

Right worshipful and well-beloved Valentine, I commend myself to you in my most humble fashion, I thank you with all my heart for the letter you sent me by John Bykerton, from which I understand that you intend to come to Topcroft in a short time, and with no other errand or business than to bring to a conclusion the business between my father and you. I would be the happiest creature alive if the business could take effect. And because you say that if you come and find matters no further on than before, you do not want to put my father and my lady my mother to any more expense or trouble for that reason for a good while afterwards, my heart is very heavy; and if you come, and nothing can be settled, then I shall be even sadder and full of sorrow.

As for myself, I have done what I can or may, God knows. I must tell you plainly that my father will part with no more money over it than £100 and 50 marks, which is a long way from fulfilling your wishes. So if you could be content with that and my poor person, I would be the merriest maiden on earth. If you do not think that would satisfy you, or that you want much more wealth, as I understood from you before, good, true and living Valentine, do not trouble to come again about it, but let it pass, and not be spoken of again, and I will be your true lover and pray for you as long as you live... No more for now, but Almightly Jesus preserve you body and soul.

By your Valentine, Margery B

LUCREZIA BORGIA
1480–1519

PIETRO BEMBO
1471-1547

For the Hammer Horror picture of Lucrezia Borgia as a monster of cruelty we have to thank her contemporary, Guicciardini, and more latterly, Victor Hugo, whose drama on the subject was turned into a successful opera by Donizetti. She was indeed the daughter of the consummately wicked Pope Alexander VI, and sister to the ruthless and unprincipled Cesare Borgia, the model for Machiavelli's notorious maxims of Italian Renaissance real-politic. However, whereas it was well-known that seven devils had hovered around her father's deathbed waiting to claim their rich prize, and that he died on the third anniversary of the day he had Lucrezia's second husband strangled, Lucrezia herself was, if anything, rather virtuous.

It says something for Renaissance standards of refinement that her third husband, Alfonso Duke of Farrara, was regarded as fairly low-life by the more exquisite of his subjects, for he was skilled on the viol, he could throw an accomplished pot, he was proficient behind a lathe, a practised foundryman, and the foremost expert on gunnery in Italy. However, Lucrezia no doubt found him horny-handed by comparison with the Venetian aesthete and man of letters, Pietro Bembo (1471–1547), best-known today for the typeface that bears his name, and for his authorship of what is regarded amongst bibliophiles as the first modern publication, De Aetna of 1495.

Their go-between was Ercole Strozzi, an extravagantly foppish and philandering cripple, stabbed to death in 1508. It would seem that the affair was as brief as it was intense. Bembo was warned off in October 1503, though their correspondence continued for some years. By 1507 Strozzi was carrying secret messages from Lucrezia to another man, Francesco Gonzaga, Marquis of Mantua, while Bembo was in Urbino, helping to inspire Castiglione's guide to being a gentleman, The Book of the Courtier. Eventually Bembo retired to Padua with a woman called Morosina, and was made a Cardinal. His love-letters are carefully turned works of art, but none the less deeply felt.

BEMBO TO BORGIA

Gazing these past days into my crystal, of which we spoke during the last evening I paid my respects to your Ladyship, I have read therein, glowing at its centre, these lines I now send to you inscribed upon this paper. It would be the sweetest consolation to me and more prized than any treasure if in exchange your Ladyship might permit me to see some thing that she may have read in hers. And yet I cannot be sure that I may hope as much, when I recall that the day before yesterday you still kept silent regarding those things of which you had proposed to speak with me. I kiss your Ladyship's hand.

BORGIA TO BEMBO

Ostellato
19 June 1503

Messer Pietromio. Concerning the desire you have to hear from me regarding the counterpart of your or our crystal as it may rightly be reputed and termed, I cannot think what else to say or imagine save that it has an extreme affinity of which the like perhaps has never been equalled in any age. And may this suffice. And let it be a gospel everlasting.

This henceforth shall be my name
f.f.

BEMBO TO f.f.

Ferrara
24 June 1503

Today I would have come to pay tribute to your Ladyship, as was my obligation or my desire – I know not which the more, for both were vast and infinite – had it not been that the other night I woke with such pain in my neck that now I can only move it if I turn my entire body, and that with difficulty, and consequently it gives me no little annoyance. I believe it was a bad strain, and certainly it was very bad of it to choose to assail me at this time. But these past hours it has begun to perceive its error and appears to be relenting and preparing to be gone; and no sooner is this accomplished than I shall straightway come to your Ladyship, which will, I deem be within two days. And should it defer its departure long I shall come in any case, as I have no desire to follow this neckache with heartache, which is wont to be much more serious – although I fear I am already affected, seeing that I have delayed more than I should wish my coming to kiss your hand. Accordingly I shall come quickly whatever happens, if only to cure myself of this second malady. Here the heat is unusually intense and for my part I have never felt it stronger – I seem to be all aflame and turned to fire. I do not know whether you feel it to the same degree. In no wise, I must suppose, for where you are there is more shade than I have here, nor can I forget that by their nature women feel the heat less than men are wont to do. Craving your favour I kiss your Ladyship's hand, and beg my dear Madonna Lisabetta to say one prayer for me to her saintly mistress.

HENRY VIII
1491–1547

Henry VIII was intellectually refined, practised in the arts of peace and war, handsome and tall. He was also as ruthlessly Machiavellian as any Renaissance prince in Europe. Mary Boleyn was only too happy to be his mistress for a while, but her sister Anne (1501–1536), when she caught the King's eye in 1526, resolved to be his queen, and this she achieved seven years later. Three years after the marriage, with no sign of a son and heir, the King was flirting with Jane Seymour, and Anne had to be not merely discarded but disposed of. Trumped-up charges of adultery and treason were brought against her and she was beheaded in 1536. The seventeen short letters from the King to Anne Boleyn were smuggled out of England by Catholic agents and are still preserved in the Vatican. If they were politically compromising at the time, the tender and almost diffident expressions of supplication in them have subsequently served to soften his image. One of her letters survives from their romance, a prettily composed come-on, written after their first meeting. The first one of Henry's that we have here, written in French for purposes of discretion, is the critical one of the series he wrote to her. Shortly afterwards she became his mistress and the subsequent letters were written in English. One of these is quite breathtaking in its indelicacy, given the courtly grace with which it is expressed.

ANNE BOLEYN TO HENRY VIII – 1527

Sire,

It belongs only to the august mind of a great King to whom Nature has given a heart full of generosity towards the sex, to repay by favours so extraordinary an artless and short conversation with a girl. Inexhaustible as is the treasury of Your Majesty's bounties, I pray [you] to consider that it cannot be sufficient to your generosity; for if you recompense so slight a conversation by gifts so great, what will you be able to do for those who are ready to consecrate their entire obedience to your desires? How great soever may be the bounties I have received, the joy that I feel in being loved by a King whom I adore, and to whom I would with pleasure make a sacrifice of my heart, if fortune had rendered it worthy of being offered to him, will ever be infinitely greater.

The warrant of maid of honour to the Queen induces me to think that Your Majesty has some regard for me, since it gives me the means of seeing you oftener, and of assuring you by my own lips (which I shall do on the first opportunity) that I am,

Your Majesty's very obliged and very obedient servant, without reserve,

Anne Boleyn

HENRY VIII TO ANNE BOLEYN – 1527

My turning over in my thoughts the contents of your last letters, I have put myself into a great agony, not knowing how to understand them, whether to my disadvantage, as some passages indicate, or to my advantage, as I interpret other passages. I beseech you now, with all my heart, to let me know your whole intention as to the love between us two; for I must of necessity obtain this answer from you, having been, for more than a year, struck with the dart of love, and not yet sure whether I shall fail, or find a place in your heart and affection; and this last point has prevented me recently from naming you my mistress, which would be inappropriate if you do not love me with more than an ordinary affection, as it denotes a special relationship which is far from ordinary. But if it pleases you to play the part of a true, loyal mistress and friend, and to give yourself body and heart to me, who will be, and has been, your most loyal servant (if your rigour does not forbid me), I promise you that not only will you deserve the name, but also that I will take you for my only mistress, casting all others, that are in competition with you, out of my thoughts and affection, and serving only you. I beg you to give an entire answer to this my uncouth letter as to what and on what I may depend. But if it does not please you to answer me in writing, let me know some place where I may have it by word of mouth, and I will go thither with all my heart. No more for fear of annoying you. Written by the hand of him who would willingly remain your

H Rex

HENRY VIII TO ANNE BOLEYN - JUNE 1528

The cause of my writing at this time (good sweetheart) is only to understand of your good health and prosperity, whereof to know I would be as glad as in manner mine own, praying God that and it be His pleasure, to send us shortly together, for I promise you I long for it, howbeit trust it shall not be long too; and seeing my darling is absent, I can no less do than to send her some flesh representing my name, which is hart's flesh for Henry, prognosticating that hereafter, God willing, you must enjoy some of mine, which He pleased I would were now . . . .

HENRY VIII TO ANNE BOLEYN - JULY 1528

Mine own sweetheart, these shall be to advertise you of the great elengeness that I find here since your departing, for I ensure you, methinketh the time longer since your departing now last than I was wont to do a whole fortnight. I think your kindness and my fervence of love causeth it, for otherwise I would not have thought it possible that for so little a while it should have grieved me; but now that I am coming toward you, methinketh my pains been half released, and also I am right well comforted, insomuch that my book maketh substantially for my matter, in writing whereof I have spent about iiij hours this day, which caused me now to write the shorter letter to you at this time, because of some pain in my head, wishing myself (specially an evening) in my sweetheart's arms, whose pretty ducks I trust shortly to kiss. Written with the hand of him that was, is, and shall be yours by his will.

H.R.

MICHELANGELO BUONARROTI
1495–1564

Michelangelo was a true 'Renaissance man' inasmuch as his greatness and nobility of spirit extended beyond his art. The man is not diminished in comparison with the art, sublime as it is. His morals were as irreproachable as his passions were powerful. We include these two letters from him as witnesses to truly sublimated passion, love letters at the most refined level. He met Vittoria Colonna (1490–1547) the widowed Marchese di Pescare in 1536, and their relationship swiftly became an intense combination of romantic ardour (on his side, anyway, conscious as he was of his own ugliness) and spiritual communion. There is a note of hurt reproach in this letter from him, one of only two surviving letters to her.

MICHELANGELO TO VITTORIA COLONNA – SPRING 1539

Signora Marchese – Seeing that I am in Rome, I do not think it was necessary to have left the Crucifix with Messer Tommao and to have made him an intermediary between your ladyship and me, your servant, to the end that I might serve you; particularly as I had desired to perform more for you than for anyone on earth I ever knew. But the great task on which I have been and am engaged has prevented me from making this known to Your Ladyship. And because I know that you know that love requires no task-master, and that he who loves slumbers not – still less had he need of intermediaries. And although it may have seemed that I had forgotten, I was executing something I had not mentioned, in order to add something that was not expected. My plan has been spoilt.

'Mal fa chi tanta fe....'

The go-between he names in this letter is Tommaso de Cavalieri, to whom Michelangelo was introduced in 1533, and who was, with Vittoria Colonna, the inspiration for much of his poetry. There is no evidence to suggest that their relationship was ever consummated, and Cavalieri was present at Michelangelo's deathbed. The following is the draft of Michelangelo's first letter to Cavalieri.

MICHAELANGELO TO CAVALIERI

Florence

28 July 1533

My dear lord – Had I not believed that I had convinced you of the immense, nay, boundless love I bear you, the grave apprehension shown by your letter that I might have forgotten you, as I haven't written to you would seem to me neither strange nor surprising. But there is nothing unusual in this, nor in being alarmed, when so many other things go wrong, lest this too should come to grief; since what your lordship says to me, I would have said to you. But perhaps you did this in order to try me, or in order to kindle anew a greater flame, if a greater were possible. But be that as it may, I realize now that I could [as soon] forget your name as forget the food on which I live – nay, I could sooner forget the food on which I live, which unhappily nourishes only the body, than your name, which nourishes body and soul, filling both with such delight that I am insensible to sorrow or fear of death, while my memory of you endures. Imagine, if the eye were also playing its part, the state in which I should find myself....

FRANCOIS I
1494–1547

The father of Diane de Poitiers (1500–1560), the Comte de Saint Vallier, was condemned to death in 1524 for supporting the Duke of Bourbon in his plot against the King, Francois 1. However, when he was awaiting execution, a horseman arrived with a reprieve, and according to the scurrilous Brantome, St. Vallier was heard to mutter, as he staggered from the scaffold, 'God save the sweet thing of my daughter which hath saved me so well' – the implication being that Diane had given herself to the King in exchange for her father's life. In fact, Diane's husband had discovered the plot and was therefore in a position to ask a favour. The note that Francois sent, after his capture at the Battle of Pavia in the same year, was addressed, not to Diane de Poitiers, as the racier commentators preferred to suggest, but to Madame de Chateaubriant:

After losing, so as to have you, all the weal I could have without you, if I lost you, be sure that I would seek no other remedy than to destroy myself, for

I should ever deem better death without memory than memory without death.
   Your unfortunate friend
   Francois

   The answer was even more succinct:

The hand whose whole body is yours.

HENRI II
1519–1559

It was Henri II, son of Francois I, who made Diane de Poitiers his mistress,
though she was eighteen years older than he was. At the age of twelve he
first wore her colours in the lists, and three years later, after the death of
her husband, she became his mistress. Even on his coronation in 1547 he
chose to wear her initials embroidered on his sleeve, to display his chivalric devotion to his lady over his conventional duty to his wife, Catherine
de Medici. In 1559 he still wore her colours when he was killed jousting
against Montgomery of his Scots Guards. The following letters were
written after she had suffered a fall from her horse in 1552.

HENRI II TO DIANE DE POITIERS – 1552

My love, I entreat you to send me word of your health for the distress in
which I am through hearing of your illness, to the end that according to that I
may do; for if you continue to be ill I would not fail to go to you to do my utmost
to do you service, even as I am bound to do, and furthermore it would not be
possible for me to live so long without seeing you; and since I was not afeared in
time past to lose the good grace of the late King in order to be with you, I would
spare no trouble to serve you in anything; and I assure you that I shall not be at
ease until the bearer of this hath returned; and for that I entreat you to send me
word in very truth how you are and when you will be able to depart. I believe
that you will be well able to think how little pleasure I have at Fontainebleau
without seeing you, for being far away from her on whom depends all my weal, it
is full hard for me to have joy, which makes me sign this letter from fear that it
may be too long and tire you to read it, and will proffer you my humble recom-
mendations to your good grace, as he that is fain to keep it for ever.

H

Madame m'amye, I thank you very humbly for the pains you have taken to send me news of you, which is the most agreeable thing to me in this world, and entreat you to keep promise with me, for I cannot live without you, and if you knew how little pastime I have here you would pity me. I will not make you a longer letter, save but to assure you that I could not come as quickly as wisheth it he who remains for ever your very humble servant.

H

Meanwhile I entreat you to keep remembrance of him who never had and never knew but one God and one love, and assure you that you shall not have shame to have granted me the name of servant. Which I entreat you to keep for me for ever.

H

SIR WILLIAM ST. LOE
DIED 1565

In 1559 Sir William St. Loe, Captain of the Queen's Guard and a doughty soldier – though with an appalling record in any office that required more subtle qualities like tact or balanced judgement – became the third husband of the beautiful and ambitious Lady Cavendish, 'Bess of Hardwick' (1520–1607). All her life her obsession was the building of great houses, and it is in wry acknowledgement of this that St. Loe used to call her 'My honest sweet Chatsworth'. Judging by his letters to her she had little difficulty persuading him to make her his sole heir at the expense of the rest of his family, and she survived an attempt on the part of his younger brother to poison her. She also survived her first stretch in the Tower in 1561–2 for being privy to a secret marriage. It was the sort of thing that made Queen Elizabeth see red, particularly as the boy in question was Edward Seymour, son of Protector Somerset (executed for getting above himself in 1552), and the girl was of royal blood, being the sister of Lady Jane Grey (executed for getting above herself in 1554).

SIR WILLIAM TO LADY SAINT-LOE

My own, more dearer to me than I am to myself, thou shalt understand that it is no small fear nor grief unto me of thy well doing that I should presently see what I do, not only for that my continual nightly dreams beside my absence hath troubled me, but also chiefly for that Hugh Alsope cannot satisfy me in what estate thou nor thine is, whom I regard more than I do William Seyntlo. Therefore I pray thee, as thou dost love me, let me shortly hear from thee, for the quieting of my unquieted mind, how thine own sweet self with all thine doeth; trusting shortly to be amongst you. All thy friends here saluteth thee. Harry Skipwith desired me to make thee and no other privy that he is sure of mistress Nell, with whom he is by this time. He hath sent ten thousand thanks unto thyself for the same: she hath opened all things unto him. To-morrow Sir Richard Sackville and I ride to London together; on Saturday next we return hither again. The queen yesterday, her own self riding upon the way, craved my horse; unto whom I gave him, receiving openly for the same many goodly words. Thus wishing myself with thyself, I bid thee, my own good servant and chief overseer of my works, most heartily farewell; by thine who is wholly and only thine, yea and for all thine while life lasteth.

From Windsor the fourth of September by thy right worshipful master and most honest husband master Sir William Seyntlo, esquire.

Commend me to my mother and to all my brothers and sisters, not forgetting Frank with the rest of my children and thine. The Amnar saluteth thee and sayeth no gentleman's children in England shall be better welcome nor better looked unto than our boys. Once again, farewell good honest sweet.

Myself or Greyves shall be the next messenger.

To my own dear wife at Chatsworth deliver this.

GEORGE TALBOT, EARL OF SHREWSBURY
1528–1590

Bess of Hardwick's last marriage was in 1568 to George Talbot, Earl of Shrewsbury, one of the richest men in England. She was still beautiful but already tough as old boots and as part of the deal she insisted that two of her own children, by her second marriage, should marry two of the Earl's offspring. On her side it was a dynastic match, as the only man she had ever loved was her second husband, William Cavendish, while for his part Shrewsbury clearly could not get enough of her. Gilbert is his son; 'Manle' or Mary is her daughter.

My dear none, having received your letter of the first of December which came in very good time, else had I sent one of these few remaining with me to have brought me word of your health, which I doubted of for that I heard not from you of all this time till now, which drove me in dumps, but now relieved again by your writing unto me. I thank you, sweet none, for your puddings and venison. The puddings have I bestowed in this wise: [a] dozen to my Lady Cobham, and as many to my L. Steward and unto my L. of Leicester: and the rest I have reserved to myself to eat in my chamber. The venison is yet at London, but I have sent for it hither.

I perceive Ned Talbot hath been sick, and [is] now past danger. I thank God I have such a none that is so careful over me and mine. God send me soon home to possess my greatest joy: if you think it is you, you are not deceived.

The plague is dispersed far abroad in London, so that the Queen keeps her Christmas here, and goeth not to Greenwich as it was meant. My Lady Cobham, your dear friend, wishes your presence here: she loves you well. I tell her I have the cause to love her best, for that she wished me so well to speed as I did: and as the pen writes so the heart thinks, that of all earthly joys that hath happened unto me, I thank God chiefest for you: for with you I have all joy and contentation of mind, and without you death is more pleasant to me than life if I thought I should long be from you: and therefore, good wife, do as I will do, hope shortly of our meeting, and farewell, dear sweet none. From Hampton Court this Monday at midnight, for it is every night so late before I go to my bed, being at play in the privy chamber at Premiro, where I have lost almost a hundred pounds, and lacked my sleep.

Your faithful husband till death,

G. Shrewsbury

THE EARL TO THE COUNTESS OF SHREWSBURY

My dear none, I have received your letter of the 8th of December, wherein appeareth your desire for my soon coming. What my desire is thereunto, I refer the same to your construsion. If I so judge of time, methinks time longer since my coming hither without you, my only joy, than I did since I married you:

such is faithful affection, which I never tasted so deeply of before. This day or to-morrow we shall know great likelihood of our despatch. I think it will be Christmas Even before I shall arrive at Tutbury. Things fall out very evil against the Scots' Queen. What she shall do yet is not resolved of.

As it chances, I am glad that I am here: for if I were not I were like to have most part of my leases granted over my head: there is such suit for leases in reversion of the Duchy. My park that I have in keeping called Morley Park is granted in reversion for thirty years, wherein I have made some stir. My good neighbour hath a promise of it, and if I can get it put in I am about to get a friend of mine to put the forest of the Peak in his book. I have offered a thousand pounds for a lease in reversion for thirty years. I must pay Denege five hundred and forty-one for his lease of Stoke. How money will be had for these matters assure you I know not. I will make such means to Mr. Mildmay for the stay of Tutbury tithe, as I will not be prevented: for it is high time, for there was never such striving and prancing for leases in reversion as be now at this present.

My L. Steward hath been sick and in danger, but now well. My L. Sheffield is departed this life ; and my L. Paget just after. Your black man is in health.

Your faithful husband till my end,

G. Shrewsbury.

From the Court this Monday the 13th of December.

Now it is certain the Scots' Queen comes to Tutbury to my charge. In what order I cannot ascertain you.

To my wife the Countess of Shrewsbury at Tutbury give this.

THE EARL TO THE COUNTESS OF SHREWSBURY

My dear none, – Of all joys I have under God the greatest is yourself: to think that I possess so faithful, and one that I know loves me so dearly, is all and the greatest comfort that this earth can give. Therefore God give me grace to be thankful to Him for His goodness showed unto me, a vile sinner.

I thank you, my sweetheart, that you are so willing to come when I will. Therefore, dear heart, send me word how I might send for you; and till I have your company I shall think long, my only joy: and therefore appoint a day, and in the meantime I shall content me with your will, and long daily for your coming. I your letters study very well; and I like them so well they could not be amended: and I have sent them up to Gilbert. I have written to him how happy he is to have such a mother as you are. Farewell, only joy. This Tuesday evening.

Your faithful one,
G. Shrewsbury

THE EARL TO THE COUNTESS OF SHREWSBURY

My Sweetheart, – Your true and faithful zeal you bear me is more comfortable to me than anything I can think upon, and I give God thanks daily for his benefits he hath bestowed on me, and greatest cause I have to give him thanks that he hath sent me you in my old years to comfort me withal. Your coming I shall think long for, and shall send on Friday your litter horses and on Saturday morning I will send my folks, because Friday they will be desirous to be at Rotherham Fair . . . . I thank you for your fat capon and it shall be baked, and kept cold and untouched until my sweetheart come; guess you who it is. I have sent you a cock that was given to me, which is all the dainties I have here.

I have written to Sellars to send every week a quarter of rye for this ten weeks, which will be as much as I know will be had there, and ten quarters of barley, which will be all that I can spare you. Farewell, my sweet true none and faithful wife.

All yours,
Shrewsbury.

All might have been well with the marriage if the Earl had not been accorded the honour of guarding and looking after Mary Queen of Scots. Queen Elizabeth knew she could rely absolutely on his courage and loyalty; she also knew that he was rich and guileless enough to bear the enormous expense the business entailed over fifteen years without complaining overmuch.

The result was a bitter family feud over money and property, set off when Bess suspected that her husband's already limited faculties were deserting him to the extent of allowing the Queen of Scots to start scheming round him. To divert attention away from a fatal political indiscretion she circulated, in 1583, rumours of a sexual indiscretion instead. Unlikely as the idea might have been, of this rather joyless and unimaginative old man being bewitched by the rapidly fading charms of the Queen of Scots, the ruse succeeded in getting him relieved of his charge with, in the end, little or no dirt sticking to his escutcheon.

He was even given the unpleasant privilege of presiding at her execution in 1587. But he never forgave his wife, and up to his death in 1590 disobeyed Queen Elizabeth's orders to re-establish good relations with her. In the context of a letter of condolence to Lord Leicester in 1584 he dismisses his wife and her daughter with a coarse pungency ' . . . . for I think neither barrel better herring of them both.'

HENRI OF NAVARRE
1553-1610

Henri of Navarre learnt the art of survival at the most dangerous centre of power Europe had seen since the end of the Roman Empire. Ruled over by Catherine de Medici and her brood of sickly effeminate sons, the French court was a glittering nest of cynicism and vicious sensuality, treachery and assassination, witchcraft and poison. Navarre's wife, Margaret of Valois, carried swinging about her skirts little reliquaries containing the embalmed hearts of those of her lovers who had been murdered or executed by her mother or her royal brothers. It was that kind of court. Navarre, who became king of France in 1610, was, by contrast, a bluff soldier with the 'common touch', compassionate and magnanimous. His one frailty was the attitude of chivalric fealty he adopted towards some of his scores of mistresses. His insistence on playing the knight errant during the civil wars, for example, and personally delivering captured standards to the feet of his beloved, very nearly cost him a campaign. However, his soldierly disregard for personal freshness and modish tailoring left him ill-equipped to triumph in the lists of love. Even in the case of the best-loved of his mistresses, Gabrielle d'Estrees (poisoned in April 1599) he was aware that he was playing second fiddle from time to time. He was assassinated in 1610.

HENRI OF NAVARRE TO GABRIELLE D'ESTREES

10 February 1593

I know not with what magic you have wrought, heart of my heart, but I never endured other severances with half the impatience the present one inflicts on me. Already it seems an age since I departed from you. No need for you to beg me to return. Every artery, every muscle in my body keeps telling me, every moment, of the bliss of beholding you and of the bitterness of separation. Believe me, my beloved Queen, never did love visit me so fiercely as it does this very hour. I kiss your beautiful hands a million times.

HENRI OF NAVARRE TO GABRIELLE D'ESTREES

17 February 1593

The pain I feel at getting no news from you continues still. I am sending La Fon to you poste-haste for I fear some accident must have befallen you. Send him back at once, dear love, I implore you. Believe me, my lovely angel, when I say that I rate the possession of your good graces above the glory of a dozen battles. Consider it a jewel in your crown that you have vanquished me, who never was completely conquered save by you, whose feet I kiss a million times.

HENRI OF NAVARRE TO GABRIELLE D'ESTREES

My sweetest love, to-morrow I shall be showering kisses by the million on those beautiful hands, Already the burdens of my troubles grows lighter now that a happiness I hold as dear as life will soon be mine. But if you are a single day later than you say, 'twill be the death of me.

Never hath absence been more grievous to me than this. To spend the month of April far from one's beloved, 'tis not to live at all.

HENRI OF NAVARRE TO GABRIELLE D'ESTREES – 1599

There's no denying it: we do love each other. Assuredly, as women go, you have not got your equal, and as for men, not one can rival me in the art of loving. My passion for you is just as great as it was when I first began to love you, my longing to see you even more desperate than then. I cherish, adore and honour you most wondrously.

ARABELLA STUART
1575–1615

Arabella Stuart was the product of Bess of Hardwick's ambition, being the only child of her daughter, Elizabeth Cavendish, who had been pushed into the arms of Charles Stuart with the connivance of his mother, Lady Lennox. This was an audacious move as he was of royal blood, his mother being the daughter of Henry VIII's sister, Margaret Tudor. The Earl of Shrewsbury, Bess of Hardwick's husband, was appalled by the match, and this date, 1574, marked the end of their marital concord.

The Queen, of course, was livid, and treated Bess to a second term in the Tower. As it turned out Arabella became a sore trial to her grandmother, her romantic nature contrasting with the old battle axe's ruthless cunning, and she lost the race for the succession to the throne of England to James VI of Scotland. The girl had not improved her chances, first by wilfully flirting with the Queen's favourite, the irresistible Earl of Essex, and then by going behind the backs of both the dying Queen and her grandmother in a vain attempt to marry into the house of Seymour, a family whose ambitions the Queen had good reason to mistrust.

Again in 1610 she was expressly forbidden by James I from marrying William Seymour, but they married anyway, to the consternation of Seymour's grandfather, whose own secret marriage fifty years earlier had ended tragically, his wife starving herself to death in despair. The two lovers were imprisoned for their contumacy and it was at this time that the following letter was written. In 1611 they effected a daring escape but Arabella was recaptured before she reached Calais and spent her last years in the Tower, where she slowly went mad.

LADY ARABELLA SEYMOUR TO MR. WILLIAM SEYMOUR

Sir, – I am exceeding sorry to hear you have not been well. I pray you let me know truly how you do, and what was the cause of it, for I am not satisfied with the reason Smith gives for it. But if it be a cold, I will impute it to some sympathy betwixt us, having myself gotten a swollen cheek at the same time with a cold. For God's sake, let not your grief of mind work upon your body. You may see by me what inconveniences it will bring one to. And no fortune, I assure you, daunts me so much as that weakness of body I find in myself, for 'si nous vivons l'age d'un veau,' as Marot says, we may by God's grace be happier than we look for in being suffered to enjoy ourselves with his Majesty's favour. But if we be not able to live to it, I, for my part, shall think myself a pattern of misfortune in enjoying so great a blessing as you so little a while. No separation but that deprives me of the comfort of you; for wheresoever you be, or in what state soever you are, it sufficeth me you are mine. Rachel wept, and would not be comforted, because her children were no more; and that indeed is the remediless sorrow, and none else. And therefore God bless us from that, and I will hope well of the rest, though I see no apparent hope. But I am sure God's book mentioneth many of his children in as great distress that have done well after, even in this world. I assure you, nothing the State can do with me can trouble me so much as this news of your being ill doth. And you see when I am troubled, I trouble you too with tedious kindness, for so I think you will account so long a letter, yourself not having written to me for this good while so much as how you do. But sweet sir, I speak not this to trouble you with writing but when you please. Be well, and I shall account myself happy in being your faithful loving wife,

Arabella.

JAMES I
1566–1625

Those people in England who had read Ronsard's encomiums to the enchanting beauty of Mary Queen of Scots would have been especially disappointed in the person and behaviour of her son James I, when he came to the throne in 1603 at the age of 37. Small, fat, unwashed, drooling and coarse, he was, like all the Stuart kings who followed him, intellectually gifted but foolish. His homosexuality only compounded his difficulties as a monarch. James died shortly after writing the second of these extraordinarily touching letters to George Villiers. It was said that he had been poisoned by Villiers himself, who was all set to do even better under Charles I than he had done as James' 'Steenie'.

JAMES I TO GEORGE VILLIERS, MARQUIS OF BUCKINGHAM – 1622

My only sweet and dear child,

I am now so miserable a coward, as I do nothing but weep and mourn; for I protest to God, I rode this afternoon a great way in the park without speaking to anybody, and the tears trickling down my cheeks, as now they do, that I can scarcely see to write. But, alas! what shall I do at our parting? The only small comfort that I can have will be to pry into thy defects with the eye of an enemy, and of every mote to make a mountain; and so harden my heart against thy absence. But this little malice is like jealousy, proceeding from a sweet root; but in one point it overcometh it, for, as it proceeds from love, so it cannot but end in love.

Sweet heart! be earnest with Kate to come and meet thee at New Hall within eight or ten days after this. Cast thee to be here tomorrow, as near as about two in the afternoon as thou canst, and come galloping hither. Remember thy picture, and suffer none of the Council to come here – for God's sake! Write not a word again, and let no creature see this letter. The Lord of heaven and earth bless thee, and my sweet daughter, and my sweet little grandchild, and all thy blessed family, and send thee a happier return – both now and thou knowest when – to thy dear dad and Christian gossip.

James R.

JAMES I TO GEORGE VILLIERS, DUKE OF BUCKINGHAM – 1625

My own sweet and dear child,

Notwithstanding of your desiring me to write yesterday, yet had I written in the evening, if at my coming in out of the park such a drowsiness had not come upon me, as I was forced to sit and sleep in my chair half an hour. And yet I cannot content myself without sending you this billet, praying God that I may have a joyful and comfortable meeting with you, and that we may make at this Christenmass a new marriage, ever to be kept hereafter; for, God so love me, as I desire only to live in this world for your sake, and that I had rather live banished in any part of the earth with you, than live a sorrowful widow-life without you.

And so God bless you, my sweet child and wife, and grant that ye may ever be a comfort to your dear dad and husband.

James R.

SIR JOHN SUCKLING
1608–1641

Sir John Suckling was one of the most gifted of the school of 'Cavalier Poets' and 'the greatest gallant of his time' (Aubrey). However, in the serious matter of trying to secure himself an heiress he threw gallantry to the winds. When Anne Willoughby refused him, Suckling somehow tricked or coerced her into signing a note saying that 'she doth love him to marry him'. As a result, Suckling was beaten up by her preferred suitor, Sir John Digby, and Suckling was censured for his failure to draw against his rival 'yielded to be the best swordsman of his time' (Aubrey). Aubrey goes on "Twas pity that this accident brought the blemish of cowardice to such an ingeniose young spark. Sir J.D. was such a hero that there were very few but he would have served in the same manner.' Again according to Aubrey, he was a great gambler and credited with the invention of 'cribbidge'. Accused by the Parliamentarians in 1641 of plotting to spring Lord Wentworth from the Tower, he fled to the Continent where he committed suicide.

Aglaura is the title of a play he had performed in 1638, set in Persia, which he wrote with two alternative endings, one tragic the other comic. The letters to 'Aglaura', who has been identified as Mary Bulkeley of Anglesey, date from this period, and they make better reading, frankly, than the play does. They are clearly related in their cadences and manner to the love-sonnet tradition – only recently ended – of Spenser, Sidney and Shakespeare and also, in their finely wrought argument, to the metaphysical poetry even then being written.

SIR JOHN SUCKLING TO ANNE WILLOUGHBY – 1633

Since Joy (the thing we all so court) is but our hopes stript of our fears, pardon me if I be still pressing at it, and like those that are curious to know their fortunes aforehand, desire to be satisfied, though it displeases me afterward. To this gentleman (who has as much in-sight as the t'other wanted eyesight) I have committed the particulars, which would too much swell a Letter: if they shall not please you, 'tis but fresh subject still for Repentance; nor ever did that make me quarrel with any thing but my owne starres. To swear new oaths from this place, were but to weaken the credit of those I have sworn in another: if heaven be to forgive you now for not believing of them then, (as sure as it was a sin) heaven forgive me now for swearing of them then (for that was double sin.) More than I am I cannot be, nor list,

Yours,

J.S.

SUCKLING TO 'AGLAURA' (MARY BULKELEY)

Since you can breathe no one desire that was not mine before it was yours, or full as soon (for hearts united never knew divided wishes), I must chide you, dear princess, not thank you, for your present; and (if at least I knew how) be angry with you for sending him a blush, who needs must blush because you sent him one. If you are conscious of much, what am I then, who guilty am of all you can pretend to, and something more – unworthiness. But why should you at all, heart of my heart, disturb the happiness you have so newly given me, or make love feed on doubts, that never yet could thrive on such a diet? *If I have granted your request!* O, why will you ever say that you have studied me, and give so great an interest to the contrary! That wretched *if* speaks as if I would refuse what you desire, or could – both which are equally impossible. My dear princess, there needs no new approaches where the breach is made already; nor must you ever ask anywhere, but of your fair self, for anything that shall concern your humble servant.

SUCKLING TO 'AGLAURA' (MARY BULKELEY)

When I receive your lines, my dear princess, and find there expressions of a passion, though reason and my own immerit tell me it must not be for me, yet is the cosenage so pleasing to me, that I, bribed by my own desires, believe them still before the other. Then do I glory that my virgin-love has stayed for such an object to fix upon, and think how good the stars were to me that kept me from quenching those flames youth or wild love furnished me withal in common and ordinary waters, and reserved me a sacrifice for your eyes. While thought thus smiles and solaces himself within me, cruel remembrance breaks in upon our retirements, and tells so sad a story that, trust me, I forget all that pleased fancy said before, and turn my thoughts to where I left you. Then I consider that storms neither know courtship nor pity, and that those rude blasts will often make you a prisoner this winter, if they do no worse.

While I here enjoy fresh diversion, you make the sufferings more by having leisure to consider them; nor have I now any way left me to make mine equal with them, but by often considering that they are not so; for the thought that I cannot be with you to bear my share is more intolerable to me than if I had borne more. But I was only born to number hours, and not enjoy them; yet can I never think myself unfortunate, while I can write myself Aglaura her humble servant.

SUCKLING TO 'AGLAURA' (MARY BULKELEY)

So much, dear –, was I ever yours, since I had first the honour to know you, and consequently so little myself, since I had the unhappiness to part with you, that you yourself, dear, without what I would say, cannot but have been so just as to have imagined the welcome of your own letters; though indeed they have but removed me from one rack to set me on another – from fears and doubts I had about me of your welfare to an unquietness within myself, till I have deserved this intelligence.

How pleasingly troublesome thought and remembrance have been to me, since I left you, I am no more able now to express, than another to have them so. You only could make every place you came in worth the thinking of; and I do think those places worthy my thought only, because you made them so. But I am to leave them, and I shall do't the willinger, because the gamester still is so much in me, as that I love not to be told too often of my losses. Yet every place will be alike, since every good object will do the same. Variety of beauty and of faces, quick underminers of constancy to others, to me will be but pillars to support it, since when they please me most, I most shall think of you.

In spite of all philosophy, it will be hottest in my climate when my sun is farthest off; and in spite of all reason, I proclaim that I am not myself, but when I am yours wholly.

SUCKLING TO 'AGLAURA' (MARY BULKELEY)

Though desire, in those that love, be still like too much sail in a storm, and man cannot so easily strike, or take all in when he pleases; yet dearest princess, be it never so hard, when you shall think it dangerous, I shall not make it difficult; though – well, love is love, and air is air; and, though you are a miracle yourself, yet do not I believe that you can work any. Without it I am confident you can never make these two, thus different in themselves, one and the self-same thing; when you shall, it will be some small furtherance towards it, that you have your humble servant,

J.S.

Whoso truly loves the fair Aglaura, that he will never know desire, at least not entertain it, that brings not letters of recommendation from her, or first a fair passport.

SUCKLING TO 'AGLAURA' (MARY BULKELEY)

Since the inferior orbs move but by the first, without all question desires and hopes in me are to be governed still by you, as they by it. What mean these fears, then, dear princess?

Though planets wander, yet is the sphere that carries them the same still; and though wishes in me may be extravagant, yet he is whom they make their motion is, you know, my dear princess, yours, and wholly to be disposed of by you.

And till we hear from you, though, according to the form of concluding a letter, we should now rest, we cannot.

SUCKLING TO 'AGLAURA' (MARY BULKELEY)

Fair Princess, – If parting be a sin, as sure it is, what then to part from you? If to extenuate an ill be to increase it, what then now to excuse it by letter? That which we would allege to lessen it, with you perchance has added to the guilt already, which is our sudden leaving you. Abruptness is an eloquence in parting, when spinning out of time is but weaving of new sorrow. And thus we thought; yet being not all able to distinguish of our own acts, the fear we may have sinned farther than we think of has made us send to you to know whether it be mortal or not.

SUCKLING TO 'AGLAURA' (MARY BULKELEY)

There was (O seldom-happy word of *was*!) a time when I was not Montferrat; and sure there was a time too, when all was handsome in my heart, for you were there, dear princess, and filled the place alone. *Were there* (O wretched word again!); and should you leave that lodging, more wretched than Montferrat needs must be your humble servant,

J.S.

Mary Bulkeley married someone else in 1639, provoking his comparison of himself in his last letter to 'Montferrat'. This is either William, Marquis of Montferrat and Canavese, who was exhibited by the citizens of Alessandria in Piedmont in an iron cage for eighteen months until his death in 1292, whence, according to Dante, he found his way to Purgatory (Canto VII), or, more probably, a character of that name in Fletcher, Field and Massinger's Knight of Malta.

CHARLES I   HENRIETTA MARIA
1600–1649   1609–1669

Henrietta Maria's unpopularity – owing to her rigid adherence to the Roman Catholic faith – certainly helped to propel her husband Charles I to the scaffold in 1649. Apart from this, however, their marriage was a great success – as soon, that is, as the Duke of Buckingham's baleful influence on the new King had come to an end when he was assassinated by stabbing in 1628. Both these letters were written in 1645, when the King's cause in the Civil War was virtually lost.

HENRIETTA MARIA TO CHARLES I

Paris

My Dear Heart,

There is one thing in your letter which troubles me much, where you would have me "keep to myself your despatches," as if you believe that I should be capable to show them to any, only to Lord Jermyn to uncipher them, my head not suffering me to do it myself; but if it please you, I will do it, and none in the world shall see them. Be kind to me, or you will kill me.

I have already affliction enough to bear, which, without your love, I could not do, but your service surmounts all. Farewell, dear heart! Behold the mark which you desire to have, to know when I desire anything in earnest.

CHARLES I TO HENRIETTA MARIA

Oxford
9 April

Dear Heart,

Though it be an uncomfortable thing to write by a slow messenger, yet all occasions of this which is now the only way of conversing with thee are so welcome to me as I shall be loth to lose any; but expect neither news nor public business from me by this way of conveyance. Yet, judging thee by myself, even these nothings will not be unwelcome to thee, though I should chide thee – which if I could I would – for thy too sudden taking alarms.

I pray thee consider, since I love thee above all earthly things, and that my contentment is inseparably conjoined with thine, must not all my actions tend to serve and please thee? If thou knew what a life I lead (I speak not in respect of the common distractions), even in point of conversation, which in my mind is the chief joy or vexation of one's life, I dare say thou wouldest pity me. For some are too wise, others too foolish, some too busy, others too reserved, many fantastic . . . .

I confess thy company hath perhaps made me, in this, hard to be pleased, but not less to be pitied by thee, who art the only cure for this disease. The end of all is this, to desire thee to comfort me as often as thou canst with thy letters. And dost not thou think that to know particulars of thy health, and how thou spendest thy time, are pleasing subjects unto me, though thou hast no other business to write of?

Believe me, sweet heart, thy kindness is as necessary to comfort my heart as thy assistance is for my affairs.

Thine

DOROTHY OSBORNE   SIR WILLIAM TEMPLE
1627–1695   1628–1699

When Dorothy Osborne met William Temple at the age of 21, his father was sitting in the 'Long Parliament' while hers commanded Guernsey for the King. They remained star-crossed lovers even when hostilities ceased, as Sir William Temple was looking out for a more copper-bottomed union for his son, and Dorothy was being besieged by an endless succession of suitors, of whom the likeliest was Henry Cromwell, son of the future Protector. Their fidelity was tried over seven long years, with one final test in the form of small-pox, which took away Dorothy's looks. They married in 1655. She died in 1695, and he four years later. Dorothy writes with greatest feeling when she is attempting to argue herself and Temple out of their apparently fruitless passion. The one surviving letter from Temple displays the man's hot-headed determination that helped to carry them through.

OSBORNE TO TEMPLE

Sir

. . . . I have expected your letter all this day with the greatest impatience that was possible, and at last resolved to go out and meet the fellow; and when I came down to the stables, I found him come, had set up his horse, and was sweeping the stable in great order. I could not imagine him so very a beast as to think his horses were to be serv'd before me, and therefore was presently struck with an apprehension he had no letter for me: it went cold to my heart as ice, and hardly left me courage enough to ask him the question; but when he had drawled it out that he thought there was a letter for me in his bag, I quickly made him leave his broom. 'Twas well 'tis a dull fellow, he could not but have discerned else that I was strangely overjoyed with it, and earnest to have it; for though the poor fellow made what haste he could to untie his bag, I did nothing but chide him for being so slow. At last I had it, and, in earnest, I know not whether an entire diamond of the bigness on't would have pleased me half so well; if it would, it must be only out of this consideration, that such a jewel would make me rich enough to dispute you with Mrs. Ch[ambers,] and perhaps make your father like me as well . . . .

OSBORNE TO TEMPLE

I have seriously considered all our misfortunes, and can see no end to them but by submitting to that which we cannot avoid, and, by yielding to it, break the force of a blow which, if resisted, brings a certain ruin. I think I need not tell you how dear you have been to me, nor that in your kindness I placed all the satisfaction of my life; 'twas the only happiness I proposed to myself, and had set my heart so much upon it that it was therefore made my punishment, to let me see that, how innocent soever I thought my affection, it was guilty in being greater than is allowable for things of this world.

We have lived hitherto upon hopes so airy that I have often wondered how they could support the weight of our misfortunes; but passion gives a strength above nature, we see it in most people; and not to flatter ourselves, ours is but a refined degree of madness. What can it be, to be lost to all things in the world but the single object that takes up one's fancy, to lose all the quiet and repose of one's life in hunting after it, when there is so little likelihood of ever gaining it, and so many more probable accidents that will infallibly make us miss on't. And which is more than all, 'tis being mastered by that which reason and religion teaches us to govern, and in that only gives us a pre-eminence over beasts ... as we have not differed in anything else, we could agree in this too, and resolve upon a friendship that will be much the perfecter for having nothing of passion in it. How happy might we be without so much as a fear of the change that any accident could bring! We might defy all that fortune could do, and putting off all disguise and constraint, with that which only made it necessary, make our lives as easy to us as the condition of this world will permit. I may own you as a person that I extremely value and esteem, and for whom I have a particular friendship, and you may consider me as one that will also be

Yours faithful

Dorothy Osborne

TEMPLE TO OSBORNE

18 May 1654

. . . . I am called upon for my letter, but must have leave first to remember you of yours. For God sake write constantly while I am here, or I am undone past all recovery. I have lived upon them ever since I came, but had thrived much better had they been longer. Unless you use to give me better measure, I shall not be in case to undertake a journey into England. The despair I was in upon the not hearing from you last week, and the belief that all my letters were miscarried (by some treachery among my good friends who, I am sorry, have the name of yours), made me press my father by all means imaginable to give me leave to go presently, if I heard not from you this post. But he would never yield to that, because, he said, upon your silence he should suspect all was not likely to be well between us, and then he was sure I should not be in condition to be alone. He remembered too well the letters I writ upon our last unhappy differences, and would not trust me from him in such another occasion. But, withal, he told me he would never give me occasion of any discontents which he could remedy; that if you desired my coming over, and I could not be content without, he would not hinder me, though he very much desired my company a month or two longer, and that in that time 'twas very likely I might have his.

Well, now, in very good earnest, do you think 'tis time for me to come or no? Would you be very glad to see me there, and could you do it in less disorder, and with less surprise, than you did at Ch[icksands]?

I ask you these questions very seriously; but yet how willingly would I venture all to be with you. I know you love me still; you promised it me, and that's all the security I can have for all the good I am ever like to have in this world. 'Tis that which makes all things else seem nothing to it, so high it sets me; and so high, indeed, that should I ever fall 'twould dash me all to pieces . . . .

How hard 'tis to think of ending when I am writing to you; but it must be so, and I must ever be subject to other people's occasions, and so never, I think, master of my own. This is too true, both in respect of this fellow's post that is bawling at me for my letter, and of my father's delays. They kill me; but patience, – would anybody but I be here! Yet you may command me over at one minute's warning. Had I not heard from you by this last, in earnest I had resolved to have gone with this, and given my father the slip for all his caution. He tells me still of a little time; but, alas! who knows not what mischances and how great changes have often happened in a little time?

For God sake let me know of all your motions, when and where I may hope to see you. Let us but scape this cloud, this absence that has overcast all my contentments, and I am confident there's a clear sky attends us. My dearest dear, adieu. I am

Yours

OSBORNE TO TEMPLE

Lord, there were a thousand things I remembered after you were gone that I should have said, and now I am to write not one of them will come into my head. Sure, as I live, it is not settled yet! Good God! the fears and surprises, the crosses and disorders of that day, 'twas confused enough to be a dream, and I am apt to think sometimes it was no more. But no, I saw you; when I shall do it again, God only knows! Can there be a more Romance story than ours would make if the conclusion should prove happy? Ah! I dare not hope it; something that I cannot describe draws a cloud over all the light my fancy discovers sometimes, and leaves me so in the dark with all my fears about me that I tremble to think on't. But no more of this sad talk.

. . . . Did not you say once you knew where good French tweezers were to be had? Pray send me a pair; they shall cut no love. Before you go I must have a ring from you, too, a plain gold one; if I ever marry it shall be my wedding ring; when I die I'll give it you again . . . .

OSBORNE TO TEMPLE

. . . . Here is a ring: it must not be at all wider than this, which is rather too big for me than otherwise; but that is a good fault, and counted lucky by superstitious people. I am not so, though: 'tis indifferent to me whether there be any 'word' in't or not; only 'tis as well without, and will make my wearing it the less observed. You must give Nan leave to cut off a lock of your hair for me, too. Oh, my heart! what a sigh was there! I will not tell you how many this journey causes; nor the fears and apprehensions I have for you. No, I long to be rid on you, am afraid you will not go soon enough: do not you believe this? No, my dearest, I know you do not, whate'er you say, you cannot doubt but I am

Yours

OSBORNE TO TEMPLE

. . . . Twill be pleasinger to you, I am sure, to tell you how fond I am of your lock. Well, in earnest now, and setting aside all compliments, I never saw finer hair, nor of a better colour; but cut no more on't, I would not have it spoiled for the world. If you love me, be careful on't. I am combing, and curling, and kissing this lock all day, and dreaming on't all night. The ring, too, is very well, only a little of the biggest. Send me a tortoise-shell one to keep it on, that is a little less than that I sent for a pattern. I would not have the rule absolutely true without exception that hard hairs are ill-natured, for then I should be so. But I can allow that all soft hairs are good, and so are you, or I am deceived, as much as you are if you think I do not love you enough. Tell me, my dearest, am I? You will not be if you think I am

THE AGE OF GALLANTRY

True love is like seeing ghosts: we all talk about it but few of us have ever seen one.
                    La Rochefoucauld: Maxims

As long as it is the Nature of Man . . . . to have a Salt Itch under the breeches, the Brimstone under the Petticoat will be necessary to lay it.
                    Bernard Mandeville: Defence of the Public Stews

Hail, wedded Love, mysterious law, true source
Of human offspring, sole propriety
In Paradise . . . .
                    Milton: Paradise Lost

Towards the end of the seventeenth century, as the grip of religion on society was loosened, love was taken less seriously. At least, love lost its other-worldly, devotional aspect. For seriously practising Protestants marriage was sacred, the manifestation of divine love on earth. But this idea was – as Protestant ideas tended to be – expedient and economical. The world was by no means well lost for love. In the 1680s the first sex-manuals were published, emphasising that good sex was the basis for a good marriage. Indeed, perhaps the most revolutionary idea at this time was that sexual pleasure should no longer be regarded as criminal.

At the extra-marital end of things the emphasis was also on realism. In France, the head tutor of a salon for the schooling of lovers, Ninon de Lenclos (1620-1705), was sending out her pupils armed with the following philosophy:

> "It takes one hundred times more intelligence to make love well than to command armies."

> "I have always sworn to my lovers to love them eternally, but for me eternity is a quarter of an hour.".

> "The woman who loves but one man will never know love."

In England in 1709 Richard Steele offered readers of *The Tatler* the following advice on how to write a love-letter – advice that runs counter to all the rules of courtly or chivalrous love:

> 'I am of the opinion, writing has lost more mistresses than any one mistake in the whole legend of love. For when you write to a lady for whom you have a solid and honourable passion, the great idea you have of her, join'd to a quick sense of her absence, fills your mind with a sort of tenderness, that gives your language too much the air of complaint, which is seldom successful...women of spirit are not to be won by mourners...If possible, therefore, divert your mistress rather than sigh for her. The pleasant man she will desire for her own sake, but the languishing lover has nothing to hope for but her pity.'

2ND EARL OF CHESTERFIELD   BARBARA VILLIERS
1633–1713   1641–1709

Philip Stanhope, the 2nd Earl of Chesterfield was one of the most fashionable rakes of the Restoration and the most serious of his many affairs was with Barbara Villiers. However, while Chesterfield was in the Tower accused of wounding a Captain Whalley in a duel, she married a worthy gentleman called Roger Palmer. This was a bit of a mistake as is indicated in her letter of 1659 to Chesterfield suggesting an elopement. The following year she became the King's mistress, and her husband, Mr Palmer, soon found himself the Earl of Castlemaine.

Evidently a good friend of Barbara Villiers was Lady Ann Hamilton, the second lover whom Chesterfield had – if we go by Pepys' information – the rather unhealthy pleasure of sharing with royalty. Pepys noted in his diary: 'Mr Povy and I in his coach to Hide Parke, being the first day of the Tour there – where many brave ladies. Among others, Castlemayne lay impudently upon her back in her coach, asleep with her mouth open. There was also my Lady Kerneeguy, once my Lady Anne Hambleton, that is said to have given the Duke of York a clap upon his first coming over, (Lord's Day, 19 March 1665).

LADY ANN HAMILTON AND BARBARA VILLIERS TO CHESTERFIELD – 1657

My Lord

My friend and I are now abed together a-contriving how to have your company this afternoon. If you deserve this favour, you will come and seek us at Ludgate Hill about three a clock at Butler's shop, where we will expect you, but lest we should give you too much satisfaction at once, we will say no more; expect the rest when you see

Your &c

BARBARA VILLIERS TO CHESTERFIELD AT TONBRIDGE – 1657

My Lord

I came just now from the Duchess of Hamilton, and there I found to my great affliction, that the Lady Ann was sent to Windsor, and the World says that you are the occasion of it. I am sorry to hear that having a kindness for you is so great a crime that people are to suffer for it; the only satisfaction that one doth receive is that their cause is so glorious that it is sufficient to preserve a tranquillity of mind, that all their malice can never discompose. I see that the fates were resolved to make me happier than I could expect, for when I came home I found a letter that came from your Lordship, which makes me believe that amongst the pleasures you receive in the place where you are which I hear affords great plenty of fine Ladies, you sometimes think of her who is

My Lord

Your &c

BARBARA VILLIERS TO CHESTERFIELD – 1657

My Lord

The Joy I had of being with you the last night, has made me do nothing but dream of you, and my life is never pleasant to me but when I am with you or talking of you, yet the discourses of the world must make me a little more circumspect, therefore I desire you not to come tomorrow but to stay till the party be come to Town. I will not fail to meet you on Saturday morning till when I remain your humble servant.

LADY ANN HAMILTON TO CHESTERFIELD – 1658

My Lord

I have too good an opinion of you, not to believe you grateful, and that made me think you would not be satisfied if I should leave you forever without a farewell, and since I shall not be in a capacity of giving you one as I would, I thought fit to send you this advertisment that you may give me some adieus with your eyes, since it is to be done no other way. I am

My Lord

Your &c

CHESTERFIELD TO LADY ANN HAMILTON – 1658

Madam

Soon after your Ladyship's departure, I came to Town and went to the Park and Spring Garden, just as some do to Westminster to see those Monuments that have contained such great and lovely persons; seriously Madam I may well make the comparison, since you that were the soul of this little world have carried all the life of it with you, and left us so dull that I have quite left off the making love to five or six at a time, and do wholly content myself with the being as much as is possible.

Madam
Your &c

BARBARA PALMER (NÉE VILLIERS) TO CHESTERFIELD - 1659

My Lord

Since I saw you I have been at home and I find the monsieur* in a very ill humour, for he says that he is resolved never to bring me to Town again, and that nobody shall see me when I am in the country. I would not have you come today, for that will displease him more, but send me word presently what you would advise me to do, for I am ready and willing to go all over the world with you, and I will obey your commands that am while I live,

Yours

CHESTERFIELD TO BARBARA PALMER - 1660

Madam

My letters have equally with my thoughts attended you from all the considerable parts of my journey, and when compassion or gratitude has probably obliged you to make a return, I have thought all my sufferings not meritorious of their recompense, but Madam, the news I have from England concerning your Ladyship makes me doubt of everything, and therefore let me intreat you to send me your Picture, for then I shall love something that is like you and yet unchangeable, and though it will have no great return of kindness, yet I am sure it will love nobody else better than your very humble servant.

CHESTERFIELD TO BARBARA PALMER - 1661

Madam

Let me not live, if I did believe that all the women on earth could have given me so great an affliction as I have suffered by your displeasure, Tis true, I ever loved you as one should do in heaven, that is, more than the world, but I

*monsieur is her husband

never thought you would have sent me there before my time. I confess I have always found you so just, and so apt to excuse the faults of your friends, that I had rather be condemned to lose the light than your kindness, but therefore do not suffer one to perish who desires only to live upon your account. Besides, naturally I hate dying, and it is one of the last things I would willingly do to show my passion, yet if you will neither answer my letters, nor speak to me before I go out of Town, it is more than an even lay that I shall never come in to it again, and then about three parts of all the love that mankind has for you, will be lost in

Your obedient servant

Lady Russell was the grand-daughter of Robert Carr, Earl of Somerset, the infamous favourite of James I, and sister to Lord William Russell, who was unjustly executed in the wake of the 'Rye House' Plot to depose the King in 1683.

CHESTERFIELD TO LADY RUSSELL – 1661.

Dearest Joy of my Life

You have obliged me more by your letter than I could have expected, for I shall ever value the least mark of your kindness above all other things. I am now dismally alone, and you may easily believe the want I have of your company, for how often do I wish to have you again in my arms, how often do I please myself with the thoughts of the joys we have had, and how often do I resolve to love you as long as I live, and yet I need not resolve it, because it is impossible for me to love you less. I am now going to Scarborough and soon after that to London, so that I am not likely to see you neither this summer nor the next winter, and God knows how old your absence in that time will make me; but I would put off these journeys, my business, or anything to have you here, Ah if I had but hold of your <*> how quickly would I pull you to me and kiss you a thousand times, but these fancies make me extravagant, and I am lost in love's labyrinth, whenever I come to mention the passion with which I am

Dearest Life

Your &c

*Word erased on original letter

CHESTERFIELD TO LADY RUSSELL – 1661

Madam

The dullness of this last cold season doth afford nothing that is new to divert you, only here is a report that I would fain know the truth of, which is, that I am extremely in love with you, pray let me know if it be true or no, since I am certain that nobody but yourself can rightly inform me, for if you intend to use me favourably and do think that I am in love with you, I most certainly am so, and if you intend to receive me coldly and do not believe that I am in love, I also am sure that I am not . . . .

MARIANNA ALCOFORADO
1640–1723

As he rode past the convent of Beja, which was one of the richest and most well-appointed in Portugal, M. Noel Bouton, afterwards Marquis of Chamilly & St. Leger (1636–1715), a captain of cavalry in the army of Louis XIV, was seen by one of the nuns. Her name was Marianna Alcoforado , and she lived in a sort of self-contained flat called a *casa*, an arrangement strictly forbidden but universally winked at – presumably for some financial consideration – by the ecclesiastical authorities. Before long the two of them were solacing each other in the *casa* – until the whiff of scandal obliged him to leave. He certainly appreciated the letters she proceeded to write to him, full of pain, grief and desire, but probably not in quite the way she meant them to be appreciated. He decided they were too good to be kept to himself and had them published almost immediately. *The Letters of a Portuguese Nun* came out in 1669 – anonymously (he may have had the proper emotional obtuseness of a soldier, but he was not a complete blackguard) and to great and lasting acclaim: Elizabeth Barret Browning's *Sonnets from the Portuguese* were based on them.

With unparalleled insight, these letters reflect – from within the experience – all the complexities and nuances of feeling that accompany an overmastering and hopeless passion. As she goes on, Alcoforado evidently becomes aware that she is writing a masterpiece of sorts, but warns Bouton against taking any credit for it.

ALCOFORADO TO BOUTON

. . . . I refuse to believe that you have forgotten me. Surely I am wretched enough without torturing myself with vain hopes! Yet why should I go out of my way to forget all the care you took to prove that you loved me? That was so precious a thing to me that it would be most thankless of me not to go on loving you as passionately as when I knew the rapture of hearing you say that you loved me. Is it possible that such happy memories should have become so cruel? Must they believe their nature and become no more than the tyrannis-ers of my heart? Alas, what a condition that heart was brought to by your last letter! I could actually feel it struggling, as it seemed, to separate itself from me and go in search of you. I was so stunned by the violence of my emotion that I lost consciousness for three hours. I fought against coming back to a life which I must lose for you since I cannot keep it for you; but in spite of myself I recov-ered at last and allowed myself the flattering belief that I was dying of love and I was comforted with the thought that my heart was no longer to be torn with grieving over your absence.

ALCOFORADO TO BOUTON

. . . . I know that my love for you is sheer madness, yet I do not at all com-plain of the violence of my emotions; I am used to the torture of them and I could not live without the pleasure that I feel in loving you in the midst of a thousand sorrows. But I am racked by a hatred and disgust for everything: my family, my friends and this convent are unbearable to me: all that I have to look at, every task I have to do, is hateful to me: I am so jealous of my passion that all my actions and duties seem to have to do with you. Yes, I begrudge every moment that is not devoted to you. Alas! what should I do without so great hatred and love to fill my heart? Could I survive the loss of this unceas-ing occupation of my thoughts, and live a calm and passionless life? I could never content myself with such unfeeling emptiness.

I have no right to speak to you of a love which disgusts you – and I will not do so again. It is very nearly a year since I gave my whole heart to you: you seemed truly and honestly to return my love and I could never have believed that my endearments would become so hateful to you that you would go five hundred leagues and run the risk of shipwreck to escape from them. I did not deserve such treatment from anybody. You can remember my modesty, my blushes and my shame, but you do not remember what made you love me in spite of yourself. The officer who is waiting for this letter has just told me for the fourth time that he wants to start. What a hurry he is in! No doubt he is deserting some miserable woman in this country!

Good-bye. It is harder for me to finish this letter than it was for you to leave me, perhaps for ever. Good-bye. I dare not call you by a thousand dear names, nor give way to my emotion without constraint. I love you a thousand times more than my life, and a thousand times more than I know. How hard, how cruel you are to me! You never write to me. I cannot help saying that again. But I am starting all over again, and the officer will be going. What does it matter? Let him go. I write more for my own sake than for yours; I am only trying to find some comfort. Also the length of this letter will frighten you and you will not read it. What have I done to be made so unhappy? Why have you poisoned my life?

ALCOFORADO TO BOUTON

. . . . It is unfaithful of me to go on living: to act as if it matters whether I live or die. O, I could die with the shame of it! For it looks as if my only true despair were in my letters. If I loved you as much as I have told you a thousand times, should I not have been dead long ago? I have deceived you, and it is you, you, who have cause to complain of me. Alas! why do you not complain? I have seen you go away, I can have no hope of your ever coming back, and yet I am alive. I have betrayed you; I entreat you to forgive me. But do not forgive me. Be a tyrant to me. Say that I do not love you violently enough. Be more difficult to please. Tell me that you wish me to die for love of you. I beseech you to help me in this way so that I may master my womanly weakness and in one supreme act of true despair make an end of all my infirmity of purpose. Such a grim ending would surely compel you to think often of me; my memory would be dear to you and you would perhaps be genuinely moved by so remarkable a death. Would it not be better than the condition to which you have brought me?

Good-bye. I could very well wish that I had never seen you. Oh, how keenly I feel what a lie that is: for I know as I write to you at this moment that I would far rather be miserable in loving you than never have seen you. Therefore I accept the sadness of my fate without complaining, since it has not been your wish to make it happier. Good-bye. Promise that you will feel some tender regret for me if I die of grief, and that the violence of my passion may at least awake in you some feeling of distaste and want of sympathy for everything else. That will be consolation enough for me; and if I must give you up for always, I should wish not to leave you to another. What greater cruelty could there be than for you to make use of my despair to enhance your attractiveness for others and as a proof that you have inspired the deepest passion in the world?

ALCOFORADO TO BOUTON

I put all my unhappiness down to my having so blindly abandoned myself to my love for you; for should I not have known that the pleasures of that love would come to an end, but that love itself would not? How could I expect you to stay in Portugal all your life and to give up your fortune and your country and think only of me? There can be no relief for my sorrow, for it only weighs me down with despair when I remember the happiness that I have had. Must my every wish prove abortive? Shall I never again see you in my room, never again experience those delirious embraces of yours? Alas! that is a vain hope; for I know too well that all the passion that filled my heart and head awoke no answering passion in you except a desire for certain pleasures which died with their achievement. In those too happy moments I ought to have called upon my reason to help me to govern the fatal excess of my joy and to warn me of the unhappiness which has now come to me. But I gave myself entirely to you and was in no mood to think of anything which might kill my happiness or hinder my full enjoyment of your impassioned avowals of love. It was such pure pleasure to know that I was with you that I could not think of your ever being separated from me. Yet I remember saying to you sometimes that you would make me unhappy; but such fears were quickly swept aside, and I was happy to sacrifice them to you and to abandon myself to the witchery of your unfaithful protestations.

I can clearly see the cure for all my sufferings: for I should soon be free from them if I no longer loved you. But what a remedy! No, I would rather suffer even more, than forget you. Alas! have I any control in the matter? I cannot reproach myself with ever having wished for a moment not to love you any more. You are more to be pitied than I am, for it is better to suffer as I do than to enjoy the faded pleasures which your French mistresses give you. I do not grudge you your indifference; I am sorry for you. I defy you to forget me entirely. I flatter myself that all the pleasures which you take without me are unsatisfying. I am happier than you are, because I have more to occupy my thoughts, for I have lately been made portress of this convent. Everyone who speaks to me thinks I am mad, and I do not know what I say to them. The nuns must be as foolish as I am, to have thought me fit for a responsible post . . . .

ALCOFORADO TO BOUTON

Even now I am trying to find an excuse for you. I quite realize that it is not usual to love a nun. Yet it seems to me that, if a man could reason calmly about his choice, he would do far better to love a nun than any other woman. Nuns have nothing to hinder them from always thinking of their love, for they are not distracted by the thousand dissipations and duties of the world...

But I am not going to prove by argument that you ought to love me: that would be foolish, since I have tried far better methods without success. I am too much reconciled to my fate to fight against it. I shall be unhappy all the rest of my life: I was unhappy even when I saw you every day. The fear that you would not be faithful to me used almost to kill me; I wanted to see you every moment, and that was impossible; I was worried by the risk you ran in coming into the convent; I nearly died when you were away with the army; I despaired because I was not more beautiful and more worthy of you; I was troubled by my obscure station in life, and often feared that the love you seemed to have for me might do you harm; I thought I did not love you well enough; I was afraid of my family's anger against you; in fact I was in just as miserable a state as I am now...

But I brought all this sorrow upon myself! At the first I too simply showed you how deeply I loved you, and you took it for granted. It needs cunning to make oneself loved, it needs a skilful choice of provocations and seductions; love by itself can never engender love. You were determined to triumph over me, and having made up your mind to it there was nothing you would not have done to achieve your desire: you were even prepared to love me if that had been necessary; but you knew that there was no need of it, and that you could succeed without feeling any passion. What base treachery! Did you think you could deceive me with absolute impunity? If anything happens to bring you back to this country, I swear that I will give you up to my family's vengeance.

But in spite of everything, I do not think I can wish you any harm....

Chamilly married a rich, plain and agreeable woman in 1677 and rose to be a Marshall of France while Alcoforado also prospered in her own field. According to her obituary 'for thirty years she did rigid penance and suffered great infirmities with much submission, desiring to have more to suffer...'

JOHN CHURCHILL   SARAH JENNINGS
1650–1722   1660–1744
LATER DUKE AND DUCHESS OF MARLBOROUGH

Marlborough broke the French hegemony in Europe that had lasted for three hundred years, with a series of crushing defeats over the armies of Louis XIV between 1702 and 1712. Meanwhile, for much of this period, his wife Sarah ruled at home, as Queen Anne's favourite. When they fell in love in 1676, it was at the court of Charles II, when a girl had to be pretty self-possessed to preserve her virtue, and the brutally severe tone of the surviving letters from her to him probably reflect her determination not to be seduced by the dashing young Colonel of Guards. It was well known that Barbara Villiers, the King's mistress, had given him £5000 for gallantly dropping from her bedroom window upon hearing the royal knuckles on the door, and that on another occasion the King had actually discovered him in her cupboard. Besides, a marriage between a pretty, penniless young woman and an able penniless young man went against all the rules. But she managed to wring from him what his equally illustrious descendant, Winston Churchill, referred to as 'the only surrender to which the Duke of Marlborough was ever forced'.

CHURCHILL TO JENNINGS

It is not reasonable that you should have a doubt but that I love you above all expression, which by heaven I do. It is not possible to do anything to let you see your power more than my obedience to your commands of leaving you, when my tyrant-heart aches me to make me disobey; but it were much better it should break than to displease you. I will not, dearest, ask or hope to hear from you unless your charity pities me and will so far plead for me as to tell you that a man dying for you may hope that you will be so kind to him as to make a distinction betwixt him and the rest of his sex. I do love and adore you with all my heart and soul – so much that by all that is good I do and ever will be better pleased with your happiness than my own; but oh, my soul, if we might be both happy, what inexpressible joy would that be! But I will not think of any content but what you shall think fit to give, for 'tis you alone I love, so that if you are kind but one minute, that will make me happier than all the world can besides. I will not dare to expect more favour than you shall think fit to give, but could you ever love me, I think the happiness would be so great that it would make me immortal.

JENNINGS TO CHURCHILL

I am as little satisfied with this letter as I have been with many others, for I find all you will say is only to amuse me and make me think you have a passion for me, when in reality there is no such thing. You have reason to think it strange that I write to you after my last, where I protested that I would never write nor speak to you more; but as you know how much kindness I had for you, you can't wonder or blame me if I try once more, to hear what you can say for your justification. But this I must warn you of – that you don't hold disputes, as you have done always, and to keep me from answering of you, and yourself from saying what I expect from you, for if you go on in that manner I will leave you that moment, and never hear you speak more whilst I have life. Therefore pray consider if, with honour to me and satisfaction to yourself, I can see you; for if it be only to repeat those things which you said so oft, I shall think you the worst of men, and the most ungrateful; and 'tis to no purpose to imagine that I will be made ridiculous in the world when it is in your power to make me otherwise.

CHURCHILL TO JENNINGS

Yours last night found me so sick that I thought I should have died, and I have now so excessive a headache that I should not stir out all day but that the Duchess has sent me word that the Duke will see me this afternoon, so that at night I shall have the happiness to see you in the drawing-room. I cannot remember what it was I said to you that you took so ill, but one thing I do assure you, that I will never say or do aught willingly that I think you may take ill. Ah, my soul, did you love so well as I, you could never have refused my letter so barbarously as you did, for if reason had bade you do it, love would never have permitted it. But I will complain no more of it, but hope time and the truth of my love will make you love better.

CHURCHILL TO JENNINGS

You complain of my unkindness, but would not be kind yourself in answering my letter, although I begged you to do it. The Duchess goes to a new play to-day, and afterwards to the Duchess of Monmouth's, there to dance. I desire that you will not go thither, but make an excuse, and give me leave to come to you. Pray let me know what you do intend, and if you go to the play; for if you do, then I will do what I can to go, if [although] the Duke does not. Your not writing to me made me very uneasy, for I was afraid it was want of kindness in you, which I am sure I will never deserve by any action of mine.

JENNINGS TO CHURCHILL

At four o'clock I would see you, but that would hinder you from seeing the play, which I fear would be a great affliction to you, and increase the pain in your head, which would be out of anybody's power to ease until the next new play. Therefore, pray consider, and without any compliment to me, send me word if you can come to me without any prejudice to your health.

A stiff-necked response from Churchill at this point has been lost.

JENNINGS TO CHURCHILL

I have done nothing to deserve such a kind of letter as you have writ to me, and therefore I don't know what answer to give; but I find you have a very ill opinion of me, and therefore I can't help being angry with myself for having had too good a one of you; for if I had as little love as yourself, I have been told enough of you to make me hate you, and then I believe I should have been more happy than I am like to be now. However, if you can be so well contented never to see me as I think you can by what you say, I will believe you; though I have not other people; and after you are satisfied that I have not broke my word, you shall have it in your power to see me or not – and if you are contented without it I shall be extremely pleased.

CHURCHILL TO JENNINGS

It would have been much kinder in you, if you had been pleased to have been so good-natured to have found time to have written to me yesterday, especially since you are resolved not to appear when I might see you. But I am resolved to take nothing ill but to be your slave as long as I live, and so to think all things well that you do.

In 1677 they were engaged, but the duel continued.

CHURCHILL TO JENNINGS

It was unkind of you to go away last night since you knew that I came for no other purpose but to have the joy of seeing you, but I will not believe it was for want of love, for you are all goodness, the thought of which makes me love you above my own soul. If you shall be in the drawing-room tonight, send me word at what hour, so that I may order it so to be there at the same hour. I am now in my chamber, and will stay there as long as I can in hopes I may hear from you.

JENNINGS TO CHURCHILL

I am willing to satisfy the world and you that I am not now in the wrong, and therefore I give you leave to come tonight – not that I can be persuaded you can ever justify yourself, but I do it that I may be freed from the troubles of ever hearing from you more.

CHURCHILL TO JENNINGS

When I left my father last night, on purpose to come and speak with you, I did not believe that you would have been so unkind as to have gone away the minute I came in, fearing that I might else have spoke to you, which indeed I should have been very glad to have done. I beg you will give me leave to see you this night, at what hour you please. Pray let me hear from you, and if you do not think me impertinent for asking, I should be glad to know what made you go away.

CHURCHILL TO JENNINGS

You are very unjust in saying that I love you less than I did, for by all that is good I think I love better than ever I did. I am very sorry that you are not well and that I shall not see you today. I was three acts at the play for no other reason but that of seeing you. I was in the drawing-room almost an hour expecting you, which Mr Berkley can witness for me, for he was with me.

After twelve years of marriage:

SARAH TO JOHN CHURCHILL

Wherever you are whilst I have life my soul shall follow you, my ever dear Lord Marl., and wherever I am I shall only kill the time, wish for night that I may sleep, and hope the next day to hear from you.

After twenty-four years of marriage:

JOHN TO SARAH CHURCHILL

It is impossible to express with what a heavy heart I parted with you when I was at the waterside. I could have given my life to have come back, though I knew my own weakness so much I durst not, for I should have exposed myself to the company. I did for a great while have a perspective glass looking upon the cliffs in hopes I might have had one sight of you.

PRINCESS MARY
1662–1694

PRINCESS ANNE
1665–1714

James II had two daughters, both of whom became Queens of England. The first, Mary, married William of Orange, who deposed her own father in 1688. The second, Anne, came to the throne on the death of William and Mary. Both conducted a passionate but totally innocent correspondence with Frances Apsley, later Lady Bathurst. We include a selection of these letters as a curiosity. The sentiments expressed are clearly genuine, but they are mixed with girlish make-believe to produce an emotional confection of singular charm. The original manuscripts are almost devoid of punctuation and anarchic in their spelling. We have chosen to sacrifice the impression of a headlong rush of sentiments for the sake of clarity.

PRINCESS MARY TO FRANCES APSLEY - 1676

Who can imagine that my dear husband can be so love-sick for fear I do not love her? But I have more reason to think that she is sick of being weary of me, for in two or three years men are always weary of their wives and look for mistresses as soon as they can get them. But I think I am pretty well assured of the love of my dear. But if I had all that is to be had in the world I should never have enough. If my dearest oh! dearest Aurelia did but show half the love to me, as if I had speech to declare, should do to her, I should be the happiest creature in the world as now I am but in indifferent happiness; for nothing in the world I am sure can so much add to my pleasure as to love and to be loved again. For my part I have more love for you than I can possibly have for all the world besides. You do not expect from me a letter like your own this morning for I am sure Mr. Dryden and all the poets in the world put together could not make such another. I pretend to nothing in this world but, if it be possible, to tell my love I have for my Aurelia, to my dearest dearest husband, and ever beg of her to accept me as her most obedient wife

Mary Clorine

PRINCESS MARY TO FRANCES APSLEY - 1676

After my prayers to almighty god I come dear husband to make peace with you for it is a strange thing for man and wife to quarrel. But I find to my great sorrow that this has been a long contriving in your head, for you have been always with my sister, grudge one minute stay with me. But now at last you have found a happy occasion for you, though a very unhappy one for me, to quarrel with me. But I am sure I take it very ill of you for so slight an occasion. I have told you all along that if I should die I could not have told it; and you may be sure that if I would have told it to anybody it had been to you my dear cruel unkind Aurelia. Not but that I think my sister does deserve your love better a great deal than I, and so doubtless she does and has according to her dessert, but since you have forsaken me quite I have still the marks that you loved me once and now I do not doubt that my happy sister has the cornelian ring unhappy I should have had. She will write to you now unkind Aurelia when you are at the house but still I hope you will not go too soon for then I should be robbed of seeing you, unkind husband, as well as of your love. But she that has it will have your heart too and your letters too. Oh thrice happy she is happier than ever I was, for she has triumph over a rival that once was happy in your love till she with her alluring charms removed unhappy Clorine from your heart. Pray Aurelia – I cannot leave that loved name yet – dear Aurelia, for this is the last time I shall call you, so answer this letter that I may have one letter of your dear hand – writing to look upon and say this gold ring this piece of cornelian ring and this letter came from the cruel fair that loved me once. Now sometimes a good fancy comes into my head that this unkindess of yours proceeds from excess of love, but oh, that good fancy is crossed when I consider with what eager haste you called my happy rival when I denied to tell you and with what coldness she fained to come, but at last how you whispered and then laughed, as if you had said, 'now we are rid of her, let us be happy,' whilst poor unhappy I sat reading of a play, my heart ready to break, for I was reading where Massanisa comes first to Sophonisba and thought that scene so like my misery it made me ready to cry. But before my happy rival I would not show my weakness, but now with Sophonisba I may cry out 'she thinks me false though I have been most true, and thinking so what may her furie do.' If I have said any nonsense pray forgive it for I think I am almost mad, but with this prayer I leave you, that in your new choice you may be most happy, that she may love you as well as I, for better I am sure she cannot. So with my prayers I leave you. Think sometimes of your unfortunate

Mary Clorine

PRINCESS MARY TO FRANCES APSLEY – 1676

Two letters already you have had today dear Aurelia from me. I hope you will read the third though you I suppose are tired with them now. I hope my pardon is sealed by you dear dear dear dear dear dear Aurelia. I may, if I can, tell you how much I love you but I hope that is not doubted. I have given you proof enough. If not I will die to satisfy you dear dear husband. If all my hairs were lives I would lose them all twenty times over to save or satisfy you . . . . I am for you all one desire, I love you with a flame more lasting than the vestal's fire. Thou art my life, my soul, my all that heaven can give: death's life with you, without you death to live. What can I say more to persuade you that I love you with more zeal than any lover can. I love you with a love that never was known by man. I have for you excess of friendship, more of love than any woman can for woman and more love than ever the constantest love had for his mistress. You are loved more than can be expressed by your ever-obedient wife, very affectionate friend, humble servant to kiss the ground where once you go, to be your dog on a string, your fish in a net, your bird in a cage, your humble trout.

Mary Clorine
Saturday three o'clock in the afternoon.

Princess Mary informs her 'husband' Frances Apsley that she is pregnant: 1678

Honslerdyck
9 August

I have a hundred thousand pardons to beg of my dear dear husband who, if I did not know to be very good and hope she loves me a little, still I could not so much as hope to be forgiven, but those considerations make me – tho very criminal for not having written since I was well again – begin to believe that so charitable a body as yourself cannot know how sorry I am for the fault and continue long angry. But if anything in the world can make amends for such a fault I hope trusting you with a secret will, which though in itself 'tis not enough, yet I tell you 'tis one. Yet I would hardly give myself leave to think on it, nor nobody leave to speak of it, not so much as to myself, and that I have not yet written the Duchess word who has always charged me to do it in all her letters. It is what I am ashamed to say, but seeing it is to my husband I may, tho I have reason to fear – because the sea parts us – you may believe it is a bastard. But yet I think upon a time of need I may make you own it, since 'tis not out of the four seas. In the meantime if you have any care of your own reputation consequently you must have of your wife's too. You ought to keep this a secret, since, if it should be known, you might get a pair of horns and nothing else by the bargain. But dearest Aurelia you may be very well assured, tho I have played the whore a little, I love you of all things in the world . . . .

PRINCESS ANNE TO FRANCES APSLEY – 1679

Bruxsells

22 September

Dear Semandra, none deserves more love from everybody than you nor none has a greater share in my heart than yourself excepting whom you know I must love better. I am not one of those who can express a great deal, and therefore it may be thought I do not love so well, but whoever thinks so is much mistaken, for tho I have not, maybe, so good a way of expressing myself as some people have, yet I assure you I love you as well as those that do, and perhaps more than some. Ever since I came I have been in haste when I write to you so that I never could say much to you. Now I think I have time and therefore will begin to write a long letter. The Park here is very pretty but not so fine as ours at St. James'. There is in it a house where there is water works to be seen and to which I went one day, and indeed they are pretty. I saw a ball at court which far surpassed my expectations for it was very well. There we had lemonade, cinnamon water and chocolate sweet-meats, all very good, and truly all the people here are very civil and won't be otherwise except one is otherwise to them. All the fine churches and monasteries you know I must not see, so can give you no good account of them, but those things which I must needs see, as their images which are in every shop and corner of the street. The more I see of those fooleries and the more I hear of that Religion the more I dislike it. There is a walk a little way of which, if it were well kept, it would be very pretty, and here's a place which they call the 'cours' where they go round the street and there is all ye company every night like Hyde Park. I can give you account of nothing else because I have seen no more, Farewell dear Semandra.

Ziphares

RICHARD STEELE
1672–1729

Richard Steele is known today as one of the founders and major contributors to 'The Tatler' and 'The Spectator'. His notes and letters to Mary Scurlock, whom he married on September 9, 1707, are those of a morally irreproachable and more or less contented spouse – and therein lies their charm. Apparently, he begged his wife not to let anyone else ever look at his letters to her when he discovered that she had kept every one, but she happily and profitably published the lot after his death. It must be said that they augment rather than diminish his reputation.

STEELE TO MARY SCURLOCK

Aug.20, 1707

Madam

I beg pardon that my paper is not [finer], but I am forced to write from a coffee-house where I am attending about business. There is a dirty crowd of busy faces all around me, talking politics and managing stocks; while all my ambition, all my wealth, is love! Love, which animates my heart, sweetens my humour, enlarges my soul, and affects every action of my life.

St. James's Coffee-House
Sept. 1, 1707

Madam

It is the hardest thing in the world to be in love, and yet attend business. As for me, all who speak to me find me out, and I must lock myself up, or other people will do it for me.

A gentleman asked me this morning, "What news from Lisbon?" and I answered, "She's exquisitely handsome." Another desir'd to know "when I had been last at Hampton-court?" I replied, "Twill be on Tuesday come se'nnight." Pr'ythee allow me at least to kiss your hand before that day, that my mind may be in some composure. Oh love!

RICHARD TO MRS STEELE

Aug.12, 1708

Madam

I have your letter, wherein you let me know, that the little dispute we have had is far from being a trouble to you; nevertheless, I assure you, any disturbance between us is the greatest affliction to me imaginable. You talk of the judgement of the world; I shall never govern my actions by it, but by the rules of morality and right reason. I love you better than the light of my eyes, or the life-blood in my heart; but, when I have let you know that, you are also to understand, that neither my sight shall be so far enchanted, or my affection so much master of me, as to make me forget our common interest. To attend my business as I ought, and improve my fortune, it is necessary that my time and will should be under no direction but my own. Pray give my most humble service to Mrs. Binns. I write all this rather to explain my own thought to you than answer your letter distinctly. I enclose it to you, that, upon second thoughts, you may see the disrespectful manner in which you treat your affectionate, faithful husband.

RICHARD TO MRS STEELE

Five in the Evening, Sept. 19, 1708

Dear Prue, I send you seven pen'orth of walnuts at five a penny, which is the greatest proof I can give you at present of my being, with my whole heart, yrs.

The little horse comes back with the boy, who returns with him for me on Wednesday evening; in the meantime, I believe, it will be well that he runs in the Park. I am Mrs. Binns's servant.

Since I writ this I came to the place where the boy was order'd with the horses; and, not finding him, sent this bearer, lest you should be in fears, the boy not returning.

P.S. There are but 29 walnuts.

RICHARD TO MRS STEELE

Sept. 30, 1710

Dear Prue, – I am very sleepy and tired, but could not think of closing my eyes till I had told you I am, dearest creature, your most affectionate and faithful husband,

Richard Steele

From the Press one in the morning.
March 28, 1715

Dear Prue, – I will do everything you desire your own way
Yours ever,
Richard Steele

Feb.16, 1716
Dear Prue, – Sober or not, I am ever yours.

GABRIEL BULLOCK

In an issue of the Spectator, dated Wednesday, March 12, 1711, Richard Steele published a love letter addressed to a Mistress Margaret Clark, discovered 'wrapped about a Thread-Paper' by a 'Lady of good sense'. However, at the end of the letter, the name of the sender was missing. The complete letter was later delivered to Steele by the antiquary Browne Willis and published on March 17. Willis had, apparently, made a copy of the original before it had been torn.

He noted: 'I have been credibly informed that Mr. William Bullock, the famous comedian, is the descendant of this Gabriel, who begot Mr. William Bullock's great grandfather on the Body of the above-mentioned Mrs. Margaret Clark.' Whether or not this surmise can be accepted, what seems sure is that Gabriel Bullock was a substantial freeholder.

To her I very much respect, Mrs. Margaret Clark.

Lovely, and oh that I could write loving Mrs. Margaret Clark, I pray you let Affection excuse Presumption. Having been so happy as to enjoy the Sight of your sweet Countenance and comely Body, sometimes when I had Occasion to buy Treacle or Liquorish Powder at the Apothecary's Shop, I am so enamoured with you, that I can no more keep close my flaming Desire to become your Servant. And I am the more bold now to write to your sweet self, because I am now my own Man, and may match where I please; for my Father is taken away; and now I am come to my Living, which is Ten Yard Land, and a House; and there is never a Yard of Land in our Field but is as well worth ten Pound a Year, as a Thief's worth a Halter; and all my Brothers and Sisters are provided for: Besides I have good Household-stuff, though I say it, both Brass and Pewter, Linnens and Woollens; and though my House be thatched, yet if you and I match, it shall go hard but I will have one half of it slated. If you shall think well of this Motion, I will wait upon you as soon as my new Clothes is made and Hay-Harvest is in. I could, though I say it, have good Matches in our Town; but my Mother (God's Peace be with her) charged me upon her Death-Bed to marry a Gentlewoman, one who had been well trained up in Sowing and Cookery. I do not think but that if you and I can agree to marry, and lay our Means together, I shall be made Grand-Jury-man e'er two or three Years come about, and that will be a great Credit to us. If I could have got a Messenger for Sixpence, I wou'd have sent one on purpose, and some Trifle or other for a Token of my Love; but I hope there is nothing lost for that neither. So hoping you will take this Letter in good part, and answer it with what care and speed you can, I rest and remain,

Yours, if my own,

Mr Gabriel Bullock

now my father is dead.

Swepson, Leicestershire.

When the Coat Carts come, I shall send oftener; and may come in one of them my self.

GEORGE NILLSON

The Spectator's correspondent, now with the bit too firmly between his teeth to regard the nice distinction between the productions of long-dead correspondents and those of his contemporaries, also forwarded to Steele, for the edification of his readers, a couple of other letters. They had been written only a few years earlier 'by a Yorkshire gentleman of a good estate', George Nillson, to one Mary Norton, with a note to the local M.P. Sir William Aysenby asking for help with his suit. One can only hope that he was successful, and that Mrs. Lucy (her of the 'stinking carcase') was foiled in her dastardly machinations. The authenticity of the letters – and by association that of Gabriel Bullock – would seem to be borne out by the fact that this number of the Spectator had to be withdrawn when it came out in book form on the deprecation of a family – presumably from Yorkshire – who felt that their privacy had suffered an unwarranted intrusion.

Madam Mary. Deare loving sweet lady, I hope you are well. Do not go to london, for they will put you in the nunnery; and heed not Mrs Lucy what she saith to you, for she will lie and cheat you. Go to another Place and we will get wed so with speed. Mind what I write to you, for if they get you to London they will keep you there, and so let us get wed, and we will both go. So if you go to London, you rueing yourself. So heed not what none of them saith to you. Let us get wed, and we shall lie together any time. I will do anything for you to my poor. I hope the devil will fail them all, for a hellish Company there be. From their cursed trick and mischievous ways good lord bless and deliver both you and me.

I think to be at York the 24 day.

19 March, 1706

Madam Mary, I hope you are well. I am sorry that you went away from York. Dear loving sweet lady, I write to let you know that I do remain faithful; and if [you] can let me know where I can meet you, I will wed you, and I will do anything to my poor; for you are a good woman, and will be a loving Mistress. I am in trouble for you, so if you will come to York I will wed you. So with speed come, and I will have none but you. So, sweet love, heed not what to say to me, and with speed come: heed not what none of them say to you; your Maid makes you believe ought.

So dear love think of Mr. George Nillson with speed; I sent you 2 or 3 letters before.

I gave Mistress Elcock some notes, and they put me in prison all the night for me pains, and none knew where I was, and I did get cold.

But it is for Mrs. Lucy to go a good way from home, for in York and round about she is known; to write any more her deeds, the same will tell her soul is black within, her carcase stinks of hell.

JONATHAN SWIFT
1667–1745

Swift, author of *Gulliver's Travels*, satirist, poet and political polemicist, harried the follies and evils of his time from behind a number of different pseudonyms, and he was equally evasive in his relations with women. The red herring is his correspondence with Esther Johnson, (the illegitimate daughter of Sir William Temple) known as the *Journal to Stella*. In fact, these letters are indeed little more than a journal, invariably addressed to both Esther and her friend Rebecca Dingley in Dublin, and in them he never slips out of an avuncular pose of cheek-tweaking banter towards the two ladies.

However, he is decidedly coy about mentioning his meetings in England with Esther Van Homrigh, known to posterity as 'Vanessa', with whom he certainly did enjoy some fourteen years of discreet passion. Whether he was secretly married to one Esther or the other is a matter for speculation. There is some evidence of a child, who died in 1731, though again, curiously, it is not firmly established which Esther was the mother. 'Vanessa' died of T.B. in 1723, 'Stella' in 1727.

Swift's letters to Vanessa can be mystifying without a key to the secret language he employed to avoid any possibility of scandal: 'Cad' is short for 'Cadenus', which means himself in relation to Vanessa, 'Governor Huff' is Vanessa, '–' means some term of endearment, 'drinking coffee' means sex, and 'so low' means her black moods. Malkin is Van Homrigh's sister.

VAN HOMRIGH TO SWIFT – 1720

Is it possible that again you will do the very same thing I warned you of so lately? I believe you thought I only rallied when I told you, the other night, I would pester you with letters. Did not I know you very well, I should think you knew but little of the world, to imagine that a woman would not keep her word whenever she promised anything that was malicious. Had not you better a thousand times throw away one hour, at some time or other of the day, than to be interrupted in your business at this rate? For I know 'tis as impossible for you to burn my letters without reading them, as 'tis for me to avoid reproving you when you behave yourself so wrong. Once more I advise you, if you have any regard for your quiet, to alter your behaviour quickly; for I do assure you I have too much spirit to sit contented with this treatment. Now, because I love frankness extremely, I here tell you that I have determined to try all manner of human arts to reclaim you, and if all those fail, I am resolved to have recourse to the black one, which it is said, never does. Now see what inconveniences you will bring both me and yourself into. Pray think calmly of it. Is it not much better to come of yourself than to be brought by force, and that, perhaps, at a time when you have the most agreeable engagement in the world? For when I undertake anything, I don't love to do it by halves. But there is one thing that falls out very luckily for you, which is that, of all the passions, revenge hurries me least, so that you have it yet in your power to turn all this fury into good humour, and, depend upon it, and more I assure you. Come at what time you please, you can never fail of being very well received.

SWIFT TO VAN HOMRIGH.

12 August, 1720

I'm vexed that the weather hinders you from any pleasure in the country, because walking, I believe, would be of good use to you and Malkin. I reckon you will return a prodigious scholar, a most admirable nursekeeper, a perfect housewife and a great drinker of coffee. I have asked, and am assured there is not one beech in all your groves to carve a name on, nor a purling stream, for love or money, except a great river, which sometimes roars, but never murmurs – just like Governor Huff. We live here in a very dull Town, every valuable creature absent, and Cad – says he is weary of it, and would rather drink his coffee on the barrenest, highest mountain in Wales, than be King here.

A fig for partridges and quails;
Ye dainties, I know nothing of ye,
But on the highest mount in Wales
Would choose in peace to drink my coffee.

What would you give to have the history of Cad and –, exactly written, through all its steps, from the beginning to this time? I believe it would do well in verse, and be as long as the other. I hope it will be done. It ought to be an exact chronicle of twelve years, from the time of spilling the coffee to drinking coffee, from Dunstable to Dublin, with every single passage since. There would be the chapter of the blister; the chapter of Madam going to Kensington; the chapter of the Colonel's going to France; the chapter of the wedding, with the adventure of the lost key; of the strain; of the joyful return; two hundred chapters of madness; the chapter of long walks; the Berkshire surprise; fifty chapters of little times; the chapter of Chelsea; the chapter of swallow and cluster; a hundred whole books of myself and 'so low'; the chapter of hide and whisper; the chapter of Who made it so? My sister's money. Cad bids me tell you, that if you complain of his puzzling you with difficult writing, he will give you enough of it.

VAN HOMRIGH TO SWIFT

Celbridge 1720

Believe me 'tis with the utmost regret that I now complain to you, because I know your good nature, such that you cannot see any human being miserable without being sensibly touched. Yet what can I do? I must either unload my heart and tell you all my griefs, or sink under the unexpressible distress I now suffer by your prodigious neglect of me. 'Tis now ten long weeks since I saw you, and in all that time I have never received but one letter from you and a little note, with an excuse. Oh –, –, –, how have you forgot me! You endeav-our by severities to force me from you; nor can I blame you, for with the utmost distress and confusion, I behold myself the cause of uneasy reflections to you. Yet I cannot comfort you, but here declare that 'tis not in the power of art, time or accident to lessen the unexpressible passion, which I have for –, –, –. Put my passion under the utmost restraint, send me as distant from you as the earth will allow, yet you cannot banish those charming ideas, which will ever stick by me, whilst I have the use of memory. Nor is the love I bear you only seated in my soul, for there is not a single atom of my frame that is not blended with it. Therefore, don't flatter yourself that separation will ever change my sentiments, for I find myself unquiet in the midst of silence, and my heart is at once pierced by sorrow and love. For Heaven's sake, tell me what caused this prodigious change in you, which I have found of late. If you have the least remains of pity for me left, tell me tenderly. No, don't tell it, so that it may cause my present death; and don't suffer me to live a life like a lan-guishing death, which is the only life I can lead, if you have lost any of your tenderness for me.

SWIFT TO VAN HOMRIGH

Gaulstown, near Kinnegad

5 July, 1721

It was not convenient, hardly possible, to write to you before now, though I had a more than ordinary desire to do it, considering the disposition I found you in last; though I hope I left you in a better. I must here beg you to take more care of your health, by company and exercise, or else the spleen will get the better of you, than which there is not a more foolish or troublesome disease; and what you have no pretences in the world to, if all the advantages of life can be any defence against it. Cad – assures me he continues to esteem and love and value you above all things, and so will do to the end of his life, but at the same time entreats that you will not make yourself or him unhappy by imaginations. The wisest men of all ages have thought it the best course to seize the minutes as they fly, and to make every innocent action an amusement. If you knew how I struggle for a little health, what uneasiness I am at in riding and walking, and refraining from everything agreeable to my taste, you would think it but a small thing to take a coach now and then, and to converse with fools or impertinents, to avoid spleen and sickness. Without health, you will lose all desire of drinking your coffee, and so low as to have no spirits...

I can say no more, being called away, mais soyez assurée que jamais personne du monde a été aimée, honorée, estimée, adorée par votre amie que vous. I drank no coffee since I left you, nor intend to till I see you again. There is none worth drinking but yours, if myself may be the judge.

Rest assured that you are the only person on earth who has ever been loved, honoured, esteemed, adored by your friend.

ALEXANDER POPE
1688–1744

Pope, who dominated the literary world of his time by his perfect tech-
nical mastery of the heroic couplet and the epigrammatic wit and invective he put into it, was provided with a physique that fuelled his poetic
invective but made normal relations with women very difficult. At four
and a half feet high, the convention of his day that one should greet a
woman with a kiss could only be a humiliating exercise. He was also
hunch-backed and spindle-shanked, with various recurring complications that rendered him an invalid for much of his life. Where he scored
was in the composition of polished epistles of extravagant flattery and
adoration. However, the letters he wrote to Martha and Teresa Blount
carry the unmistakeable signs of a deeper and more committed regard.
In 1717 he settled an annuity of £40 on Teresa, the more high-spirited
and spendthrift of the two – until she married – which seems to have
spoiled their relationship. Martha, as is evident from his last letter to
her, he loved to his dying day.

POPE TO TERESA BLOUNT

7 August 1716

Madam – I have so much Esteem for you, and so much of the other thing,
that were I a handsome fellow I should do you a vast deal of good: but as it is,
all I am good for is to write a civil letter, or to make a fine Speech. The truth
is, that considering how often & how openly I have declared Love to you, I am
astonished (and a little affronted) that you have not forbid my correspondence, & directly said, *See my face no more.* It is not enough, Madam, for your
reputation, that you keep your hands pure, from the Stain of Such Ink as
might be shed to gratify a male Correspondent; Alas! while your heart con-
sents to encourage him in this lewd liberty of writing, you are not (indeed you
are not) what you would so fain have me think you, a Prude! I am vain enough
to conclude (like most young fellows) that a fine Lady's Silence is Consent,
and so I write on.

But in order to be as Innocent as possible in this Epistle, I'll tell you news.
You have asked me News a thousand times at the first word you spoke to me,
which some would interpret as if you expected nothing better from my lips:
And truly 'tis not a sign Two Lovers are together, when they can be so imperti-

nent as to enquire what the World does? All I mean by this is, that either you or I cannot be in love with the other; I leave you to guess which of the two is that stupid & insensible Creature, so blind to the others Excellencies and Charms . . . .

POPE TO TERESA AND MARTHA BLOUNT – 1717

Mapledurham

Dear Ladies, – I think myself obliged to desire, you would not put off any Diversion you may find, in the prospect of seeing me on Saturday, which is very uncertain. I Take this occasion to tell you once for all, that I design no longer to be a constant Companion when I have ceas'd to be an agreeable one. You only have had, as my friends, the priviledge of knowing my Unhappiness; and are therefore the only people whom my Company must necessarily make melancholy. I will not bring myself to you at all hours, like a Skeleton, to come across your diversions, and dash your pleasures: Nothing can be more shocking than to be perpetually meeting the Ghost of an old acquaintance, which is all you can ever see of me.

You must not imagine this to proceed from any Coldness, or the least decrease of Friendship to you. If You had any Love for me, I should be always glad to gratify you with an Object that you thought agreeable. But as your regard is Friendship & Esteem; those are things that are as well, perhaps better, preserv'd Absent than Present. A Man that you love is a joy to your eyes at all times; a Man that you Esteem is a solemn kind of thing, like a Priest, only wanted at a certain hour to do his Office: 'Tis like Oil in a Salad, necessary, but of no manner of Taste. And you may depend upon it, I will wait upon you on every real occasion, at the first summons, as long as I live.

Let me open my whole heart to you: I have sometimes found myself inclined to be in love with you: and as I have reason to know from your Temper & Conduct how miserably I should be used in that circumstance, it is worth my while to avoid it: It is enough to be Disagreeable, without adding Fool to it, by constant Slavery. I have heard indeed of Women that have had a kindness for Men of my Make; but it has been after Enjoyment, never before; and I know to my Cost you have had no Taste of that Talent in me, which most Ladies would not only Like better, but Understand better, than any other I have.

I love you so well that I tell you the truth, & that has made me write this Letter. I will see you less frequently this winter, as you'll less want company. When the Gay Part of the world is gone, I'll be ready to stop the Gap of a vacant hour whenever you please. Till then I'll converse with those who are more Indifferent to me, as You will with those who are more Entertaining. I wish you every pleasure God and Man can pour upon ye; and I faithfully promise you all the good I can do you, which is the Service of a Friend, who will ever be Ladies, Entirely Yours.

POPE TO TERESA BLOUNT – [1717/18]

> Mapledurham
>
> 21 February

Madam, – I am too much out of order to trouble you with a long letter. But I desire to know what is your meaning to resent my complying with your request, & endeavouring to serve you in the way you proposed, as if I have done you some great injury? You told me if such a thing was the secret of my heart, you should entirely forgive and think well of me. I told it, & find the contrary – You pretended so much generosity, as to offer your Services in my behalf: the minute after, you did me as ill an office as you could, in telling the party con-cerned, it was all but an Amusement occasione'd by my Loss of another Lady.

You expressed your self desirous of increasing your present income upon Life: I proposed the only method I then could find, & you encourag'd me to proceed in it – when it was done, you received it as if it were an Affront. – Since when, I find the very thing, in the very manner you wished, & mention it to you; You don't think it worth an answer.

If your meaning be, that the very things you ask, and wish, become Odious to you, when it is I that comply with 'em, or bring 'em about; pray own it, & deceive me no longer with any thought, but that you Hate me. My Friendship is too warm & sincere to be trifled with; therefore if you have any meaning, tell it me, or you must allow me to take away That which perhaps you don't care to keep.

> Your humble Servant. A.P.

I shall speedily obey you in sending the Papers you order'd; which when I do, Be pleas'd to sign the enclos'd receipt, & return it by the bearer of 'em.

POPE TO MARTHA BLOUNT

25 March, 1744

Dear Madam, – Writing is become very painful to me, if I would write a letter of any length... I assure you I do not think half so much of me as of you, and when I grow worst I find the anxiety for you doubled.

Would to God you would Quicken your haste to settle, by reflecting what a pleasure it would be to me, just to see it, and to see you at ease; & then I could contentedly leave you to the Providence of God, in this Life, & resign my Self to it in the other! I have little to say to you when we meet; but I love you upon unalterable Principles, which makes me feel my heart the same to you as if I saw you every hour. adieu.

VOLTAIRE
1694–1778

If there is a literary equivalent of Mozart, then that man would have to be Voltaire, born Francois Marie Arouet. According to Goethe he was the greatest writer of all time. James Boswell informed Rousseau – rather tactlessly – that Voltaire's conversation was the most brilliant he had ever heard. For much of his long life he was the most influential man in Europe, producing an enormous quantity of work as philosopher, poet, playwright, novelist, historian, social reformer and political activist. His letters alone fill 60 volumes. He was always susceptible to women. At the age of seventy he produced a closely annotated edition of the complete works of Corneille in twelve volumes in order to raise a dowry for Corneille's grand-daughter.

Fifty years earlier he was ready to offer his own hand to a girl of distinctly less illustrious forebears. He had been packed off to The Hague in the fond hope that his fancy literary ideas might be stifled amongst a more stolid people than the Parisians. When he announced his intention to marry his mistress, Olympe Du Noyer, the barely literate daughter of a resourceful woman who edited a scurrilous anti-French news-sheet entitled *La Quintessance des nouvelles historiques, critiques, politiques, morales et galantes*, he was confined to his lodgings. Following a secret exchange of letters she called on him dressed as a man, but they were discovered before they could elope, and he was bundled back to Paris. Three years later, when he was beaten up and imprisoned for insulting the Chevalier de Rohan, her letter was found on him. He was still writing to her thirty years later.

VOLTAIRE TO OLYMPE DU NOYER

28 November 1713

I am a prisoner here in the name of the king, but they have the power only to take my life, not my love for you. Yes, my adorable beloved, I will see you this evening, even if this puts my head on the block. For god's sake don't talk to me in such mournful terms as those of your letter; live, and be discreet: beware of your mother, for she is your cruellest enemy. What do I say! Beware of everybody, trust nobody, be ready as soon as the moon appears, I will leave the hotel incognito, I will take a coach or chaise, we will go like the wind to Schevelin [Scheveningen], I will bring ink and paper, we will write our letters. But if you love me, console yourself; gather all your virtue and presence of mind, control yourself when you are with your mother, try to bring your portrait, and be sure that not even the greatest sufferings will prevent me from serving you. No, nothing is capable of detaching me from you: our love is based on virtue, it will last as long as our life. Order the cobbler to go for a chaise; but no, I don't want you to trust him. Be ready at four o'clock, I will wait for you near your street. Farewell, there is nothing I will not risk for you, you deserve much more. Farewell, my dear heart.

DU NOYER TO VOLTAIRE

6 December 1713

In the uncertainty in which I am whether I shall have the pleasure of seeing you this evening I warn you that it wasn't la Vruijere who was yesterday at our place; 'twas a misunderstanding by the cobbler's wife who alarmed us for nothing at all. My mother does not suspect at all that I have spoken to you and thank heaven she thinks that you have already left. I won't speak to you of my health, it's what worries me least and I think too much about you to have the time to think of myself. I assure you my dear heart that if I doubted your tenderness my troubles would rejoice me. Yes, my dear child, life would be too great a burden if I did not have the tender hope of being loved by what is dearest to me in all the world. Do what you can so that I can see you this evening; you need only descend into the kitchen of the cobbler and I assure you that you have nothing to fear, for our maker of Quintessances thinks that you are already half-way to Paris, so that if you want to I shall have the pleasure of seeing you this evening; and if it cannot be allowed me to go tomorrow to mass at the house, I will beg M. de la Bruyere to show me the chapel – curiousities is permitted to women – and then *as if nothing were the matter* I will ask him if they yet had any news of you and since when you were gone. Don't refuse me this favour, my dear Arouet, I ask it of you in the name of what is most tender, that is, in the name of the love I have for you. Farewell my amiable child, I adore you and I swear to you that my love will last as long as my life.

Dunoyer

> Voltaire fell in love with his niece, Marie Louise Denis in 1741, shortly before her husband's early death, which, it must be said, was sincerely lamented by Voltaire, probably even more so than by Denis' ever-calculating widow. He was besotted with her though he was soon made aware that she was a bad apple, and he finally, regretfully, dismissed her – with ample provision – on 1 March 1768 after one outrage too many. She had seduced a young writer under their roof and encouraged him to steal and publish a satire on Calvinism that he was keeping under lock and key as potentially damaging to relations with Geneva. These early love-letters are translated from the Italian.

VOLTAIRE TO MME. DENIS – DECEMBER 1745

I don't know yet when my affairs will allow me to leave a place I abhor. The court, society, the great ones of the earth bore me. I shall be happy only when I can live with you. Your company, and better health would make me happy. A thousand kisses. My soul kisses yours, my prick and my heart are in love with you. I kiss your pretty bottom and all your adorable person.

VOLTAIRE TO MME. DENIS – DECEMBER 1745

You have written me a ravishing letter, which I have kissed. I am not surprised that you write so well in Italian. It is very right and proper that you should be expert in the language of love. Good heavens! How do you manage? Are so many charms really buried in disuse? You, not going to bed with anyone? Oh my dear one, you insult your god. You tell me that my letter gave pleasure even to your senses. Mine are like yours, I could not read the delicious words you wrote me without feeling inflamed to the depths of my being. I paid your letter the tribute I should have liked to pay to the whole of your person. The pleasures of the senses pass and flee in the twinkling of an eye, but the affection that binds us, the mutual confidence, the pleasures of the heart, the sensual joys of the soul, are not destroyed and do not perish thus. I will love you until death.

You will find here in my bedroom the four tickets for 'Armide' by Lully. I should like to come and lay them at your feet and then to make the journey from Paris to Versailles with my dear Denis. Good-bye, a thousand kisses.

VOLTAIRE TO MME. DENIS – OCTOBER 1746

My dear, I had already heard of the great victory of our proud Saxon Maurice over poor Prince Charles, Prince of Lorraine, always on the war-path and always beaten. Thanks be given to our Saxon Achilles. I feel like drinking his health with you. But I beg you to be sober and to make me sober. I ask your leave to bring my limpness. It would be better to have an erection, but whether I have an erection or not, I will always love you, you will be the only consolation of my life.

VOLTAIRE TO MME. DENIS – 1747

True to my laudable habit I have not digested, but the heart rejoices when the stomach annoys. What! You are writing me verse, my dear! Well, let us put it to music. Rameau is coming here, he will sing you his act in his hoarse voice. Be here about two o'clock if you can. You are adorable, and I love you with all my heart. If you want to dine here I will send out for whatever you fancy, and we will have ices. A thousand kisses.

V.

JAMES BOSWELL
1740–1795

Boswell, diarist and biographer of Dr Johnson, got his sentimental education, like so many of his countrymen, abroad. Indeed, he received the final touches, consisting of some expert tuition in sexual technique from Rousseau's mistress, Therese le Vasseur, on the journey home from Paris to London in 1766. His first continental flirtation was in Utrecht with the legendary 'Belle de Zuylen', Isabella van Serooskerken van Tuyll, known to posterity simply as 'Zelide', a woman of formidable intellectual gifts, who evidently enjoyed Boswell's good-natured vanity, even in the following ungallant, hedged–about opening gambit for her hand. It is the letter of a man who is smitten and wishes he wasn't. It should be said that his primary blunder is to have interpreted her open affection for veiled adoration.

BOSWELL TO ZELIDE
(Written in French)

9 July 1764

. . . . As you and I, Zelide, are perfectly easy with each other, I must tell you that I am vain enough to read your letters in such a manner as to imagine that you really was in love with me, as much as you can be with any man. I say was, because I am much mistaken if it is not over before now. Reynst had not judged so ill. You have no command of yourself. You can conceal nothing. You seemed uneasy. You had a forced merriment. The Sunday evening that I left you, I could perceive you touched. But I took no notice of it. From your conversation I saw very well that I had a place in your heart, that you regarded me with a warmth more than friendly. Your letters showed me that you was pleasing yourself with having at last met with the man for whom you could have a strong and a lasting passion. But I am too generous not to undeceive you. You are sensible that I am a man of strict probity. You have told me so.

I thank you. I hope you shall always find me so. Is it not, however, a little hard that I have not a better opinion of you? Own, Zelide, that your ungoverned vivacity may be of disservice to you. It renders you less esteemed by the man whose esteem you value. You tell me, "I should be worth nothing as your wife. I have no subaltern talents." If by these talents you mean the domestic virtues, you will find them necessary for the wife of every sensible man. But there are many stronger reasons against your being my wife; so strong that, as I said to you formerly, I would not be married to you to be a king. I know myself and I know you. And from all probability of reasoning, I am very certain that if we were married together, it would not be long before we should be both very miserable. My wife must be a character directly opposite to my dear Zelide, except in affection, in honesty, and in good humour. You may depend upon me as a friend. It vexes me to think what a number of friends you have. I know, Zelide, of several people that you correspond with. I am therefore not so vain of your corresponding with me . . . .

. . . . Perhaps I judge too hardly of you. I think you have no cordiality, and yet you are much attached to your father and to your brothers. Defend yourself. Tell me that I am the severe Cato. Tell me that you will make a very good wife. Let me ask you then, Zelide, could you submit your inclinations to the opinion, perhaps the caprice of a husband? . . . . Could you give spirits to your husband when he is melancholy? I have known such wives, Zelide. What think you? Could you be such a one? If you can, you may be happy with the sort of man that I once described to you. Adieu.

I had sealed this letter. I must break it up and write a little more. I charge you, once for all, be strictly honest with me. If you love me, own it. I can give you the best advice. If you change, tell me. If you love another, tell me. I don't understand a word of your mystery about a certain gentlman whom you think of three times a day. What do you mean by it? – Berlin is a most delightful city. – I am quite happy. I love you more than ever. I would do more than ever to serve you. I would kneel and kiss your hand if I saw you married to the man that could make you happy. Answer me this one question: If I had pretended a passion for you (which I might easily have done, for it is not difficult to make us believe what we are already pleased to imagine) – anwer me: would you not have gone with me to the world's end? Supposing then that I had been disinherited by my father, would you not have said, "Sir, here is my portion. It is yours. We may live genteelly upon it." Zelide, Zelide, excuse my vanity. But I tell you you do not know yourself if you say that you would not have done thus . . . .

> In 1765 Boswell arrived in Italy in a fever of erotic anticipation, noting in his diary that Italian women 'are so debauched that they are hardly to be considered moral agents'. On January 13 he wrote an inflamed

avowal of undying passion to the Countess Burgaretta after she had apparently suggested that certain 'arrangements' might be made. The following day he changed tack and sent her a short note: 'Today I feel better. My passion abates; and for that reason I still have hopes that you will make the 'arrangement' of which you spoke.' A few days later the Boswell charm was again in action, this time in pursuit of the Countess Skarnavis. Unfortunately, he again made the mistake of getting to the point all too prematurely. With Porzia Sansedoni, late mistress of his friend Lord Mountstuart, Boswell went so far as to make his pitch for her favours before he had even met her – another learning experience.

BOSWELL TO PORZIA SANSEDONI
(*Written in French*)

25 August 1765

. . . . I foresaw it even before I came here when my Lord Mountstuart drew me a picture of your character. I found in you the very person my romantic soul had imagined; and that soul has begun to indulge in hopes that the time is come, at last, to enjoy the felicity of which it believed itself worthy.

But I see I am not born to be happy I have declared my feelings towards you, and have learned that you are unable to reciprocate them. It is true, I have the honour to be not distasteful to you. You have displayed for me an esteem – I would even say a sort of tenderness – by which I am deeply flattered. But you insist that the delicacy of your attachment to my Lord precludes you from giving thought to any other man. I have told you, in all sincerity, how much I admired this romantic sentiment. But I have ventured to recall to you that it was a little too extravagant. My Lord is so formed that he is incapable of fidelity himself, and does not expect it from you; and believe me, Madame, did I imagine that my Lord would be vexed by your according me your friendship, there is nothing I would not endure sooner than to obtain it at the cost of a delicate point of honour. But I believe, on the contrary, my Lord would be generous enough to desire that his friend should possess the happiness he sighs for. It appears to me natural that you should be able to accord me a share of that love you have for my Lord, since, like yourself, I am a part of him. Ah, if that could happen, how much closer would be the bonds which knit me to my amiable friend, penetrated, as we should both be, with the same sentiments for yourself; beloved, as we should both be, by la cara Porzia! How beautiful would be the mixture of tender feeling between the three of us!

BOSWELL TO PORZIA SANSEDONI

Siena

6 September 1765

. . . . I wish it were over. What a romantic idea! Yes, I could wish it were in the past; for it is not the ecstasy of a moment but the delicious memory of a whole lifetime that I so ardently desire. O dear, dear Madame, excuse, I entreat you, these extravagant ideas. I have entire confidence in you. I yield myself completely to you. Dispose of me as you will. I am nothing, independently of you; thus you are completely mistress of an honest Scot whose heart and soul breathe nothing but adoration for you.

Permit me to add one word more. To show you the delicacy of my ideas as to the proof which I desire from you, I should like to be with you late at night, and, in a modest darkness, to receive a tender pledge of your favour for an eternal friend. And, Madame, on the word of a man of honour, I shall never ask another. There you have the true romantic. I swear by everything that is sacred that after that single proof, no friend will be more respectful than I, or more chaste. I shall regard you with the liveliest gratitude. I shall adore you as my beneficient goddess and you will have in me the noblest of friends.

I entreat you, dear, dear Madame, think seriously of this, for never again will you find yourself in such circumstances as these. Consider well the nature of my passion. Consider well the generosity of my ideas. Your act, which it fills me with transport to picture, will but interrupt for a moment your romantic fidelity to my Lord, to grant a sublime and eternal happiness to his worthy friend.

Adieu, most adorable of women. I am wholly yours,

J. Boswell

P.S. If you do not forbid it, I shall wait upon you a moment at five. You ought to see me like that, for a moment, every day.

P.P.S. Read this letter with care. It contains very, very romantic sentiments.

BOSWELL TO PORZIA SANSEDONI

Siena
5 September 1765

Good morning, dear Mme. Sansedoni, I am very well and gay. And although I have some suspicions that you like me better when I am a melancholy cavalier, I refuse to dissimulate, even with a view to recommending myself to you. I refuse to feign a sadness I do not feel. If your heart declares itself for me, I shall be the happiest of mortals; and I shall think of you all my life with transport. If that cannot be, I have enough sense to be able to acquiesce in having failed to achieve the *impossible*. I shall, none the less, be your friend. I shall think of you all my life with tender esteem.

Judge, then, dear Madame. Be sincere. My resolution is fixed. I am myself. I am the proud Boswell. I am no wretched suppliant for your pity. No, Madame. I am a man who adores you and lays claim to your attachment. If you cannot love me, do nothing. I go.

The little favours which you granted me last evening ravished me. Ah, Madame, you have never seemed so beautiful to me as when you took off your glove and extended me your hand to kiss with romantic ardour. You said that I had accustomed you to think – you would not tell me what thoughts. Think on, dear Madame; think those thoughts, and perhaps you will come to think more strongly. I will be with you between eleven o'clock and noon *to talk of my Lord*. Thank Heaven I am so well. Adieu.

> Girolama Piccolomini, wife of the mayor of Siena, was Boswell's only real conquest in Italy. Unfortunately, she did not get over him after his return to Scotland and continued to write letters over which he wept crocodile tears while he soberly pitched for the hand of the girl next door, a Miss Blair. The match would enlarge the family estate very satisfactorily. However, she lost patience with his inability to avoid catching recurrent doses of V.D., and eventually he was fortunate enough to secure as his wife a penniless but good-natured cousin, Peggie Montgomerie, in 1769.

PICCOLOMINI TO BOSWELL
(*Written in Italian*)

Siena

14 February 1766

Dear, dearest Boswell, – If you knew how many times I have sent to the post-office to ask if there was a letter from you, you would not repay me by saying that for several weeks you have been unable to write to me. Ah, how well I know that phrase! I know also with certainty that when one cannot express the sentiments of the heart, it is a clear sign that they are not really felt; on the contrary, when one loves one never lacks words. I could write to you from morning to night without ever stopping; and though I did not tell you things that were well expressed I should still tell you things that were as sincere and loving as though you had never left me . . . .

Passion consumes itself in enjoyment but constancy endures for ever, and will be mine even when I shall have become convinced that you have not a shred of affection left for me. So my entire consolation consists in thinking myself superior to the mass of men, who are directed for the most part only by the impulses of the machine . . . .

I remain as I was when we were in the darkness in the large room. By the way, do you remember the little room? Do not our transports there come back to your mind? I long to go there now to get away from my guests for a while; besides, I am in the same state as then. Yes, I am going there now, now, and you will be kind enough to meet me and assuage my desires. Oh – Heaven, to how strong a transport have I abandoned myself! . . . .

It is time now to break off, but first I must tell you that La Porzia has banished all notions of fidelity to my Lord, for she is making conquests right and left at a terrible rate.

In reading over this postscript, I find that physical passion has taken possession of my senses, and that I can no longer truthfully say, as I did above, that I do not love you through impulses of the machine. Confess at least that even at this great distance you do terrible things to me. Oh, *coquin*, if one day you also learn what real passion is!

. . . . You write our language very well; the only fault I find is that you show so little tenderness. Good-bye – really, this time. I love you; that's all. And you, how do you love me? Believe me, I have written this page in a genuine state of distraction, but finally I have recovered a little from my seizure and ask your forgiveness. I am, with all respect, yours to command . . . .

Only one word more: do you still have the ribbon I gave you, worked by my own hands? I always carry your fan, in spite of the terribly cold weather.

———————————————

90

THE AGE OF ROMANCE

The spot where she stood seemed to him unapproachable holy ground.
Anna Karenina: Tolstoy

She only said, 'My life is dreary,
    He cometh not,' she said;
She said, 'I am aweary, aweary,
    I would that I were dead!'
Mariana: Alfred, Lord Tennyson

Reader, I married him.
Jane Eyre: Charlotte Bronte

The worldly, decorous epicureanism of Ninon de Lenclos degener-
ated amongst the aristocracy of the eighteenth century into a coarse
and cynical scoring of sexual conquests. Choderlos de Laclos' novel *Les
Liasons Dangereuses* of 1782 exposed this libertinism to such an effect as
to be a contributing factor to the French revolution. In fact, literature at
the end of the eighteenth century was changing the emotional climate
of Europe. According to Sainte-Beuve, "Rousseau was like a meteor
which fired the heads and hearts of women, and kindled their imagination". His *La Nouvelle Heloise*, together with Sterne's *Sentimental
Journey*, Richardson's *Clarissa*, and a strain of morbid 'Gothick' literature educated a whole generation in how to *feel*.

How one was supposed to feel was 'natural'. All one had to do was to
listen to one's heart. As can be imagined, this notion produced some of
the most unnatural language in the annals of sentimental literature.
Rousseau's advice on how to write a love-letter is singularly unhelpful:
"Begin without knowing what you are going to say, and finish without
knowing what you have said."

The Romantic Age was not kind to women. They were expected to
be 'feminine' at all times and as sexually passive as possible. They were
ethereal, spiritual beings, and a man had to make himself worthy of
them. The old chivalric code was back, but in an over-literal form – it
became possible, for example, for a gentleman to shoot himself rather
than to write and tell his chaste fiancée that he had a social disease.

Women were, in fact, almost too refined to live, and it was in death,
or in the process of dying, that they seemed – to the romantic spirit – to
be at their most attractive. One role that they threw themselves into
with enthusiasm was that of 'muse'. Again, however, this could be taken
over-literally. In 1834, Heinrich Stieglitz returned home to find a note
from his wife, Charlotte, saying that she had committed suicide in order
to shock his enervated poetic powers into new life. She was lying on the
bed dressed in white with a dagger in her heart.

ELIZABETH LINLEY
1754–1792

At the fashionable resort of Bath in 1770, the singer Elizabeth Linley was the sensation of the Assembly Rooms. In the morally delicate position – for a woman – of appearing in public as a performer, she was the object of candidly carnal propositions as well as more honourable ones. When Captain Matthews announced his intention of taking her by force, the wily Richard Brinsley Sheridan (1751–1816), future playwright, politician and wit, helped her to escape to France, and in doing so won her heart. Sheridan then fought a duel with Matthews. However, Sheridan's father, an actor-manager, would not allow his son to marry into a family of mere musicians, while Mr Linley was adamant that his profitable daughter should not be thrown away on a pauper. The lovers met in grottos and corresponded secretly, calling each other Horatio and Delia. Sheridan fought a second duel with Matthews, in which he was seriously wounded, and the lovers were married in 1773. Only Eliza's side of the correspondence has survived, but her letters have a teenage enthusiasm which Sheridan, a grudging correspondent at the best of times, is unlikely to have matched. She is thrilled with the plot of her romance, though she toys with the idea that a tragic denouement might have done just as well.

LINLEY TO SHERIDAN

11 o'clock

Though I parted from you so lately, and though I expect to see you again so soon, yet I cannot keep my fingers from the pen but I must be plaguing you with my scrawl. Oh, my dearest love, I am never happy but when I am with you. I cannot speak or think of anything else. When shall we have another happy half hour? I declare I have not felt real joy since I came from France before this evening. Perhaps now while I am writing and amusing myself by expressing the tender sentiments which I feel for you, you are flirting with Miss W, or some other handsome girl . . . .

I really think Charles suspected something this evening. He looked amazingly knowing this evening when I came down. Deuce take his curious head. I wish he would mind his own business and not interrupt us in our stolen pleasures. Is it not amazing, my dear Love, that we should always have so great an inclination for what is not in our possession?...

Let me see, what have I more to say? – nothing but the same dull story over and over again – that I love you to distraction, and that I would prefer you and beggary before any other man and a throne. I will call you Horatio – that was the name you gave yourself in that sweet poem – write to me then, my dear Horatio, and tell me that you are equally sincere and constant...

My hand shakes so at this moment I can scarce hold the pen. My father came into my room this moment, and I had just time to stuff the letter behind the glass. 'Twas well he did not take much notice of me, for I was .... Goodbye. God bless – I will . . . .

LINLEY TO SHERIDAN

12 o'clock

You unconscionable creature to make me sit up this time of the night to scribble nonsense to you, when you will not let me hear one word from you for this week to come. Oh, my dear, you are the Tyrant indeed. Yet do not fancy I would do this if it was not equally agreeable to myself. Indeed, my dearest love, I am never happy except when I am with you or writing to you. Why did you run away so soon tonight? Tho' I could not enjoy your conversation freely, yet it was a consolation to me that you was so near me.

My mother and me called on Miss Roscoe this evening, when we talked a great deal about you. Miss R. said she was sure you and I should make a match of it. Nay, she said the whole world was of the opinion that we should be married in less than a month. Only think of this, bright Heavens! God bless you, my dear, dear love. I am so weary I must go to bed. There is but one thing that could keep me awake and that is your company. Once more adieu . . . .

Upon my knees, half naked, once more I am going to tire you with my nonsense. I could not bear to see this little blank without filling it up. Though I do not know with what, as I have almost exhausted the Budget of news which I had collected since our long absence. I do insist that you write to me, you lazy wretch, can't you take so small a trouble? I can receive your letter by the same method. My sister is very impatient that I don't come into bed, but I feel more happiness in this situation, tho' I am half froze than in the warmest bed in England . . . .

LINLEY TO SHERIDAN

I cannot resist the opportunity of thanking my dearest Horatio for his concern for me. Believe me I have not been in my senses these two days, but the happy account of your recovery has perfectly restored them. Oh! my dearest love when shall I see you? I will not ask you to write as I am sure it must hurt you. I am going to Wells tomorrow. I am obliged to be there before my father returns, and I expect him very soon. I shall be happy till I hear from you there. Oh! my Horatio, I did not know till now how much I loved you. Believe me had you died, I should certainly [have] dressed myself as a man and challenged M. He should have killed me or I would have revenged you and myself. I cannot stay to write more as Mr. P. is waiting. I suppose you can trust him. I will not write again till I hear from you at Wells as I do not know how to direct safely. God in heaven bless you my dearest Horatio and restore you once more to health to happiness and the arms of your Eliza.

JULIE DE L'ESPINASSE
1732-1776

Mlle de L'Epinasse was literally consumed by love, and the letters she wrote to the Comte de Guibert in her last months make terrifying reading. Illegitimate – and it did not help that her father was also her brother–in–law – she had resigned herself to moving into a convent when she was taken up by her aunt, Madame du Deffand, whose salon was one of the most influential intellectual centres of Paris. She was not pretty, being disfigured by smallpox, but her charm soon earned her a salon of her own.

In 1766 her heart was captured by a Spanish diplomat, the Marquis of Mora, and her regard was fully and chastely reciprocated. But when ill-health drove him away, she fell under the spell of the Comte de Guibert, an acclaimed military theorist and minor play-wright. Later, she discovered that the day they became lovers, de Mora was struck down with the illness that killed him in June 1774. Guibert's marriage in June 1775 – even she acknowledged that it was necessary, for the dowry – sealed her tragic fate. Her letters to Guibert represent to an extreme degree the romantic reproach levelled at the old order:

'You have tastes, but no passions; you have a mind, but no character. In a word, it seems as if nature had studied to bring together the aptest combinations to make you happy and to make you amiable.' (Dec. 1775)

Rousseau and Sterne were encouraging a whole generation to enjoy their misery, and gave expressive wings to what evidently came naturally to her anyway.

'I am ready to thank Heaven for the misery which overwhelms me and is killing me, since it leaves me the soft sensibility and profound passion which make one accessible to everyone who is suffering, who has known grief, who is tormented by the pleasure and the misery of love. Yes, my friend, you are happier than I, but I have more pleasure than you . . . .'(Dec. 1775)

We begin with a letter from Guibert in which he attempts to throw off the mantle of the villain of Richardson's best-selling novel,*Clarissa*.

GUIBERT TO L'ESPINASSE – MAY 1775

What do you want? What do you demand? You draw a picture of me and of my conduct which makes me shudder. You set me at the side of Lovelace, and all the scoundrels of romance. It is a barbarous toil, and I cannot imagine how you had the strength to carry it out.

I look at myself, I search my own heart, and my heart reassures me. No, I am not as guilty towards you as you imagine. You gratuitously credit me with the intention of tormenting you, of devoting your life to misery, of wanting to make you live on a passion which would satisfy my vanity. You tell me that I have turned and turned again the dagger in your wounds. Is this revolting picture true, good Heavens! So, I delight in your tears, in your convulsions, in your plans of suicide, and in that wretched feeling which binds you hand and foot to life? I feed upon them and you give me the mind of an executioner? I might easily be revolted and indignant; but I love and I forgive. I love you now, I have loved you, I have been carried off my feet. I have tried to console you. I would have given, and I would still give, my blood for you. Such are my crimes. Read my letters over again, judge me, put yourself back in the circumstances in which your heart and mine were, and then see whether I am a villain. But, thanks to Hell, you turn everything into gall and poison; you have sworn to feed my soul on them, you want to make the misery which does not come from me fall heavily on it, you do not let me breathe a moment. Hatred would not be more cruel than your activity.

My friend, calm yourself, calm yourself, I beg you. My heart and my health need rest. I have been dreadfully tired by my day. Your letter that I only opened at 2 o'clock has made me ill. My head aches. I am in great discomfort. I should need sleep to calm my woes and above all, my thoughts, which mean always you, first of all. Oh, sleep, sleep yourself too, my friend. May Heaven send us both peaceful sleep and a happier awakening.

L'ESPINASSE TO GUIBERT

Sunday evening, 15 October 1775

The blow which you have struck me has reached my heart, and my body is giving way, I feel it. I do not want either to alarm, or to interest you, but I feel that I am dying of it; there is now no source of help left me in the world, for even supposing the impossible, that you were to become free again, and were to me what I had longed for, it would be too late; the roots of life are attacked, and I perceive it without regret and without terror. My friend, you have prevented me from killing myself, and you are causing my death! How inconsistent! But I forgive you; in a little while it will be all the same. Heavens, I do not want to reproach you; if you saw into my heart, it is far from wanting to hurt you, or to bring a moment's bitterness into your life!

No, though I am in the depths of misery, though I feel that I am a victim because I have loved, though I feel as blameworthy as I am unhappy, I find in my heart only the most lively desire for your happiness; your interests are still first in the life which is slipping from me. Good-bye, my friend; you see, I am not cross; but there are places, there are things which leave me nothing but grief. Write to me; tell me what you are doing, tell me if you are pleased; if the thing which interests you has turned out as you wished. In short, my friend, find, if you can, a little sweetness in dropping a few moments of pleasure into a heart which is deeply wounded and yet entirely yours.

L'ESPINASSE TO GUIBERT

Wednesday, after midnight, December 1775

Yes, my dear Edmond, I still feel all the trouble, all the annoyance, all the pain which attach to a deep affection and an impossible situation, and I feel every moment that my heart is becoming inaccessible to pleasure.

Yes, my friend, I await you, I want you, my heart and my thoughts follow you, you arrive and often my heart stays cold, physical suffering takes up all my attention; I should like to be all yours, and they are stronger than you or I. Oh! what a horrible thing is the decomposition of one's mechanism.

L'ESPINASSE TO GUIBERT

Tuesday, 6.00 p.m. January 1776

During the few days left to me I want you not to be able to spend one without remembering that you are loved to distraction by the most wretched of creatures. Yes, my friend, I love you; I want this bitter truth to pursue you, to disturb your happiness; I want the poison which has preserved my life, which is consuming it, and no doubt will put an end to it, to flood your heart with that painful sensibility which will at least dispose you to regret one who has loved you most tenderly and passionately.

L'ESPINASSE TO GUIBERT

Tuesday, 4 o'clock, May 1776

My friend, I love you; that is a sedative which stupefies my pain. It rests only with you to change it into a poison, of all poisons the most rapid and violent.

Alas! I feel so sick of life, that I am ready to beg your pity and generosity to grant me that relief. It would put an end to a painful agony which will soon weigh heavy on your mind.

Oh! my friend, let me owe repose to you; in virtue's name, be cruel once. I am sinking. Good-bye.

CATHERINE THE GREAT, EMPRESS OF RUSSIA
1729–1796

Catherine the Great was sensually apt from an early age, as she confessed in her memoirs: 'as soon as I was alone I climbed astride my pillows and galloped in my bed until I was quite worn out'. When she seized power from her husband in 1762 she ensured that she would never have to make do with pillows again. From the letters which she wrote to a succession of stalwart favorites, however, it is clear that her prodigious appetite was accompanied by great kindness and affection. Her passion was often ardently reciprocated, even into her late middle age.

Colonel Peter Zavadovskii, at 37, had only a brief run with the ball from January 1776 to June 1777, and despite being staggeringly well-paid for his eighteen months' stint, never really got over her. In her love-notes to him, Catherine switches easily from ardent young girl, to indulgent sugar-mummy, to solicitous mother, and finally to testy spouse working late at the office.

CATHERINE TO ZAVADOVSKII

Petrusa, you laugh at me, yet I am out of my mind over you. I love your smile immemorably.

Petrusa dear, all will pass, except my passion for you.

You are Vesuvius itself: when you least expect it an eruption appears; but no, never mind, I shall extinguish them with caresses. Petrusa dear!

My advice is – stay with me: 2) believe it when I say something; 3) do not quarrel hourly about trifles; 4) reject hypochondriac thoughts and replace them with amusing ones; 5) Conclusion: all this feeds love, which without amusement is dead, like faith without kind deeds.

There's your answer.

Petrusa, you have gone out of your mind! What nonsense! Where will you go? I feel nothing except affection; I show you nothing except some affection; and yet here are your conclusions! How well you use logic! Petrusa, you are unjust in regard to me; I do not seek causes to become angry, and indeed I am not angry by nature, even the little irascibility in me changes with one glance from you. Dear little darling, truly you jest. What do you lock yourself in the room for? Truly hypochondria is good for nothing. Give me back my dear Petrusa, do not lock him away: me loves the dark-haired man; but leave the wrathful master home. Darling, if you do not wish to be deemed mean, then come with a caress.

Petrusa, dear, I coughed less tonight than in the last ones, now occasionally after a strong sweat. Darling, keep healthy and love us at least a little, if a lot is not possible. However, it is your choice, but I love you as strongly as today's wind was rich in snow.

Petrusa, in your ears a cry of falsehood has taken root, for you do not enter into my station at all. I have set myself the rule to be assiduous to state affairs, to lose the least time possible, but whereas a time of relaxation is absolutely necessary for life and health, so these hours are dedicated to you, and the time remaining belongs not to me, but to the Empire, and if I do not use this time as I ought to, then in me will take root against myself and others my own indignation, dissatisfaction, and *mauvaise humeur* from the feeling that I am spending time in idleness and not as I ought to. Ask Pr[ince] Or [lov] whether I have not been this way long since. Yet you immediately cry out and blame it on lack of affection. It is not from that, but from an orderly division of time between state affairs and you. See for yourself, what other diversion do I have except strolling. This I must do for health.

Petrushinka, I rejoice that you have been healed by my little pillows, and if my caress facilitates your health, then you will never be sick. Dear little darling, you have no fault before me; stretch out your arms, I shall embrace you. Being dear, as you are, you have no cause to change yourself. I am extraordinarily contented with you and hour by hour honour you on par with the love that will be with you irrevocably. Dearest, dear darling, you are born for me, and our feelings for the most part, and especially in endearment are essentially the same; your soul when it flies toward me, then it is met midway enroute from my [side].

To a person most valuable and dear, who however is extremely, extremely mistaken, when he attributes the commotion of thought to boredom, I beg you that you not be mistaken in me, never ascribe to me the qualities of base and weak souls; the tsar knows how to reign, but when he has nothing but tedium the whole day, then he is tedious; he is all the more tedious when a dear visage looks on stupidly and the tsar, instead of merriment, gets from it a supplement of tedium and vexation. All this is past and forgotten.

ROBERT BURNS
1759–1796

On December the 30th 1787 Robert Burns wrote to a friend 'I am at this moment ready to hang myself for a young Edinburgh widow'. The woman in question was Agnes McLehose – not in fact a widow but separated from her husband. She had contrived a meeting with the young lion of Edinburgh society on December 4th, but a nasty fall from a coach immediately afterwards incapacitated him sufficiently to divert him from his usual direct strategy of seduction to a full-blown epistolary romance instead. He should have realised she was determined to keep him at arm's length when she suggested they should address one another as if they were Arcadian shepherds of conventional fantasy – Sylvander and Clorinda – though it may be of significance that shortly after his death she referred to the poet's letters to her as appearing 'under the signature of Clitander'. However, she kept her virtue, and Burns had to make do with her maidservant, Jenny Clow instead. In March 1788 Burns married Jean Armour, who had borne him twin girls, both dying within weeks. Jenny Clow later gave him a son. As for Mrs McLehose, she provided the inspiration for many of his best known lyrics, including *Ae fond kiss*.

BURNS TO McLEHOSE

21 January, 1788

I am a discontented ghost a perturbed spirit. Clarinda, if ever you forget Sylvander, may you be happy, but he will be miserable.

O, what a fool I am in love! – what an extravagant prodigal of affection! Why are your sex called the tender sex, when I never have met with one who can repay me in passion? They are either not so rich in love as I am, or they are niggards where I am lavish.

O Thou, whose I am, and whose are all my ways! Thou see'st me here, the hapless wreck of tides and tempests in my own bosom: do Thou direct to thyself that ardent love, for which I have so often sought a return, in vain, from my fellow-creatures! If Thy goodness has yet such a gift in store for me, as an equal return of affection from her who, Thou knowest, is dearer to me than life, do thou bless and hallow our band of love and friendship; watch over us, in all our outgoings and incomings, for good; and may the tie that unites our hearts be strong and indissoluble as the thread of man's immortal life!

BURNS TO McLEHOSE

24 January 1788

"Unlavish Wisdom never works in vain"

I have been asking my reason, Clarinda, why a woman, who for native genius, poignant wit, strength of mind, generous sincerity of soul, and the sweetest female tenderness, is without a peer; and whose personal charms have few, very, very few parallels, among her sex; why, or how she should fall to the blessed lot of a poor hairumscairum Poet, whom Fortune has kept for her particular use to wreak her temper on, whenever she was in ill-humour. One time I conjectured that as Fortune is the most capricious jade ever known; she may have taken, not a fit of remorse, but a paroxysm of whim, to raise the poor devil out of the mire, where he had so often and so conveniently served her as a stepping-stone, and give him the most glorious boon she ever had in her gift, merely for the maggot's sake, to see how his fool head and his fool heart will bear it. At other times I was vain enough to think that Nature, who has a great deal to say with Fortune, had given the coquettish goddess some such hint as, "Here is a paragon of Female Excellence, whose equal, in all my former compositions, I never was lucky enough to hit on, and despair of ever doing so again; you have cast her rather in the shades of life; there is a certain Poet, of my making; among your frolicks, it would not be amiss to attach him to this master-piece of my hand, to give her that immortality among mankind which no woman of any age ever more deserved, and which few Rhymesters of this age are better able to confer."

Evening, 9 o'clock

I am here, absolutely unfit to finish my letter – pretty hearty after a bowl, which has been constantly plied since dinner, till this moment. I have been with Mr. Schetki, the musician, and he has set it finely. – I have no distinct ideas of any thing, but that I have drunk your health twice tonight, and that you are all my soul holds dear in this world.

Sylvander

McLEHOSE TO BURNS

Thursday Forenoon, January 24th

Sylvander, the moment I waked this morning, I received a summons from Conscience to appear at the Bar of Reason. While I trembled before this sacred throne, I beheld a succession of figures pass before me in awful brightness! Religion, clad in a robe of light, stalked majestically along, her hair dishevelled, and in her hand the Scriptures of Truth, held open at these words – "If you love me, keep my commandments." Reputation followed: her eyes darted indignation, while she waved a beautiful wreath of laurel, intermixed with flowers, gathered by Modesty in the Bower of Peace. Consideration held her bright mirror close to my eyes, and made me start at my own image! Love alone appeared as counsel in my behalf. She was adorned with a veil, borrowed from Friendship, which hid her defects, and set off her beauties to advantage. She had no plea to offer, but that of being the sister of Friendship, and the offspring of Charity. But Reason refused to listen to her defence, because she brought no certificate from the Temple of Hymen! While I trembled before her, Reason addressed me in the following manner: – "Return to my paths, which alone are peace; shut your heart against the fascinating intrusion of the passions; take Consideration for your guide, and you will soon arrive at the Bower of Tranquillity."

Sylvander, to drop my metaphor, I am neither well nor happy today: my heart reproaches me for last night. If you wish Clarinda to regain her peace, determine against everything but what the strictest delicacy warrants.

I do not blame you, but myself. I must not see you on Saturday, unless I find I can depend on myself acting otherwise. Delicacy, you know, it was which won me to you at once: take care you do not loosen the dearest, most sacred tie that unites us? Remember Clarinda's present and eternal happiness depends upon her adherence to Virtue. Happy Sylvander! that can be attached to Heaven and Clarinda together. Alas! I feel I cannot serve two masters. God pity me!!

Thursday night
Your letter – I should have liked had it contained a little of the last one's seriousness. Bless me! You must not flatter so; but it's in a 'merry mood," and I make allowances. Part of some of your encomiums, I know I deserve; but you are far out when you enumerate "strength of mind" among them. I have not even an ordinary share of it – every passion does what it will with me; and all my life, I have been guided by the impulse of the moment – unsteady, and weak! . . . .

Friday morning
My servant (who is a good soul) will deliver you this. She is going down to Leith, and will return about two or three o'clock. I have ordered her to call then, in case you have ought to say to Clarinda today . . . .

BURNS TO McLEHOSE

25 January 1788
Clarinda, my life, you have wounded my soul. – Can I think of your being unhappy, even tho' it be not described in your pathetic elegance of language, without being miserable? Clarinda, can I bear to be told from you, that "you will not see me tomorrow night – that you wish the hour of parting were come"! Do not let us impose on ourselves by sounds: if in the moment of fond endearment and tender dalliance, I perhaps trespassed against the *letter* of Decorum's law; I appeal, even to you, whether I ever sinned in the very least degree against the *spirit* of her strictest statute. – But why, My Love, talk to me in such strong terms; every word of which cuts me to the very soul? You know, a hint, the slightest signification of your wish, is to me a sacred command. – Be reconciled, My Angel, to your God, your self and me; and I pledge you *Sylvander's honour*, an oath I dare say you will trust without reserve, that you shall never more have reason to complain of his conduct. – Now, my Love, do not wound our next meeting with any averted looks or restrained caresses: I have marked the line of conduct, a line I know exactly to your taste, and which I will inviolably keep; but do not *you* show the least inclination to make boundaries: seeming distrust, where you know you may confide, is a cruel sin against Sensibility. –

"Delicacy, you know it, was which won me to you at once – *take care* you do not loosen the dearest most sacred tie that unites us" – Clarinda, I would not have stung *your* soul, I would not have bruised *your* spirit, as that harsh crucifying, "Take care," did *mine*; no, not to have gained heaven! Let me again appeal to your dear Self, if Sylvander, even when he seemingly half-transgressed the laws of Decorum, if he did not shew more chastised, trembling, faltering delicacy, than the MANY of the world do in keeping these laws.

O Love and Sensibility, ye have conspired against My Peace! I love to madness, and I feel to torture! Clarinda, how can I forgive myself, that I ever have touched a single chord in your bosom with pain! would I do it willingly? Would any consideration, any gratification make me do so? O, did you love like me, you would not, you could not deny or put off a meeting with the Man who adores you; who would die a thousands deaths before he would injure you; and who must soon bid you a long farewell! –

I had proposed bringing my bosom friend, Mr Ainslie, tomorrow evening, at his strong request, to see you; as he only has time to stay with us about ten minutes, for an engagement; but – I shall hear from you: this afternoon, for mercy's sake! for till I hear from you I am wretched. – O Clarinda, the tie that binds me to thee, is entwisted, incorporated with my dearest threads of life!

Sylvander

BURNS TO McLEHOSE – MARCH 1793

I suppose, my dear Madam, that by your neglecting to inform me of your arrival in Europe, a circumstance which could not be indifferent to me, as indeed no occurrence relating to you can – you meant to leave me to guess and gather that a correspondence I once had the honor and felicity to enjoy, is to be no more. – Alas, what heavy laden sounds are these – "no more!" – The wretch who has never tasted pleasure, has never known woe; but what drives the soul to madness, is the recollection of joys that are "no more!" – But this is not language to the world. – They do not understand it. But, come, ye children of Feeling & Sentiment; ye whose trembling bosom chords ache, to unutterable anguish, as recollection gushed on the heart! Ye who are capable of an attachment, keen as the arrow of Death, and strong as the vigour of Immortal Being – Come! and your ears shall drink a tale – but hush! – I must not, can not tell it! Agony is in the recollection, and frenzy is in the recital!

I present you a book: may I hope you will accept of it. – I dare say you have brought your books with you. – The fourth volume of the Scots Songs is published: I will also send it you. –

Shall I hear from you? But first, hear me! No cold language – no prudential documents – I despise Advice, and scorn Control – If you are not to write such language, such sentiments, as you know I shall wish, shall delight to receive; I conjure you, By wounded Pride! By ruined Peace! By frantic disappointed Passion! By all the many ills that constitute that sum of human woes – A BROKEN HEART! – To me be silent for ever ! ! ! – If you insult me with the unfeeling apothegms of cold-blooded Caution, May all the – but hold – a Fiend could not breath a malevolent wish on the head of MY Angel!

Mind my request! – If you send me a page baptised in the font of sanctimonious Prudence – By Heaven, Earth and Hell, I will tear it into atoms! – Adieu! May all good things attend you!

R.B.

WOLFGANG AMADEUS MOZART
1756–1791

Mozart was a musical genius unparalleled in European history, who married, in 1782 in Vienna, a cheerful, unreflective and nondescript young woman from a musical family, Constanze Weber. She bore him six children (two of whom survived) and outlived him by over 50 years. These letters show that his love for her, after seven years of marriage, was total and passionate. The first was written before the marriage and reveals him as a prudish stickler for etiquette. The later letters show that this ludicrous fussiness outside marriage goes with an extraordinary freedom within marriage.

MOZART TO CONSTANZE WEBER

Vienna, 29 April 1782

Dearest, Most Beloved Friend!

Surely you will still allow me to address you by this name? Surely you do not hate me so much that I may be your friend no longer, and you – no longer mine? And even if you will not be my friend any longer, yet you cannot forbid me to wish you well, my friend, since it has become very natural for me to do so. Do think over what you said to me to-day. In spite of all my entreaties you have thrown me over three times and told me to my face that you intend to have nothing more to do with me. I (to whom it means more than it does to you to lose the object of my love) am not so hot-tempered, so rash and so senseless as to accept my dismissal. I love you far too well to do so. I entreat you, therefore, to ponder and reflect upon the cause of all this unpleasantness, which arose from my being annoyed that you were so impudently inconsiderate as to say to your sisters – and, be it noted, in my presence – that you had let a *chapeau* measure the calves of your legs. No woman who cares for her honour can do such a thing. It is quite a good maxim to do as one's company does. At the same time there are many other factors to be considered – as, for example, whether only intimate friends and acquaintances are present – whether I am a child or a *marriageable* girl – more particularly, whether I am already betrothed – but, above all, whether only people of my own social standing or my social inferiors – or, what is even more important, my social superiors are in the company? If it be true that the Baroness herself allowed it to be done to her, the case is still quite different, for she is already past her prime and cannot possibly attract any longer – and besides, she is inclined to be promiscuous with her favours. I hope, dearest friend, that, even if you do not wish to become my wife, you will never lead a life like hers. If it was quite impossible for you to resist the desire to take part in the game (although it is not always wise for a man to do so, and still less for a woman), then why in the name of Heaven did you not take the ribbon and measure your own calves *yourself* (as *all self-respecting women* have done on similar occasions in my presence) and not allow a *chapeau* to do so? – why, I myself *in the presence of others* would never have done such a thing to you. I should have handed you the ribbon myself. Still less, then, should you have allowed it to be done to you by a stranger – a man about whom I know nothing. But it is all over now; and the least acknowledgement of your somewhat thoughtless behaviour on that occasion would have made everything all right again; and if you will not make a grievance of it, dearest friend, everything will still be all right. You realise now how much I love you. *I do not fly into a passion as you do.* I think, I reflect and I feel. *If you will but surrender to your feelings,* then I know that this very day I shall be able to say with absolute confidence that Constanze is the virtuous, honourable, prudent and loyal sweetheart of her honest and devoted

Mozart

MOZART TO CONSTANZE

Berlin

19 May 1789

Oh, how glad I shall be to be with you again, my darling! But the first thing I shall do is to take you by your front curls; for how on earth could you think, or even imagine, that I had forgotten you? How could I possibly do so? For even supposing such a thing, you will get on the very first night a thorough spanking on your dear little kissable arse, and this you may count upon.

MOZART TO CONSTANZE

Berlin

23 May 1789.

On Thursday, the 28th, I shall leave for Dresden, where I shall spend the night. On June 1st I intend to sleep in Prague, and on the 4th – the 4th – with my darling little wife. Arrange your dear sweet nest very daintily, for my little fellow deserves it indeed, he has really behaved himself very well and is only longing to possess your sweetest... Just picture to yourself that rascal; as I write he crawls onto the table and looks at me questioningly. I, however, box his ears properly – but the rogue is simply ... and now the knave burns only more fiecely and can hardly be restrained. Surely you will drive out to the first post-stage to meet me? I shall get there at noon on the 4th.

MOZART TO CONSTANZE

Vienna

6 June. 1791

I have this moment received your dear letter and am delighted to hear that you are well and in good spirits. Madame Leutgeb has laundered my nightcap and neck-tie, but I should like you to see them! Good God! I kept on telling her, '*Do let me show you how she (my wife) does them!*' – But it was no use. I am delighted that you have a good appetite – but whoever gorges a lot, must also shit a lot – no, walk a lot, I mean. But I should not like you to take *long walks* without me. I entreat you to follow my advice exactly, for it comes from my heart. Adieu – my love – my only one. Do catch them in the air – those 2999½ little kisses from me which are flying about, waiting for someone to snap them up. Listen, I want to whisper something in your ear – and you in mine – and now we open and close our mouths – again – again and again – at last we say: 'It is all about Plumpi – Strumpi –' Well, you can think what you like – that is just why it's so convenient. Adieu. A thousand tender kisses. Ever your

Mozart

GEORGE, PRINCE OF WALES (LATER GEORGE IV)
1762–1830

In 1795 George, Prince of Wales, was married to Caroline of Brunswick. It was a marriage made in Hell. On their first meeting, having embraced her, he tottered back, and calling over the Earl of Malmesbury, muttered 'Harris, I am not well; pray get me a glass of brandy'. What made it worse was that he had already, in 1785, married – morganatically – someone else. This was Mrs Fitzherbert, a twice-widowed Roman Catholic, celebrated in the song, *The Lass of Richmond Hill* – though more matron than lass, being six years older than he was.

Their preliminary correspondence is couched in the conventional language of decorous passion then still in fashion, with much striking of emotional poses and the usual fancy names: George becomes 'Telemachus', while she adopts the name 'Margeritta'; and the Goethean theme is continued when George addresses her – otherwise unaccountably – as 'Charlotte'. The 'Werter' with whom George is pleased to compare himself rather favourably is of course the hero of Goethe's novel *The Sorrows of Young Werther*, which taught a whole generation that the noblest thing a young man could do was to shoot himself in the head for love.

As for Mrs Fitzherbert, she wheels on Shakespeare in an attempt to inspire her prince with the example of the reform of Prince Hal. She was wasting her time.

However, he always felt himself to be a hero in his own mind. In later life, around the dinner table, his imagination would sometimes run away with him to such an extent that the Duke of Wellington was obliged to remind him gently that he had not in fact been present at the Battle of Waterloo.

I was drawn to the Steine this evening by a party who drank tea with us and would not excuse me, (tho' I was really too ill to go out) because it was generally believed that your Royal Highness in imitation of a ridiculous Frenchman was to run a race backwards! Oh! that you had a Mentor to guard you from those numerous perils that around you wait! – the greatest of which are your present companions. As I beheld you the other day like another Harry:–

'Rise from the ground like feathered Mercury,
And vaulted with such ease into your seat
As if an angel drop'd down from the clouds;
To turn and wind a fiery Pegasus.
And witch the world with noble horsemanship.'

I could not avoid continuing the comparison, and wishing that you would sometimes use that Prince's words:–

'Reply not to me with a fool born jest,
For Heaven doth know, so shall the world perceive;
That I have turn'd away my former self,
So will I those that kept me company.'

Adieu! – if I am too free remember it is your own condescension that draws on you the remarks of
                    Margaritta.

You admire Shakespeare, I perceive! he is indeed an author that all people of taste must love to enthusiasm; I have read this play with attention, and a time may come when I may likewise surprise my subjects, if my better genius, which shines forth in the sweet form of the haughty, yet lovely Margaritta will deign to add her influence; which like the sun may draw some latent blossom from an expiring plant, that otherwise would sink into obscurity.
                    Hal

GEORGE, PRINCE OF WALES TO MRS. FITZHERBERT

Are you then sensible my amiable Margaritta, of an increase of that passion I wish to awaken in your gentle heart. Let me flatter myself that you will one day feel a tender friendship for me. Even reason devoid of passion will authorise this wish, and why need Edmund* be forgot? why so frequently mention the lamented man? yet you may love his memory and esteem the living.

Do not suppose yourself wrong in indulging me with your letters neither; I entreat you compare me not to the weak – the passionate Werter. If my passion is less ardent – it is better founded; – for who can equal my Charlotte.

After Mrs Fitzherbert had initially avoided his attentions by fleeing to the continent, and any idea of official sanction for their marriage had been firmly ruled out, George was described by his friend Charles James Fox as 'rolling on the floor, striking his forehead, tearing his hair, falling into hysterics, and swearing that he would abandon the country, forgo the Crown, sell his jewels and plate, and scrape together a competence to fly with the object of his affections to America'. He clearly felt the same in 1799, when he dispatched a letter from Windsor Castle, marked 'Private. Mrs. Fitzherbert, to be delivered into her own hands only.'

12 June

Oh God! Oh God! Who has seen the agony of my soul and knowest the purity of my intentions, have mercy, have mercy on me: turn once more I conjure thee, the heart of my Maria, to me, for whom I have lived and for whom I will die. You know not what you will drive me to from despair, you know you are my wife, the wife of my heart and soul, my wife in the presence of my God: 'tis the only only reprieve left . . . . I will . . . . relinquish everything for you, rank, situation, birth, and if that is not sufficient, my life shall go also . . . .

Wednesday morn. Four o'clock. It is now two hours since I wrote the above; I have calm'd myself . . . . The wretched experiences of the last five years have made life only desirable in one shape to me and that is in you. I am wrapped up in you entirely; after 17 years' attachment nothing can alter me, shake me or change me. Alike yours in life or in death.

*Mrs Fitzherbert's late husband.

And now, God bless you, my Maria, my only life, my only love, thine unalterably thine, George P.

Oh! my heart, my heart, but I am composed and calm. Whatever your answer may be and whatever the consequence, still my blessings with my love will ever attend thee my Maria. *Thy* George P.

LORD NELSON
1785–1805

Horatio Nelson, an operatic figure, young, romantic, one-eyed, his empty sleeve pinned to his bemedalled breast, was loved in his own person (even by the man he cuckolded) as no Englishman has been loved before or since. At Portsmouth in 1805, when he was on his way to Trafalgar, people fell on their knees as he passed. Dying in the hour of total victory, his last words express the man: his vanity – 'Don't throw me overboard'; his unashamed affection for his friends – 'Kiss me Hardy'; his passion – 'Take care of my dear Lady Hamilton'; and finally his patriotism – 'Thank God I have done my duty'.

Looking at the *ménage a trois* between Lord and Lady Hamilton and Admiral Nelson it is difficult to credit the harmony of their life together, but it seems that the earthy passion of Emma and Nelson was matched only by the unalloyed affection for them both of old Lord Hamilton. They maintained a bizarre fiction of a 'pure and platonic' relationship even when Emma produced a sudden crop of children. Even in a loud, colourful and unbridled age, Nelson and Lady Hamilton were a social embarrassment. At about the time the following letter was written, a Swedish diplomat remarked that she was the fattest woman he had ever laid eyes upon.

LORD NELSON TO LADY HAMILTON

Wednesday 29th January 1800

Separated from all I hold dear in this world what is the use of living if indeed such an existance can be called so, nothing could alleviate such a Separation but the call of our Country but loitering time away with nonsense is too much, no Separation no time my only beloved Emma can alter my love and affection for You, it is founded on the truest principles of honor, and it only remains for us to regret which I do with the bitterest anguish that there are any obstacles to our being united in the closest ties of this Worlds rigid rules, as We are in those of real love. Continue only to love Your faithful Nelson as he loves his Emma. You are my guide I submit to You, let me find all My fond heart hopes and wishes with the risk of my life I have been faithful to my word never to partake of any amusement or to sleep on Shore. Thursday Janry 30th We have been Six days from Leghorn and no prospect of our making a passage to Palermo, to me it is worse than death. I can neither Eat or Sleep for thinking of You my dearest love, I never touch even pudding You know the reason. No I would Starve sooner. My only hope is to find You have Equally kept Your promises to Me, for I never made You a promise that I did not as strictly keep as if made in the presence of heaven, but I rest perfectly confident of the reallity of Your love and that You would die sooner than be false in the smallest thing to Your Own faithful Nelson who lives only for his Emma, friday I shall run Mad we have had a gale of Wind that is nothing but I am 20 Leagues farther from You than Yesterday noon. Was I master notwithstanding the weather I would have been 20 Leagues nearer but my Commander In Chief knows not what I feel by absence, last Night I did nothing but dream of You altho' I woke 20 times in the Night. In one of my dreams I thought I was at a large Table You was not present, Sitting between a Princess who I detest and another. They both tried to Seduce Me and the first wanted to take those liberties with Me which no Woman in this World but Yourself ever did. The consequence was I knocked her down and in the moment of bustle You came in and taking Me in Your embrace wispered I love nothing but You My Nelson. I kissed You fervently And we enjoy'd the height of love. Ah Emma I pour out my Soul to You. If you love any thing but Me You love those who feel not like your N. Sunday Noon fair Wind which makes me a little better in hopes of seeing You my love My Emma to morrow. Just 138 Miles distant, and I trust to find You like myself. for no love is like Mine towards You.

LORD BYRON
1788–1824

Whenever the arrival of Lord Byron was announced amongst any company in Europe, the ladies present flushed, palpitated, and even on occasion, fainted. Inexperienced girls were seriously advised not to look him in the eye. He was strikingly good-looking but rather short, and stout, with a pronounced limp on account of his club foot. His appeal derived from the obviously autobiographical elements in the 'Byronic hero' of his poetry: a surly type, given to dark thoughts about his own wickedness. Fortunately he preserved the letters he received from various distraught ladies, many of them – the letters, that is – of considerable bulk. 'When a woman takes up a pen', he observed wearily 'she never knows when to lay it down again'. He would also, when he could, secure a lock of hair as a memento. He even managed to purloin a few strands of Lucrezia Borgia's hair from the Ambrosiana library in Milan, where he had admired her correspondence with Pietro Bembo.

In 1812 he received a tress from Lady Falkland, ten years his senior (who had recently lost her husband in a duel). Her conviction that she was the object of his secret longings was uncorroborated by anything whatsoever in his personal communication and was based solely on her supposed evidence of it in his poetry. What she could not know was that no woman was ever suffered to call him 'George'.

LADY FALKLAND TO BYRON

12 June 1812.

Surely I cannot be mistaken! Byron, my adored Byron, come to me. I shall feel each hour an age until you are pressed to a heart as ardent and warm as your own . . . . Tell me, my Byron, if those mournful tender effusions of your heart to that Thyrza* whom you lamented as no more – were not intended for myself? I should not have been vain enough to support it had not the date exactly corresponded with a severe illness under which I was at that time suffering. Your Farewell address in September, 1809[†] also I think to be intended for me.

. . . . But now, my Byron, if you really believe I could add to or constitute your happiness, I will most joyfully accept your hand – but remember I must be loved exclusively – your heart must be all my own . . . . I could not, my beloved Byron, brook a second time to be slighted by my husband . . . .

---

*It seems that in writing the lines 'To Thyrza' Byron had been thinking of a choir boy he had been besotted with at Cambridge, called Edlestone. [†]'To Florence'.

LADY FALKLAND TO BYRON

13 July 1812

I have again read your Romaunt, and feel more than ever convinced that
in Greece, Cadiz, Florence, etc. I may trace myself – in Athens – Falkland
your old ally – in the 'Maid of Athens' your own Christina. ...You believe that
my affections are buried with Falkland in the tomb. Banish all apprehension
on that account – I had long ceased to respect or esteem him. It is not a love-
less heart I offer you, but a heart whose every throb beats responsive to your
own.

LADY FALKLAND TO BYRON – FEBRUARY 1813

I cannot any longer endure this dreadful agony of mind. Do you wait until
I write again to yourself, my best beloved Byron. I would have done this
sooner, but Mr. Corbett* told me that you would insult me – of this I never felt
a fear – and from your own note which he read to me – not one word of which
I could or did believe. Oh no, the feelings of the heart are indeed reciprocal
and hearts and minds will act in unison. Why, my adored boy, don't you return
my affection as you did? What have I done to forfeit it? Pray do tell me,
George . . . .

> After three months Byron had generally had enough of any woman, and
> Lady Caroline Lamb was no exception as far as he was concerned.
> However, she was not so easily thrown off and embarrassed him in
> public with a long series of escapades, culminating in a hysterical and
> bloody scene at a grand ball. Her well-known impression of him – 'mad,
> bad and dangerous to know' – summed up her own character much
> more accurately than his.
> The first of these two letters from Byron – witty, to the point, exas-
> perated, even in the heat of a fresh passion – is incontrovertibly his own
> composition, but the other is very likely a forgery by Lady Caroline
> herself. The dubious letter was written after she had had a scene with
> her husband, and had carried out her threat to run off to her lover. Sir
> William, who took an aristocratically tolerant attitude towards his wife's
> affairs, had told her that Byron would never take her in, and indeed,
> Byron had despatched her back to the bosom of her family, where her

*Byron's lawyer

mother had had a fit. And all in front of the servants. If it were a forgery – and she managed to fool his publisher by imitating his hand on another occasion – her motive would have been to have evidence of Byron's continuing attachment, and also his willingness to elope, which would have dignified her behaviour a little.

Later she would impersonate Byron more extensively in the form of the eponymous hero of her novel, *Glenarvon*. By April 1813 he was so sick of her that he wished never to see her again until they might 'be chained together in Dante's Inferno'. And after she died in 1827, more or less insane, her husband could be heard to mutter 'Shall I meet her in another world?'

BYRON TO LADY CAROLINE LAMB

Sy. Even

April, 1812

I never supposed you artful, we are *all* selfish, nature did that for us, but even when you attempt deceit occasionally, you cannot maintain it, which is all the better, want of success will curb the tendency. – Every word you utter, every line you write proves you to be either *sincere* or a *fool*, now as I know you are not the one I must believe you the other. I never knew a woman with greater or more pleasing talents, *general* as in a woman they should be, something of everything, & too much of nothing, but these are unfortunately coupled with a total want of common conduct. – For instance the *note* to your *page*, do you suppose I delivered it? or did you mean that I should? I did not of course. – Then your heart – my poor Caro, what a little volcano! that pours *lava* through your veins, & yet I cannot wish it a bit colder, to make a *marble slab* of, as you sometimes see (to understand my foolish metaphor) brought in vases tables &c. from Vesuvius when hardened after an eruption. – To drop my detestable tropes & figures you know I have always thought you the cleverest most agreeable, absurd, amiable, perplexing, dangerous fascinating little being that lives now or ought to have lived 2000 years ago. – I wont talk to you of beauty, I am no judge, but our *beauties* cease to be so when near you, and therefore you have either some or something better. And now, Caro, this nonsense is the first and last compliment (if it be such) I ever paid you, you have often reproached me as wanting in that respect, but *others* will make up the deficiency . . . . All that you so often *say*, I *feel*, can more be said or felt? – This same prudence is tiresome enough but one must maintain it, or what can we do to be saved? – Keep to it. –

[written on cover] If you write at all, write as usual – but do as you please, only as I never see you – Basta!

'LORD BYRON' TO LADY CAROLINE LAMB

August 1812

My dearest Caroline,

If tears which you saw and know I am not apt to shed, – if the agitation in which I parted from you, – agitation which you must have perceived through the *whole* of this most *nervous* affair, did not commence until the moment of leaving you approached, – if all I have said and done, and am still but too ready to say and do, have not sufficiently proved what my real feelings are, and must ever be towards you, my love, I have no other proof to offer. God knows, I wish you happy, and when I quit you, or rather you, from a sense of duty to your husband and mother, quit me, you shall acknowledge the truth of what I again promise and vow, that no other in word or deed, shall ever hold the place in my affections, which is, and shall be most sacred to you, till I am nothing. I never knew till *that moment* the *madness* of my dearest and most beloved friend; I cannot express myself; this is no time for words, but I shall have a pride, a melancholy pleasure, in suffering what you yourself can scarcely conceive, for you do not know me. I am about to go out with a heavy heart, because my appearing this evening will stop any absurd story which the event of the day might give rise to. Do you think *now* I am *cold* and *stern* and *artful*? Will even *others* think so? Will your *mother* even – that mother to whom we must indeed sacrifice much, more, much more on my part than she shall ever know or can imagine? 'Promise not to love you!' ah, Caroline, it is past promising. But I shall attribute all concessions to the proper motive, and never cease to feel all that you have already witnessed, and more than can ever be known but to my own heart, – perhaps to yours. May God protect, forgive, and bless you. Ever, and even more than ever,

Your most attached, Byron

PS – These taunts which have driven you to this, my dearest Caroline, were it not for your mother and the kindness of your connections, is there anything on earth or heaven that would have made me so happy as to have made you mine long ago? and not less *now* than *then*, but *more* than ever at this time. You know I would with pleasure give up all here and all beyond the grave for you, and in refraining from this, must my motives be misunderstood? I care not who knows this, what use is made of it, – it is to *you* and to *you* only that they are *yourself* [sic]. I was and am yours freely and most entirely, to obey, to honour, love – and fly with you when, where, and how you yourself *might* and *may* determine.

Harriette Wilson was the only one of Byron's admirers to have pursued a more disreputable and scandalous career than he had. It is not just that she was a *demi-monde*. Her memoirs, published in 1825, were a fund-raising exercise whereby she invited half the British Establishment to stump up if they hoped *not* to find their names in the book as con-quests or clients. Byron, if he had been alive then, would, no doubt, have joined with Wellington in his famous retort 'Publish and be damned!' – not only because the poet's reputation was way beyond redemption anyway, but also because, unlike Wellington, his connec-tion with her had been purely epistolary. He did, however, perhaps uniquely amongst her male acquaintance, give her money out of sheer kindness rather than lust, guilt or fear. Her love-letters to him are among the best he received.

BYRON TO HARRIETTE WILSON

April 1814

. . . . You tell me that you wished to know me better, because you liked my writing. I think you must be aware that a writer is in general very different from his productions, and always disappoints those who expect to find in him qualities more agreeable than those of others; I shall certainly not be lessened in my vanity, as a scribbler, by the reflection that a work of mine has given you pleasure; and, to preserve the impression in its favour, I will not risk your good opinion, by inflicting my acquaintance upon you.

Very truly your obliged servant,

B

HARRIETTE WILSON TO LORD BYRON

I have received the 1000 francs and must repeat my very sincere thanks to you, dear Lord Byron; though it was too bad to cut me off with such a shabby short letter and such an excuse – just to choose the very moment when the Horse was waiting and the divorce going on. However it is a very *nice dear* little letter, written more after my style than your own and, if you were not aware of it, so much the more flattering to me – I love the little cramped hand too now, and know every turn of it.

Pray, dear Lord Byron, think of me a little now and then (I don't mean as a woman, for I shall never be a woman to you) merely as a *good little Fellow* who feels a warmer interest in all that happens to you and all that annoys you than anybody else in the world. Forget me when you are *happy*; but in gloomy moments, chilly miserable weather, bad razors and cold water, perhaps you'll recollect and write to me. You can easily judge by a woman's scribbling whether her heart is with it, and you *know* I love you *honestly* and *dearly*. Alas! I can never prove it by any sacrifice . . . .

I am truth and nothing but the truth. I looked at you for half an hour together one night and while studying your very beautiful countenance I could fancy a new sensation produced by the warm pressure of your lips to mine, beyond what my nature could endure – wild and eager as your peotry – terrifying by its power to *wither* and destroy me.

Jupiter was all powerful in a cloud and *ladies* have been known to admire a *Horse*, but there is a *quieter, better,* more voluptuous feeling for a *woman,* and *you can't give it to her.*

Besides, I never loved any but blue eyes. Are you as dark as at the Masquerade, or were you painted? Nothing, I suppose, will ever bring you to Paris, not even your friend *T. Moore*; yet I *will* hope that we shall one day (some twenty years hence) take a pinch of snuff together before we die; and as you watch me, in my little pointed cap, *spectacles*, bony ankles and thread stockings, stirring up and tasting my *pot au feu*, you'll imagine Ponsonby's Worcester's and Argyle's *Angelick Harriette!!*

I have made a new conquest lately – Lord Francis Cunningham; but I *hate boys* so I have been setting him to hunt and pull out my *grey hairs* to destroy his *Illusions*. He found *ten* and I did not know I had one. 'Better get a *Monkey*,' you'll say, than a fine young *blue*-eyed man of one and twenty. What a fool he must be! When you and I meet, I shall set you to work at the *brown ones*, for I mean to attack them as soon as the grey predominates. It is more dignified to keep to one colour, n'est-ce-pas? . . . .

I trust and hope 'at this present writing' you are out of your scrape, or I shall be the more sorry because I know you did not love *her* enough to make the scrape worth while. Pray, dearest, let *me* love you, *tell me to love you*.

I am at a very *harmless* distance, you know . . . .

. . . . Au reste – *try me* and make haste, for this wet weather and pain in my side will very soon finish me. I am like the late old Duke of Queensbury almost, who told Lord Yarmouth and myself one evening we went to call on him five months before his death, that 'he had not lost' (Oh, but you'll be so *disgusted with me!* But I must go on now, you know) 'that he had not lost *one drop* of that *precious Balsam* for the last *eight years*,' and that if he did he should bring on his spasms (*anti-frisky* ones, of course) for the next *forty hours*.'

I am very sorry I *began* it; it's a *beastly* story . . . .

Farewell, dearest Lord Byron; I shall not *dare* venture to bore you with any more stupid letters, but I only wish you knew but half how devotedly I am

Votre Affectionée

Beau Page

God bless you; nobody knows anything about loving you but myself.

> Byron needed a generous and strong-minded wife with a sense of humour, and unfortunately Annabella Milbanke whom he married in 1815 was not that quality of woman. He referred later to their honeymoon as a 'treaclemoon'. However, this was not quite the way he saw her when he was writing his desperate appeals to her not to go through with the separation. She remained coldly proof to anything he wrote to or for her, (no other woman failed to respond to his poem 'Farewell...') and the precise reason for this is hard to locate. It is possible that it lies in an act of love that had seemed reasonable enough to him, given that she was in the advanced stages of pregnancy, but had been, to her, unforgiveable in its criminal depravity.
>
> That he was committing incest with his half-sister, Augusta Leigh, would certainly have put the lid on it when her suspicions were confirmed. And before she went to visit her parents, whence she sent him her last love letter, she had explored the possibility of having him committed as a dangerous lunatic. But she began proceedings for their separation only a few days after this affectionate note was sent off. The 'good goose' is Augusta.

January.16 1816

Dearest Duck

We got here quite well last night, and were ushered into the kitchen instead of the drawing-room, by a mistake that might have been agreeable enough to hungry people...Dad...and Mam long to have the family party completed...Such a *sitting*-room or *sulking*-room all to yourself. If I were not always looking for B, I should be a great deal better already for the country air...Love to the good goose, and everybody's love to you both from hence. Ever thy most loving

Pippin . . . . Pip-ip

BYRON TO LADY BYRON

8 February 1816

All I can say seems useless – and all I could say – might be no less unavailing – yet I still cling to the wreck of my hopes – before they sink forever. – Were you then *never* happy with me? – did you never at any time or times express yourself so? – have no marks of affection – of the warmest *and* most reciprocal attachment passed between us? – or did in fact hardly a day go down without some such on one side and generally on both? – do not mistake me – [two lines crossed out] I have not denied my state of mind – but you know it's causes – & were those deviations from calmness never followed by acknowledgement & repentance? – was not the last which occurred more particularly so? – & had I not – had we not – the days before & on the day when we parted – every reason to believe that we loved each other – that we were to meet again – were not your letters kind? – had I not acknowledged to you all my faults & follies – & assured you that some had not – & would not be repeated? – I do not require these questions to be answered to me – but to your own heart. – The day before I received your father's letter – I had fixed a day for rejoining you – if I did not write lately – Augusta did – and as you had been my proxy in correspondence with her – so did I imagine – she might be the same for me to you. – Upon your letter to me – this day – I surely may remark – that it's expressions imply a treatment which I am incapable of inflicting – and you of imputing to me – if aware of their latitude – & the extent of the inferences to be drawn from them. – This is not just – but I have no reproaches – nor the wish to find cause for them. – Will you see me? – when & where you please – in whose presence you please: – the interview shall pledge you to nothing – & I will say & do nothing to agitate either – it is torture to correspond thus – & there are things to be settled & said which cannot be written. – You say "it is my disposition to deem what I *have worthless*" – did I deem *you* so? – did I ever so express myself to you – or of you – to others? – You are much changed within these twenty days or you would never have thus poisoned your own better feelings – and trampled upon mine.

ever yrs. most truly & affectionately

B

BYRON TO LADY BYRON

5 February 1816

Dearest Bell – No answer from you yet – perhaps it is as well – but do recollect – that all is at stake – the present – the future – & even the colouring of the past: – The whole of my errors – or what harsher name you choose to give them – you know – but I loved you – & will not part from you without your *own* most express & *expressed* refusal to return to or receive me. – Only say the word – that you are still mine in your heart – and "Kate! – I will buckler thee against a million" –

ever yours dearest most

B

On April the 8th 1816, after his separation from his wife, Byron and his half-sister were cut by London society gathered that evening at Lady Jersey's. The only friendly face there was that of Miss Mercer Elphinstone (1788-1867), who remarked 'You had better have married me. I would have managed you better'. They had engaged in an intermittent correspondence as friends for several years, but it was only in his last letter to her that he was able to hint at a more turbulent regard; untill then he had been afraid, given that she was immensely wealthy, of his motives being misunderstood.

As he fled abroad a few days later, he sent some small present to her with the message: 'Tell her that had I been fortunate enough to marry a woman like her, I should not now be obliged to exile myself from my country.' Nicknamed 'the Fop's Despair' for her collection of marriage offers, she eventually lived happily ever after with the dashing Comte de Flahaut de la Billarderie.

LORD BYRON TO MARGARET MERCER ELINSTONE

11 April 1816

Dear Miss Mercer

I thank you truly for kind acceptance of my memorial – more particularly as I felt a little apprehensive that I was taking a liberty of which you might disapprove. – A more useless friend you could not have – but still a very sincere and by no means a new one – although from circumstances you never knew – (nor would it have pleased you to know) – how much. – These having long ceased to exist – I breathe more freely on this point – because *now* no motive can be attributed to me with regard to you of a selfish nature – at least I hope not. – I know not why I venture to talk thus – unless it be – that the time is come – when whatever I may say – can not be of importance enough to give offence – & that neither my vanity nor my wishes ever induced me at any time to suppose that I could by any chance have become more to you than I now am. – This may account to you for that which – however little worth accounting for – must otherwise appear inexplicable in our former acquaintance – I mean – those 'intermittents' at which you used to laugh – as I did too – although they caused me many a serious reflection. – But this is foolish – perhaps improper – yet it is – or rather – was the truth – and has been a silent one while it could have been supposed to proceed from hope or presumption: – I am now as far removed from both by irrevocable circumstances as I always was by my own opinion & by yours – & I soon shall be still further if further be possible – by distance. – I cannot conclude without wishing you a much happier destiny – not than *mine is* – for that is nothing – but than mine ever could have been – with a little common sense and prudence on my part: – no one else has been to blame – it may seem superfluous to wish *you* all this – & it would be so if our happiness always depended on ourselves – but it does not – a truth which I fear I have taught rather than learned however unintentionally.

ever most truly yrs.
Byron

In Italy Byron fell headlong for the seventeen year old Contessa Guiccioli. According to Venetian social mores this was quite allowable, and to begin with the old Count Alessandro was content with Byron's role as his wife's 'Cavalier Servente'. However, as the affair got out of hand, she separated from her husband. Just for once Byron did the decent thing and was intending to marry her when he set off for the wars in Greece where he was to die of a fever at Missolonghi. Their letters are translations from the Italian. To put his passion into perspective we include a letter written during this period to Augusta Leigh (which she passed on to his wife, with the comment: 'He is surely...a Maniac').

BYRON TO TERESA GUICCIOLI

22 April 1819

You vowed to be true to me and I will make no vows to you; let us see which of us will be the more faithful. Remember that, when the time comes that you no longer feel anything for me, you will not have to put up with my reproaches; I shall suffer, it is true, but in silence. I know only too well what a man's heart is like, and also, a little, perhaps, a woman's; I know that Sentiment is not in our control, but is what is most beautiful and fragile in our existence. So, when you feel for another what you have felt for me, tell me so sincerely – I shall cease to annoy you – I shall not see you again – I shall envy the happiness of my rival, but shall trouble you no more. This however I promise you: You sometimes tell me that I have been your *first* real love – and I assure you that you shall be my last Passion. I may well hope not to fall in love again, now that everything has become indifferent to me. Before I knew you – I felt an interest in many women, but never in one only. Now I love *you*, there is no other woman in the world for me.

You talk of tears and of our unhappiness; my sorrow is within; I do not weep. You have fastened on your arm a likeness that does not deserve so highly; but yours is in my heart, it has become part of my life, of my soul; and were there another life after this one, there too you would be mine – without you where would Paradise be? Rather than Heaven without you, I should prefer the Inferno of that Great Man buried in your city, so long as you were with me, as Francesca was with her lover.

My sweetest treasure – I am trembling as I write to you, as I trembled when I saw you – but no longer – with such sweet heart-beats. I have a thousand things to say to you, and know not how to say them, a thousand kisses to send you – and, alas, how many Sighs! Love me – not as I love you – for that would make you too unhappy, love me not as I deserve, for that would be too little – but as your Heart commands. Do not doubt me – I am and always shall be your most tender lover.

Byron

25 April 1819

My Treasure – my life has become most monotonous and sad; neither books, nor music, nor *Horses* (rare things in Venice – but you know that mine are at the Lido) – nor dogs – give me any pleasure; the society of women does not attract me; I won't speak of the society of men, for that I have always despised. For some years I have been trying systematically to avoid strong passions, having suffered too much from the tyranny of Love. *Never to feel admiration* – and to enjoy myself without giving too much importance to the enjoyment in itself – to feel indifference toward human affairs – contempt for many, but hatred for none, – this was the basis of my philosophy. I did not mean to love any more, nor did I hope to receive Love. You have put to flight all my resolutions – now I am all yours – I will become what you wish – perhaps happy in your love, but never at peace again. You should not have re-awakened my heart – for (at least in my own country) my love has been fatal to those I love – and to myself. But these reflections come too late. You have been mine – and whatever the outcome – I am, and eternally shall be, entirely yours.

Venice

17 May 1819

My dearest Love – I have been negligent in not writing, but what can I say. Three years absence – & the total change of scene and habit make such a difference – that we have now nothing in common but our affections and our relationship.

But I have never ceased nor can cease to feel for a moment that perfect and boundless attachment which bound & binds me to you – which renders me utterly incapable of *real* love for any other human being – what could they be to me after *you?* My own XXX [Short word crossed out] we may have been very wrong – but I repent of nothing except that cursed marriage – & your refusing to continue to love me as you had loved me – I can neither forget nor quite *forgive you* for that precious piece of reformation – but I can never be other than I have been – and whenever I love anything it is because it reminds me in some way or other of yourself – for instance I not long ago attached myself to a Venetian for no earthly reason (although a pretty woman) but because she was called XXXX [short word crossed out] and she often remarked (without knowing the reason) how fond I was of the name. – It is heart-breaking to think of our long Separation – and I am sure more than punishment enough for all our sins – Dante is more humane in his "Hell" for he places his unfortunate lovers (Francesca of Rimini & Paolo whose case fell a good deal short of *ours* – though sufficiently naughty) in company – and though they suffer – it is at least together. – If ever I return to England – it will be to see you – and recollect that in all time – & place – and feelings – I have never ceased to be the same to you in heart – Circumstances may have ruffled my manner – & hardened my spirit – you may have seen me harsh & exasperated with all things around me; grieved & tortured with *your new resolution*, – & the soon after persecution of that infamous fiend who drove me from my Country & conspired against my life – by endeavouring to deprive me of all that could render it precious – but remember that even then *you* were the sole object that cost me a tear? and *what tears!* do you remember *our* parting? I have not spirits now to write to you upon other subjects – I am well in health – and have no cause of grief but the reflection that we are not together – When you write to me speak to me of yourself – & say that you love me – never mind common-place people & topics – which can be in no degree interesting – to me who see nothing in England but the country which holds *you* – or around it but the sea which divides us. – They say absence destroys weak passions – & confirms strong ones – Alas! *mine* for you is the union of all passions & of all affections – Has strengthened itself but will destroy me – I do not speak of *physical* destruction – for I have endured & can endure much – but of the annihilation of all thoughts feelings or hopes – which have not more or less a reference to you & to *our recollections*.

Ever dearest

BYRON TO TERESA GUICCIOLI

Ravenna
4 August 1819

My Treasure: Your reproaches are unjust; – Alessandro and your father being present – and I not being able then to clasp you to my heart – I kissed your hand and hurried away, so as not to show my suffering, which would only too clearly have revealed the whole, whole truth! I vow that I love you a thousand times more than when I knew you in V[enice]. You know it – you feel it. *Think*, my love, of *those* moments – delicious – dangerous – but – *happy*, in every sense – not only for the pleasure, more than ecstatic, that you gave me, but for the danger (to which you were exposed) that we fortunately escaped. The hall! Those rooms! The open doors! The servants so curious and so near – Ferdinando – the visitors! how many obstacles! But all overcome – it has been the real triumph of Love – a hundred times Victor.

Farewell – my only Treasure – my one Hope. Farewell – I kiss you untiringly from my heart – and am ever yours.

BYRON TO TERESA GUICCIOLI

Filetto

10 October 1820

My only Love for ever!!! + + + I was infinitely glad to get your works – I have read one or two of them – *but how astounded I am!* One must know them to know you. The experience of a year and a half did not tell me as much about you as reading *two of your pages*. I must confess to you that this increase of light on the subject is to your disadvantage; I do not mean as to your genius, for that must be adored in silence, but as to *morals*, of which it is permissible even for a simple mind like mine to speak, and must indeed be spoken of without reserve between Friends.

Here then, briefly, are my reflections. – I believed you to be sincere; now I shall not be able to affirm it with such assurance. – I believed you to be sensitive to misfortune, but *never* affected by it; this opinion I still have and must have, in order to esteem and love you; but you have written one thing that, in my opinion, might give the impression that in some moments of your life you showed a certain weakness of character. It is your *Farewell*, and the *Sketch from Private Life* that make me think so. In these there is more than talent, tenderness and Love; more than was proper towards a woman who had offended you; and besides it is completely in contradiction with all that you have told me about your feelings for your wife. – I do not blame you for having felt such a tenderness, it only hurts me that you should have concealed the truth from me; or if indeed you did not feel it, that you should so have deceived the World. Believe me, Byron, your *Farewell* in particular does not give any idea of your independent character. It gives the impression of a guilty man *asking for pity;* or at least, too proud to ask for it openly, but hoping that his prayer for it will be understood; and this is a situation which never should be yours! I assure you that I can hardly persuade myself that this *Farewell* is Byron's. But if it is, and the sentiment expressed in it is sincere, I cannot understand how the proudest, the coldest, of Englishwomen could refrain from coming to throw herself into your arms and beg for mutual forgiveness. – Oh, I no longer understand anything – knowledge of the human heart is very difficult, and perhaps will always be unattainable by me. I will rest on this conviction; asking you meanwhile to forgive my frankness, which however I shall never give up as long as I shall be your friend – that is to say as long as I live. I will say no more to you about this subject.

Come *whenever you like* – I cannot and do not wish to force your inclinations. – I am sorry, because I had a great deal to say to you.

Your true Friend and Lover for Ever
Teresa G.G.

EUGENE DELACROIX
1799–1863

Delacroix was the leading painter of the French romantic movement, his works being notable for their scale and energy, as also for their sensuality and orientalism. One other feature of his painting is his impeccable observation of horses, which he developed in England, where he also picked up an English manner – *le phlegme Anglais* – and a plain, English style of dress. It may even be said that the only real passion of his life was for an English girl, Elizabeth Salter, a servant of one Mrs Lamb who lodged with his sister in Paris over the winter of 1817–18 while engaged on legal business. To his friend J.B. Pierret he wrote (Dec 1817) 'This evening, with the help of my dictionary, I made up a wretched letter which will say things as best it can. I don't understand it too well myself and Heaven knows if somebody else will...' The reference to himself as 'Yorick' is a tribute to the enduring success of Sterne's *Sentimental Journey* of 1768.

DELACROIX TO ELIZABETH SALTER – DECEMBER 1817

[Draft]

You must excuse me for all the mistakes and errors of linguage of this letter. I am not instructed in the English tongue: But if you apprehend what I say to you, I shall be sufficiently fortunate. When the heart speak, it is unnecessary to speak correctly. O happy, happy Yorick if you should hold it to be true that I tell; happy moreover if you should condescend to answer to me; while I cannot to see you, I will read over again the your loved hand's characters. El you shall laugh perhaps at my faulty speech: But alas, whilst my mind is full of thoughts, and should wish to express them to you, my pen is cold. At the time I think to my E, it seems to me, it to be easy to speak of her charms, But I cannot find the words. Comfort me, Prithee; tell to me that you do not despise me, and love me a little, little, little. I will kiss your letter and I will keep him on my heart. I kiss your hand, and cheek, and fine eyes, and cherry lips. Call me your you will be my beloved E. What I felt when my sister had troubled us! I have seen you only a little moment; and I expect ardently to morrow.

Farewell! I hope that you will embellish my dreams till the next day.

Your Eug

DELACROIX TO ELIZABETH SALTER – DECEMBER 1817

[Draft]

I not seen you E and you forget me absolutely. Often I have expected you and you have contemned my advertissements. I conceive you are wearied to see me in stairs to the face of the whole house, and I confess it not please me much. Yet, if we could understand we could find the means to frame even any swift moments. I not have lost memory of this happy evening when all babblers and troublesome were removed. You not remember probably last friday; but I have that present to my mind and I resent better for the want of so welcome occasion. Often, when I go near the kitchen I hear your fits of laughing, and I laugh in no wise. You ask me perhaps what matter is it to me. I will only answer such is my temper. Pardon me that caprice and my fantastical humour. I frame great many purposes to see you easily but needless . . . . I cannot call again to my mind that fortunate friday without a middle start of pleasure. The security of our company added over to the delight of your view. Oh my lips are arid, since had been cooled so deliciously. If my mouth could be so nimble to pronounce your linguage, as to savour so great sweetness, I not should be so wearied when I endeavour to speak or to write you. Pardon me if I call again to your memory the happiness which you have granted me. Not reproach me that, yet are so rare the Delights of Life. I beg you a favour: not refuse me. When Ch. L . . . . will be go out and when also L . . . . I conjure you make me known of that. Sometimes you will say it to me on the stairs: or if it not may be, you will have complaisance to say you have something to tell me: and I shall know what it signifies. You will not omit, you will tell me Sunday a thing which interest me. I am sure you laugh at it and you prepare to amuse me with trifflings. You are a cruel person which play afflicting the anothers. Nevertheless not be angry at it; I am a pitiful Englishman and I bet I have told in this write a multitude of impertinence, it must therefore pardon me in considera-tion of my good intentions. Thought of me.

I will go out this evening. Prithee come a few. I hope God will remove ours enemies. I beg him for that. My whisker not sting more.

JOHN KEATS
1795–1821

John Keats achieved in his very short life perhaps the greatest body of lyric poetry in the English language. He met Fanny Brawne (1800-1865) in 1818 and they were engaged within a few months. Before he died in Rome he asked for her letters to be placed in his grave. After his death she wore mourning for seven years, thus proving his tormenting fear that she was 'a little inclined to the Cressid' quite groundless. As may be deduced from the following letters her position as the object – with the emphasis on 'object' – of Keats' sublime romantic passion, was not an enviable one.

KEATS TO FANNY BRAWNE

27 July 1819
Sunday Night.

My sweet Girl,

I hope you did not blame me much for not obeying your request of a Letter on Saturday: we have had four in our small room playing at cards night and morning leaving me no undisturb'd opportunity to write. Now Rice and Martin are gone and I am at liberty. Brown to my sorrow confirms the account you give of your own ill health. You cannot conceive how I ache to be with you: how I would die for one hour - for what is in the world? I say you cannot conceive; it is impossible you should look with such eyes upon me as I have upon you: it cannot be. Forgive me if I wander a little this evening, for I have been all day employ'd in a very abstract Poem and I am in deep love with you – two things which must excuse me. I have, believe me, not been an age in letting you take possession of me; the very first week I knew you I wrote myself your vassal; but burnt the Letter as the very first time I saw you I thought you manifested some dislike to me. If you should ever feel for Man at the first sight what I did for you, I am lost. Yet I should not quarrel with you, but hate myself if such a thing were to happen – only I should burst if the thing were not as fine as a Man as you are a Woman. Perhaps I am too vehement, then fancy me on my knees, especially when I mention a part of your Letter which hurt me; you say speaking of Mr Severn 'but you must be satisfied in knowing that I admired you much more than your friend'. My dear love, I cannot believe there ever was or ever could be any thing to admire in me especially as far as sight goes – I cannot be admired, I am not a thing to be admired. You are, I love you; all I can bring you is a swooning admiration of your Beauty. I hold that place among men which snubnos'd brunettes with meeting eyebrows do among women – they are trash to me – unless I should find one among them with a fire in her heart like the one which burns in mine. You absorb me in spite of myself – you alone: for I look not forward with any pleasure to what is call'd being settled in the world; I tremble at domsestic cares – yet for you I would meet them, though if it would leave you the happier I would rather die than do so. I have two luxuries to brood over in my walks, your Loveliness and the hour of my death. O that I could have possession of them both in the same minute. I hate the world: it batters too much the wings of my self-will, and would I could take a sweet poison from your lips to send me out of it. From no others would I take it. I am indeed astonish'd to find myself so careless of all charms but yours – remembering as I do the time when even a bit of ribband was a matter of interest with me. What softer words can I find for you after this – what it is I will not read. Nor will I say more here, but in a Postscript answer any thing else you may have mentioned in your Letter in so many words - for I am distracted with a thousand thoughts. I will imagine you Venus to-night and pray, pray, pray to your star like a Heathen.

Your's ever, fair Star,
John Keats

My seal is mark'd like a family table cloth with my Mother's initial F for Fanny: put between my Father's initials. You will soon hear from me again. My respectful Compts to your Mother. Tell Margaret I'll send her a reef of best rocks and tell Sam I will give him my light bay hunter if he will tie the Bishop hand and foot and pack him in a hamper and send him down for me to bathe him for his health with a Necklace of good snubby stones about his Neck.

KEATS TO FANNY BRAWNE

May 1820
My dearest Girl,
I wrote a Letter for you yesterday expecting to have seen your mother. I shall be selfish enough to send it though I know it may give you a little pain, because I wish you to see how unhappy I am for love of you, and endeavour as much as I can to entice you to give up your whole heart to me whose whole existence hangs upon you. You could not step or move an eyelid but it would shoot to my heart – I am greedy of you. Do not think of anything but me. Do not live as if I was not existing – Do not forget me – But have I any right to say you forget me? Perhaps you think of me all day. Have I any right to wish you to be unhappy for me? You would forgive me for wishing it, if you knew the extreme passion I have that you should love me – and for you to love me as I do, you must think of no one but me, much less write that sentence. Yesterday and this morning I have been haunted with a sweet vision – I have seen you the whole time in your shepherdess dress. How my senses have ached at it! How my heart has been devoted to it! How my eyes have been full of Tears at it! Indeed I think a real Love is enough to occupy the widest heart – Your going to town alone, when I heard of it was a shock to me – yet I expected it – promise me you will not for some time, till I get better. Promise me this and fill the paper full of the most endearing names. If you cannot do

so with good will, do my Love tell me – say what you think – confess if your heart is too much fastened on the world. Perhaps then I may see you at a greater distance, I may not be able to appropriate you so closely to myself. Were you to loose a favourite bird from the cage, how would your eyes ache after it as long as it was in sight; when out of sight you would recover a little. Perhaps if you would, if so it is, confess to me how many things are necessary to you besides me, I might be happier, by being less tantalized. Well may you exclaim, how selfish, how cruel, not to let me enjoy my youth! to wish me to be unhappy! You must be so if you love me – upon my Soul I can be contented with nothing else. If you could really what is called enjoy yourself at a Party – if you can smile in peoples faces, and wish them to admire you *now*, you never have nor ever will love me – I see *life* in nothing but the certainty of your Love – convince me of it my sweetest. If I am not somehow convinc'd I shall die of agony. If we love we must not live as other men and women do – I cannot brook the wolfsbane of fashion and foppery and tattle. You must be mine to die upon the rack if I want you. I do not pretend to say I have more feeling than my fellows – but I wish you seriously to look over my letters kind and unkind and consider whether the Person who wrote them can be able to endure much longer the agonies and uncertainties which you are so peculiarly made to create – My recovery of bodily health will be of no benefit to me if you are not all mine when I am well. For god's sake save me – or tell me my passion is of too awful a nature for you. Again God bless you.

J.K.

No – my sweet Fanny – I am wrong. I do not want you to be unhappy – and yet I do, I must while there is so sweet a Beauty – my loveliest my darling! Good bye! I kiss you – O the torments!

ALEXANDER PUSHKIN
1799–1837

Pushkin, Russia's greatest poet, followed the custom of the Russian nobility in devoting much of his youth to pursuing married ladies and fighting duels. He met Anna Petrovna Kern when in exile in North Russia, banished on account of his atheism. His love-letters are all in

French, the conventional language of gallantry, and it is significant that his letters to his wife, after his marriage in 1831, would all be in Russian. His beautiful wife attracted admirers like flies, most notably, and in the end scandalously, a young French émigré, D'Anthese-Heeckeren. In the inevitable duel Pushkin was mortally wounded.

PUSHKIN TO ANNA PETROVNA KERN

From Mikhaylovskoe to Riga
13 August 1825

. . . . What do I care about your character? I don't care a straw – should pretty women have character? The essential things are their eyes, their teeth, their hands, and their feet (I would have added a heart, but your girl cousin has discredited that word too much). You say that it is easy to come to know you; did you wish to say to love you? I am sufficiently of that opinion and I am even the proof of it. I have behaved with you like a boy of 14 – it is shameful. But since I no longer see you, I am little by little regaining the ascendant which I had lost, and I employ it to scold you. If we ever see each other again, promise me...No, I do not want your promises, and, besides, a letter is so cold; there is no force nor emotion in an entreaty by mail, and a refusal has neither charm nor voluptuousness. Hence good-bye – and let us talk of something else. How is your husband's gout coming along? I hope he had a good attack of it on the second day after your arrival. If you knew what aversion mixed with respect I feel for that man! Divine one, in heaven's name see to it that he gambles and has the gout, the gout! That is my only hope . . . .

PUSHKIN TO ANNA PETROVA KERN

From Mikhaylovskoe to Riga
28 August 1825

Here is a letter for your aunt; you may keep it for her if she by chance is no longer in Riga. Tell me, is it possible to be as flighty as you are? How could a letter addressed to you have fallen into hands other than yours? But, since what is done is done, let us talk of what we shall have to do.

If your husband wearies you too much, leave him – but do you know how? Leave all the family there, take post horses for Ostrov, and come . . . . where? To Trigorskoe? Not at all. To Mikhaylovskoe! Here is the fine project which has been plaguing my imagination for the past quarter of an hour. But can you conceive of how happy I would be? You will tell me: "And the hullabaloo, and the scandal?" The devil with it! When a woman leaves her husband, the scandal is already complete; the rest is nothing or very little. But won't you admit that my project is romantic? And once Kern is dead, you are as free as the air . . . . Now then, what do you say about it? Didn't I tell you that I was in the mood to give you a bold and striking piece of advice!

Let us speak seriously; that is, coldly: shall I see you again? The idea that I shall not makes me shudder. You will tell me: "Console yourself." Very well, but how? Fall in love? Impossible. First I would have to forget your twitches. Go abroad? Strangle myself? Get married? All these things present great difficulties; I am loath to do any of them . . . . Oh! by the way, how am I going to get your letters? Your aunt is opposed to this correspondence, so chaste, so innocent (and how else . . . . at 250 miles?). Our letters will probably be intercepted, read, commented upon, and then burned with ceremony. Try to disguise your handwriting, and I shall see to the rest. But write me, and a lot, lengthwise and crosswise and diagonally (a geometrical term). This is what diagonal means. But above all give me the hope of seeing you again. If not, really, I shall try to fall in love with somebody else. I am much more amiable by the post than face to face, am I not? Well, if you come, I promise to be extremely amiable – I shall be gay on Monday, exalted on Tuesday, tender on Wednesday, light-hearted on Thursday, and on Friday, Saturday, and Sunday I shall be whatever will please you, and all the week at your feet. Farewell.

28 August
Do not unseal the enclosed letter. That is not nice. Your aunt would get angry.

PUSHKIN TO HIS WIFE, NATALIA

Boldino
30 October 1833
Yesterday I received both your letters, dear heart; I thank you. But I must read the Riot Act to you a little. You seem only to think now of flirting – but look here; it is not the fashion any more and is considered as the mark of bad

bringing-up. There is little sense in it. You are pleased that men run after you –
much cause for pleasure! Not only you, but Praskowja Petrowna could succeed
with ease in getting all the unmarried pack of loafers to run after her. When
the trough is there, the pigs come of their own accord. Why do you need to
receive men who make love to you in your house? One can never know what
sort of people one may come across. Read the Ismailov fable of Foma and
Kusma. Foma entertains Kusma with caviar and herring. Kusma wished to
drink after that. But Foma gave him nothing; whereupon the guest gave the
host a sound thrashing. From this the poet draws the moral lesson; You pretty
women! do not give your adorers a herring to eat, if you have no intention of
giving them something to drink afterwards; for you could easily come across a
Kusma. Do you see? I beg of you, to arrange no academical dinners in my
house. . . .

And now, my angel, I kiss you, as if nothing had happened, and thank you,
that you have elaborately and sincerely described your entire life of pleasure.
Have a good time, little wife, but do not overdo it and do not forget me altogether. I can hardly hold out any longer – so keen am I to see you *coiffée a la
Ninon*; you must look delicious. Why did you not think before of this old
strumpet and copy her coiffure? Write to me, what successes you have at balls
. . . . And my angel, please, please, do not flirt too outrageously. I am not
jealous, and I know that you will not overstep the utmost limits, but you know
how I dislike everything which smells of our Moscow "young ladies," who do
not surpass the *il faut*, who are what one calls in English "vulgar." . . . . If I find
on my return, that your dear, simple aristocratic tone has changed, I shall get a
divorce, I swear to you, and become a soldier out of grief. You ask me, how I
do, and whether I have become handsomer. To begin with, I am growing a
beard, whiskers, and moustache which are an ornament to man; when I go out
into the street, they call me uncle; secondly, I wake up at 7 o'clock, drink
coffee, and lie in bed till 3 o'clock. Lately I started writing, and have scribbled
a lot of stuff; at 3 o'clock I go riding, at 5 I take a bath, and then comes my
dinner - potatoes and buckwheat. Till 9 o'clock I read. Thus the day passes,
and every day is alike.

SARAH AUSTIN
1793–1867

Sarah Austin was a model Victorian wife and mother. More, she was one of those Englishwomen who take charge in a crisis, whether in fire-fighting, or looking after the victims of the shipwreck of a convict ship near Boulogne (for which she was given an award by the Humane Society) or fearlessly succouring the victims of an outbreak of plague in Malta. And she stood by her brilliant but hopelessly ineffectual husband through all the miserable frustrations and vicissitudes of their married life. All her life she laboured as a translator, mostly from the German, and in her last years prepared her late husband's notes for publication – work that he had been too indolent to do for himself – which earned him a lasting reputation in the legal profession. However, at the age of 39 she had fallen passionately in love with the author of a book she was translating. Over a few months she had poured out a torrent of sensual longing to a man she had never met.

Her letters were only preserved because Hermann von Puckler-Muskau (1784-1871) preserved *all* the letters of his lady-friends, arranged in alphabetical order (she came after Aschbrock). He was an eccentric adventurer, best-selling travel-writer and an important land-scape gardener. Though he was an aristocrat, he was well-known in England (nick-named 'Prince Pickling Mustard') as a twenty-four carat bounder who had agreed on a divorce with his wife, Lucie, in order to pay off the gardeners by bringing a rich English girl into their house-hold. Having failed in this enterprise he re-married Lucie, his fortunes bolstered by the enormous success of his books, particularly in the trans-lation by Sarah Austin – even though she had cut out all the salacious passages, of which there were a great many, apparently. Whatever made Sarah fall for him was whatever makes any pure sweet English girl fall for a dissolute and caddish foreigner. His real wickedness was not that he wanted her body (he was a bit past it anyway) but that his real motive for the correspondence was, as her letter of July 18 1832 suggests – replying to a request for a snippet of pubic hair – almost an academic curiosity. The letters were written in German.

PUCKLER-MUSKAU TO AUSTIN – APRIL 1832

. . . . If you have the power of imagination to imitate me in everything we can conquer all the disadvantages of our separation in a truly unusual fashion. But you must banish every womanly reticence, for since ours is merely a

written exchange, it demands intense belief, and you can give yourself over
unreservedly . . . .

15 October 1832

. . . . If what I hear and conceive of you is true, I am as Rosalind says, 'just
as high as your heart – that is for my head to be there.' My throat is too small
and always was so, my shoulders wide and well formed and my waist extremely
slender in proportion to the expanse above and below. My bosom is not
extremely large and prominent but round and firm. But I tell you the hips and
all below them are singularly handsome, I believe I might say perfect. An old
medical friend of mine once came behind me in the street and said, 'there can
be but one such back as that in England. I knew it was you.' From my usual
good health too I have a remarkably fine elastic muscle, 'clean-limbed' as
jockies say, knee and ankle sharply turned, and calf and thigh firm, round and
accurately formed . . . .

3 June 1823

. . . . I do not think all violation of promises and vows, wrong – nay criminal – but those given in our marriages are so impracticable of observance, that
what man does observe them? Like all overstrained attempts at compelling
virtue it defeats itself. This institution (of which *au reste* I am an ardent
admirer) wants entire remodelling. Is not neglect, unkindness, indifference as
much a violation of the vow as infidelity? Can a man be said to 'love and
cherish' a woman for whose comfort, advantage, happiness, he shews not the
least solicitude, and whose devoted efforts to please him he receives with
sullen apathy, or worse? Yet this, or corresponding conduct on the part of a
woman, is accounted no infraction of the treaty!

Now for the proposition you make to me as to the manner of our meeting;
–if ever we meet; you know not half I could dare, or half I could imagine, for
the man I love. I have thought and felt it all. It should be as you wish. I want
not to act any reserves or scruples. If I love you at all I love you entirely.
Besides you are right. I could not look on a face I never saw and say, that is
mine, though it seems to me I could wake in your arms and feel that I was at

home. All these preliminaries are however needless. We cannot meet – at least not for years – and years will change us sadly, in one way or another. This summer it is decreed that we all go to Polvellan in Cornwall – the place whence I wrote you my first mad letters – so gaily! We shall go and return together. So no hope of Bonn for this year. Another perhaps, and only perhaps, and even then I may be so surrounded as to make our meeting impossible; for I take for granted you would not choose to see me always in the presence of others. I could not bear that.

I am almost sorry to hear of your longing and begin to wish you did not love me so much. I would not cost you one uneasy thought, love. Don't let it go to your head. You would very likely be disappointed in me – you who have had so much beauty and talent and pleasure. Your fancy is wonderful and I love you for it and did from the first. I would fantasize with you to the limits of possibility, and beyond. I would humour you in your wildest vagaries and desires, – but do not let it trouble your repose. You are in command of yourself – that's good my friend – keep in command – I do not wish to usurp. My love is far more tender than demanding. All I ask is that yours may be the same but you will tell me that is not in man's nature. Alas, do I know it? I must go. Good night. I kiss your hair and your portrait.

AUSTIN TO PUCKLER-MUSKAU

18 July 1832

I am not entirely satisfied with your last letter. There was very little *coeur*, very little tenderness in it, and *without that*, how would I like a request which it required a thousand folds of tenderness to envelop. Now you will cry out about prudery, as you wish. You would not find me a prude, dearest, but I should be profoundly wounded and afflicted by any thing that seemed like cold, hard sensuality.

Are you angry that I did not send you what you asked for? It was not prudery – for I cannot conceive the thing I would refuse you in the outpouring of fondness. But there was some thing, I can hardly define what, that wounded me in the manner of asking – some thing that looked like trying what you could make me do. Such a trial of your power over a confiding, enthusiastic heart I should *hate* you for. I should give you that, as I would a hand, an eye, my heart's blood, if we were once bound together in love, but in the same manner . . . .

and not, beloved, in the spirit of a wanton. Whatever were a source of pleasure to you would be sacred in my eyes. It comes over me like an icy shudder, Good God, if I am writing thus, and write the tears gushing from my eyes, to one who does not, cannot understand me – to one whose heart is hardened and seared by debauchery! If that were so, miserable world it be for *me*, – more miserable for *you*. Sometimes I fear your Mephistopheles nature . . . .

THE REV. CHARLES KINGSLEY
1819–1875

The Rev. Charles Kingsley is best known today as the author of 'The Water Babies' and other popular novels. In his time he was also known as a leading exponent of 'muscular Christianity' and a social reformer (though when, in later life, he became the Queen's favourite parson, he soft-pedalled on the social reform). He was first converted by Fanny Grenfell, a well-to-do Tractarian with whom he fell in love. However, the Tranctarian notion that the body was evil and celibacy the ideal was an inconvenient one for lovers. So in his turn Kinglsey had to convert her away from these Romish notions to the idea of the holiness of matter as expounded by F. D. Maurice.

If the body was holy, this did not mean that it was to be indulged. Kingsley resorted to scourging himself, sleeping on the floor once a week and regular fasting in order to keep himself pure until their marriage in January 1844. Even then they agreed that they would defer full consumma- tion for the first month of their marriage. As far as he was concerned, heaven was going to consist of eternal congress with Fanny – 'those thrilling writhings are but dim shadows of a union which shall be perfect' – and this imaginatively religious approach to sex seems to have contributed very largely to the success of their marriage. As Fanny lay dying in 1875 he quickly succumbed to pneumonia, so neither had to wait very long for the other.

In the first of the extracts that follow he proposes a kind of imaginary intimacy conducted on a purely spiritual plane combined with prayer. The second was written after their first meeting following their engagement. His wedding gift that Fanny proposes they look at before going to bed on their first night, is his biography of St. Elizabeth, which contained his own illus- trations of this Hungarian saint's very unpleasant matyrdom. We can only surmise that Fanny examined these picures – of naked women, clearly mod- elled on herself, being tortured or murdered – in the eccentric spirit in which they were meant.

Sunday night. Helston.

2 October 1843

Darling! Darling baby! I received your letter today – I cannot say that it made me unhappy. All its confessions were but pledges of love. I see you love me enough to weep freely on my bosom. Are you lowered in my eyes! No! So you did not use much voluntary mortification? Well! God saw, perhaps, that the involuntary chastisement of sickness would be more beneficial to you than the lash, and scourge, and vigil. He knew best doubtless, and this treatment has done its work – for how you are improved. I can see in your few letters the working of a humility and health and soberness...And so you only abstained from inflicting pain because I commanded! Did I not know your heart? I feared your old morbid melancholy venting itself in physical self-torture, as it did with the old ascetics. When you are in my arms you may mortify yourself as you will – I shall fear no extravagances then...

Matter is holy – awful glorious matter. Let us never use those words animal and brutal in a degrading sense. Our animal enjoyments must be religious ceremonies...When you go to bed tonight, forget that you ever wore a garment, and open your lips for my kisses and spread out each limb that I may lie between your breasts all night (Canticles 1, 13)...At a quarter past eleven lie down, clasp your arms and every limb around me, and with me repeat the Te Deum aloud . . . .

24 October 1843

My darling baby...What can I do but write to my naughty baby who does not love me at all and who of course has forgotten me by this time? But I have not forgotten her, for my hands are perfumed with her delicious limbs, and I cannot wash off the scent, and every moment the thought comes across me of those mysterious recesses of beauty where my hands have been wandering, and my heart sinks with a sweet faintness and my blood tingles through every limb for a moment and then all is still again in calm joy and thankfulness to our loving God. And I ask myself – Is it not all a dream? No! We are delivered safe! Home at last! Glory to God! And every loving moment I feel a strange freedom and lightness. Oh happy me! My dear dear wife! I will pray much tonight – for all our friends...for your freedom from these spasms (for which I love you more, for they show that your very body yearns for married love) . . . . Kiss me my wife! Charles.

GRENFELL TO KINGSLEY

Sat. 9 Dec 1843

My own darling husband – Your letter of yesterday has just come and is such a comfort to me...My protector, my shield, my refuge, my all in all! How shall we spend our wedding day? – you desire me to tell you. Why, we shall arrive at Cheddar about five to find dinner ready. We shall then have been 2½ hours in the journey with people. Instead of being able to cry on your bosom when I turn away from my sisters and home I shall have to dry my tears and remember that other eyes are upon me, besides yours. It will be a self-denying beginning to our married life – painful but salutary. Then we shall be at Cheddar as I said at dinner, and I will sit very near you, but before dinner have a long, long kiss – and after dinner we shall be very weary...for how can one sleep the night before such a parting as the 9th of Jan?

So after dinner I shall perhaps feel worn out so I shall just lie on your bosom and say nothing but feel a great deal, and you will be very loving and kiss me and call me your poor child. And then we shall read psalms – perhaps not tho' till we go up to bed – but you will perhaps show me your Life of Saint Elizabeth, your wedding gift, and we will not arrange our rooms till Wednesday... for my heart will want healing. And then after tea we will go up to rest! We will undress and bathe and then you will come to my room, and we will kiss and love very much and read psalms aloud together, and then we will kneel down and pray in our night dresses. Oh! What solemn bliss! How hallowing! And then you will take me up in your arms, will you not? And lay me down in bed. And then you will extinguish our light and come to me! How I will open my arms to you and then sink into yours! And you will kiss me and clasp me and we will both praise God alone in the dark night with His eye shining down upon us and His love enclosing us. After a time we shall sleep! . . . .

And yet I fear you will yearn so for fuller communion that you will not be so happy as me. And I too perhaps shall yearn, frightened as I am! But every yearning will remind me of our self-denial, your sorrow for sin, your strength of repentance. And I shall glory in my yearning, please God! O God let it be so!

For I am weak, And my beloved would be weak but for Thee! Strengthen us, that we repine not at the self-inflicted fast which Thy Spirit suggested, a fast in the midst of plenty. One bitter drop in a cup overflowing with sweetness, all from Thee. The food from Thee, the soil from ourselves. Blessed Lord strengthen us. Charles, dearest one, I pray thus because I will confess to you that at moments I have wavered. Only momentary waverings! And then the humiliation of feeling that I repine at what should be my glory – even your self-denial! Darling! Do you ever waver? If you do, do not wrestle against the feeling, but thank God even with an unthankful heart for giving you grace to make the resolution, and ask for strength to keep it. Oh! if we could not only take our burdens to the foot of the Cross, but leave them there, as Jesus himself invites us to do, how lightly should we tread...

God bless you my beloved. This day month! Pray God to preserve us till then – Your own own Fanny.

ROBERT BROWNING   ELIZABETH BARRETT
1812–1889   1806–186

A childhood injury rendered Elizabeth Barrett a lifelong invalid and the Victorian way with invalids was to confine them permanently indoors. It is therefore unlikely that she would ever have met Robert Browning if her poetry had not drawn from him, on January 10, 1845, a letter of esteem and admiration which, in retrospect, reads like a genuine love letter. The relationship blossomed slowly but surely from this point – it took four months of solid Victorian correspondence before they actually met. But the courtship was threatened from the first by Elizabeth's jealous and tyrannical father, and it came under increasing strain until the two of them made the decision to elope. Elizabeth Barrett left the suffocating gloom of Wimpole Street for Pisa with her beloved and, for the last 15 years of her life she was never separated from him. Her father later remarked: 'I have no objection to the young man, but my daughter should have been thinking of another world.'

In the very opening of this celebrated correspondence there is already a strange intimation of the love that is to develop between the two poets. It is as though two seeds are being planted in receptive soil.

Friday 10 January 1845

I love your verses with all my heart, dear Miss Barrett, – and this is no off-hand complimentary letter that I shall write, – whatever else, no prompt matter-of-course recognition of your genius and there a graceful and natural end of the thing: since the day last week when I first read your poems, I quite laugh to remember how I have been turning and turning again in my mind what I should be able to tell you of their effect upon me – for in the first flush of delight I thought I would this once get out of my habit of purely passive enjoyment, when I do really enjoy, and thoroughly justify my admiration– perhaps even, as a loyal fellowcraftsman should, try and find fault and do you some little good to be proud of hereafter! – but nothing comes of it all – so into me has it gone, and part of me has it become, this great living poetry of yours, not a flower of which but took root and grew – oh, how different that is from lying to be dried and pressed flat and prized highly and put in a book with a proper account at top and bottom, and shut up and put away . . . . and the book called a 'Flora', besides! After all I need not give up the thought of doing that, too, in time; because even now, talking with whoever is worthy, I can give a reason for my faith in one and another excellence, the fresh strange music, the affluent language, the exquisite pathos and true new brave thought – but in this addressing myself to you, your own self, and for the first time, my feeling rises altogether. I do, as I say, love these books with all my heart – and I love you too: do you know I was once not very far from seeing – really seeing you? Mr. Kenyon said to me one morning would you like to see Miss Barrett? – then he went to announce me, – then he returned . . . . you were too unwell – and now it is yeàrs ago – and I feel as at some untoward passage in my travels – as if I had been close, so close, to some world's-wonder in chapel or crypt, only a screen to push and I might have entered, but there was some slight . . . . so it now seems . . . . slight and just-sufficient bar to admission, and the half-opened door shut, and I went home my thousands of miles, and the sight was never to be!

Well, these Poems were to be – and this true thankful joy and pride with which I feel myself

Yours ever faithfully,
Robert Browning.

Saturday, January 1845

I thank you, dear Mr. Browning, from the bottom of my heart. You meant to give me pleasure by your letter – and even if the object had not been answered, I ought still to thank you. But it is thoroughly answered. Such a letter from such a hand! Sympathy is dear – very dear to me: but the sympathy of a poet & of such a poet, is the quintessence of sympathy to me! Will you take back my gratitude for it? – agreeing too that of all the commerce done in the world, from Tyre to Carthage, the exchange of sympathy for gratitude is the most princely thing?

For the rest you draw me on with your kindness. It is difficult to get rid of people when you once have given them too much pleasure – that is a fact, & we will not stop for the moral of it. What I was going to say . . . . after a little-natural hesitation . . . . is, that if ever you emerge without inconvenient effort from your 'passive state,' & will tell me of such faults as rise to the surface & strike you as important in my poems (for of course, I do not think of troubling you with criticism in detail) – you will confer a lasting obligation on me, and one which I shall value so much, that I covet it at a distance. I do not pretend to any extraordinary meekness under criticism – and it is possible enough that I might not be altogether obedient to yours. But with my high respect for your power in your Art, your experience as an artist, it would be quite impossible for me to hear a general observation of yours on what appear to you my master-faults, without being the better for it hereafter in some way. I ask for only a sentence or two of general observation – and I do not ask even for that, so as to teaze you – but in the humble, low voice, which is so excellent a thing in women – particularly when they go a-begging. The most frequent general criticism I receive, is I think, upon the style . . . . 'if I would but change my style!'– But that is an objection (isn't it?) to the writer bodily? Buffon says, and every sincere writer must feel, that 'Le style c'est l'homme'– a fact, however, scarcely calculated to lessen the objection with certain critics. –

Is it indeed true that I was so near to the pleasure and honour of making your acquaintance? – and can it be true that you look back upon the lost opportunity with any regret? – But, ... you know . . . . if you had entered the 'crypt,' you might have caught cold, or been tired to death, & wished yourself 'a thousand miles off'– which wd have been worse than travelling them. It is not my interest however to put such thoughts in your head about its being 'all for the best' – and I would rather hope (as I do) that what I lost by one chance I may recover by some future one. Winters shut me up as they do a dormouse's eyes: in the spring, we shall see & I am so much better that I seem turning round to the outward world again. And in the meantime I have learnt to know your voice, not merely from the poetry but from the kindness in it.

I am writing too much, notwithstanding, – and notwithstanding that I am writing too much, I will write of one thing more. I will say that I am your debtor, not only for this cordial letter & for all the pleasure which came with it, but in other ways, & those the highest: & I will say that while I live to follow this divine art of poetry, ... in proportion to my love for it & my devotion to it, I must be a devout admirer & student of your works. This is in my heart to say to you & I say it.

And, for the rest, I am proud to remain

Your obliged & faithful

Elizabeth B. Barrett

GUSTAVE FLAUBERT
1821–1880

Flaubert, having been deliberately celibate for two years, clapped eyes on Louise Colet in 1846 as she was posing for the sculptor, James Pradier, and two days later Flaubert was in her bed. She was a few years older than he was, married, a journalist and minor poet, and something of a feminist. As a novelist Flaubert was a perfectionist, religiously devoted to 'le mot juste', and there was a monkish ambivalence to his passion that could not but irritate his lover. However, the love-letters of the 'Hermit of Croisset', carefully preserved by Colet after their nine years relationship, remain one of the treasures of nineteenth century French literature.

FLAUBERT TO COLET

Croisset

August 6 - 7 1846

I am shattered, numb, as though after a long orgy; I miss you terribly. There is an immense void in my heart. Formerly I was calm, proud of my serenity. I worked keenly and steadily from morning to night. Now I cannot read, or think, or write. Your love has made me sad. I can see you are suffering;

I foresee I will make you suffer. Both for your sake and for my own. I wish we had never met, and yet the thought of you is never absent from my mind. In it I find an exquisite sweetness. Ah! How much better it would have been to stop short after our first ride together! I had forebodings that things would turn out as they have! The next day, when I didn't come to Phidias', it was because I already felt myself sliding down the slope. I wanted to stop: what pushed me? So much the worse! So much the better! God did not give me a merry constitution; no one senses more keenly than I the wretchedness of life. I believe in nothing – not even in myself, which is rare. I devote myself to Art because it gives me pleasure to do so, but I have no faith whatever in beauty, any more than in anything else. So the part of your letter in which you speak of patriotism, poor darling, would have made me laugh if I had been in a gayer mood. You will think that I am hard, I wish I were. All those who cross my path would benefit from my being so, and so would I, with my heart that's been cropped close – like meadow grass in autumn by all the passing sheep. You would not believe me when I told you I was old. Alas, yes, for every sensation that enters, my soul turns sour, like wine poured into jars too often used. If you knew all the inner forces that have consumed me, all the mad desires that have passed through my head, everything I have tried and experienced in the way of sensations and passions, you would see that I am not so young! It is you who are a child, you who are fresh and new, you whose candour makes me blush. The grandeur of your love fills me with humility; you deserved someone better than I. May lightning strike me, may all possible curses fall upon me if ever I forget that! You ask me whether I despise you because you gave yourself to me too quickly. Have you really been able to suspect that? Never, never: whatever you do, whatever may happen, I am devoted to you for life, to you, to your daughter, to anything and anyone you wish. That is a vow. Remember it. Use it. I make it because I can keep it.

Yes, I desire you and I think of you. I love you more than I loved you in Paris. I can no longer do anything; I keep seeing you in the studio, standing near your bust, your long curls stirring on your white shoulders, your blue dress, your arm, your face – everything. Ah! Now *strength* is beginning to circulate in my blood. You seem to be here; I am on fire, my nerves tremble...you know how...you know the heat of my kisses.

Ever since we said we loved each other, you have wondered why I have never added the words 'for ever'. Why? Because I always sense the future, the antithesis of everything is always before my eyes. I have never seen a child without thinking that it would grow old, nor a cradle without thinking of a grave. The sight of a naked woman makes me imagine her skeleton. As a result, joyful spectacles sadden me and sad ones affect me but little. I do too much inward weeping to shed outward tears – something read in a book moves me more than a real misfortune. When I had a family, I often wished I had none, so that I might be freer, free to live in China or among savages. Now that my family is gone, I long for it, and cling to the walls that still retain the imprint of its shadow. Others would be proud of the love you lavish on me, their vanity would drink its fill of it, and their male egotism would be flattered to its inmost depths. But after the moments of frenzy have passed, my heart swoons with sadness, for I say to myself: "She loves me and I love her too, but I do not love her enough. If she had never known me, she would have been spared all the tears she is shedding." Forgive me, forgive me in the name of all the rapture you have given me. But I have a presentiment of immense unhappiness for you. I fear lest my letters be discovered, that everything become known. *I am sick and my sickness is you.*

You think that you will love me for ever, child. For ever! What presumption on human lips! You have loved before, have you not? So have I. Remember that you have said "for ever" before. But I am bullying you, hurting you. You know that my caresses are fierce. No matter: I should rather inject some disquiet into your happiness now than deliberately exaggerate its extent, as men always do, to make you suffer the more when it ends – who knows? You will thank me later, perhaps, for having had the courage not to be more tender. Ah! If I lived in Paris, if every day of my life could be passed at your side – yes, then I'd let myself be swept away by this current, without crying for help! I should find in you, for my heart, my body and my mind, a daily gratification that would never weary me. But apart, destined to see each other only rarely, how frightful! What a prospect! What can we do? Still – I cannot imagine how I was able to leave you. But that is how I am; there you see my wretched character. If you were not to love me, I should die; but you do love me, and I am writing you to stop. I am disgusted by my own stupidity. But in whatever direction I look I see only unhappiness! I wish I might have come into your life like a cool brook to refresh its thirst, not as a devastating torrent. At the thought of me your flesh would have thrilled, your heart smiled. Never curse me! Ah, I shall love you well before loving you no longer. I shall always bless you – your image will stay with me, all imbued with poetry and tenderness, as last night was bathed in the milky vapour of its silvery mist...

I owe you a frank explanation of myself, in response to a page of your letter which makes me see that you harbour illusions about me. It would be cowardly of me (and cowardice is a vice that disgusts me, in whatever aspect it shows itself) to allow these to persist.

My basic character, whatever anyone may say, is that of the mountebank. In my childhood and my youth I was wildly in love with the stage. I should perhaps have been a great actor if I had happened to be born poorer. Even now, what I love above all else, is *form*, provided it be beautiful, and nothing beyond it. Women whose hearts are too ardent and whose minds too exclusive do not understand this religion of beauty, beauty considered apart from emotion. They always demand a cause, an end. I admire tinsel as much as gold: indeed, the poetry of tinsel is even greater, because it is sadder. The only things that exist for me in the world are splendid poetry, harmonious, well-turned, singing sentences, beautiful sunsets, moonlight, pictures, ancient sculpture, and strongly marked faces. Beyond that, nothing. I would rather have been Talma than Mirabeau, because he lived in a sphere of purer beauty. I am as sorry for caged birds as for enslaved human beings. In all of politics, there is only one thing that I understand: the riot. I am as fatalistic as a Turk, and believe that whether we do everything we can for the progress of humanity, or nothing at all, makes no whit of difference. As for that "progress," I have but an obtuse comprehension of muddy ideas. I am completely out of patience with everything pertaining to that kind of language. I despise modern tyranny because it seems to me stupid, weak, and without the courage of its convictions. But I have a deep cult of ancient tyranny, which I regard as mankind's finest manifestation. I am above all a man of fantasy, caprice, lack of method. I thought long and *very seriously* (don't laugh, it is a memory of my best hours) of becoming a Mohammedan in Smyrna. The day will come when I will go and settle somewhere far from here, and nothing more will be heard of me. As for what ordinarily touches men most closely, and for me is secondary – I mean physical love – I have always kept it separate from this other. I heard you jeer at J.J. on this account the other day: his case is mine exactly. You are the only woman whom I have both loved and possessed. Until now I used women to satisfy desires aroused in me by other women. You made me untrue to my system, to my heart, perhaps to my nature, which, incomplete in itself, always seeks the incomplete.

I loved one woman from the time I was fourteen until I was twenty, without telling her, without touching her; and after that I went three years without feeling sexual desire. At one time I thought I should continue so until I died, and I thanked God. I wish I had neither body nor heart, or rather, I wish I might be dead, for the figure I cut on this earth is infinitely ridiculous. That is what makes me mistrustful and fearful of myself.

You are the only woman to whom I have dared to try to give pleasure, the only one, perhaps, to whom I have given it. Thank you, thank you for that! But will you understand me to the end? Will you be able to bear the burden of my spleen, my manias, my whims, my prostrations and my wild reversals? You tell me, for example, to write you every day, and if I don't you will reproach me. But the very idea that you want a letter every morning will prevent me from writing it. Let me love you in my own way, in the way my nature demands, with what you call my originality. Force me to do nothing, and I will do everything.

FLAUBERT TO COLET

Croisset
Midnight. Aug. 8-9.

My deplorable mania for analysis exhausts me. I doubt everything, even my doubt. You thought me young, and I am old. I have often spoken with old people about the pleasures of this earth, and I have always been astonished by the brightness that comes into their lacklustre eyes; just as they could never get over their amazement at my way of life, and kept saying "At your age! At your age! You! You!" Take away my nervous exaltation, my fantasy of mind, the emotion of the moment, and I have little left. That's what I am underneath. *I was not made to enjoy life.* You must not take these words in a down-to-earth sense, but rather grasp their metaphysical intensity. I keep telling myself that I'll bring you misfortune, that were it not for me your life would have continued undisturbed, that the day will come when we shall part (and I protest in advance). Then the nausea of life rises to my lips, and I feel immeasurable self-disgust and a wholly Christian tenderness for you.

At other times – yesterday, for example, when I had sealed my letter – the thought of you sings, smiles, shines, and dances like a joyous fire that gives out a thousand colours and penetrating warmth. I keep remembering the graceful, charming, provocative movement of your mouth when you speak – that rosy, moist mouth that calls forth kisses and sucks them irresistibly in. What a good idea I had, to take your slippers. If you knew how I keep looking at them! The bloodstains are fading: is that their fault? We shall do the same: one year, two years, six, what does it matter? Everything measurable passes, everything that can be counted has an end. Only three things are infinite: the sky in its stars, the sea in its drops of water, and the heart in its tears. Only in that capacity is the heart large; everything else about it is small. Am I lying? Think, try to be calm. One or two shreds of happiness fill it to overflowing, whereas it has room for all the miseries of mankind.

By the way – so we'll christen the blue dress together. I'll try to arrive some evening about six. We'll have all night and the next day. We'll set the night ablaze! I'll be your desire, you'll be mine, and we'll gorge ourselves on each other to see whether we can be satiated. Never! No, never! Your heart is an inexhaustible spring, you let me drink deep, it floods me, penetrates me, I drown. Oh! The beauty of your face, all pale and quivering under my kisses! But how cold I was! I did nothing but look at you; I was surprised, charmed. If I had you here now...Come, I'll take another look at your slippers. They are something I'll never give up; I think I love them as much as I do you. Whoever made them, little suspected how my hands would tremble when I touch them. I breathe their perfume; they smell of verbena – and of you in a way that makes my heart swell.

Adieu, my life, adieu my love, a thousand kisses everywhere. Phidias has only to write, and I will come. Next winter there will no longer be any way for us to see each other, but if Phidias writes between now and the beginning of the winter I'll come to Paris for at least three weeks. Adieu, I kiss you in the place where I *will* kiss you, where I wanted to; I put my mouth there, je me roule sur toi, mille baisers. Oh! donne-m'en, donne'm'en!

FLAUBERT TO COLET

Monday, 10 p.m. September 14, 1846

If I were in Paris...how I would love you! I would sicken, die, stupefy myself, from loving you; I would become nothing but a kind of sensitive plant which only your kisses would bring to life. No middle course! Life! And life is precisely that: love, love, sexual ecstasy. Or, something which resembles that but is its negation: namely, the Idea, the contemplation of the Immutable – in a word, Religion, in the broadest sense. I feel that you are too lacking in that, my love, I mean, it seems to me that you do not greatly adore Genius, that you do not tremble to your very entrails at the contemplation of the beautiful. It is not enough to have wings: they must bear you aloft. One of these days I will write you a long literary letter. Today I finished *Sakountala*. India dazzles me. It is superb. My studies of Brahminism this winter have nearly driven me crazy. There have been moments when I thought I'd lost my wits...

FLAUBERT TO COLET

Croisset,

Friday 10 p.m. September 18, 1846

You tell me, my angel, that I have not initiated you into my inner life, into my most secret thoughts. Do you know what is most intimate, most hidden, in my heart, and what is most authentically myself? Two or three modest ideas about art, lovingly brooded over; that is all. The greatest events of my life have been a few thoughts, a few books, certain sunsets on the beach at Trouville, and talks five or six hours long with a friend now married and lost to me. I have always seen life differently from others, and the result has been that I've always isolated myself (but not sufficiently, alas!) in a state of harsh unsociability, with no exit. I suffered so many humiliations, I so shocked people and made them indignant, that I long ago came to realize that in order to live in peace one must live alone and seal one's windows lest the air of the world seep in. In spite of myself I still retain something of this habit. That is why I deliberately avoided the company of women for several years. I wanted no hindrance to my innate moral precept. I wanted no yoke, no influence. In the end I no longer desired women's company at all. Stirrings of the flesh, throbbings of the heart, were absent from my life, and I was not even conscious of my sex. As I told you, I had an overwhelming passion when I was little more than a child. When it ended I decided to divide my life in two parts: to put on one side my soul, which I reserved for Art, and on the other my body, which was to live as best it could. Then you came along and upset all that. So here I am, returning to a human existence!

You have awakened all that was slumbering, or perhaps decaying, within me! I have been loved before, and intensely, though I'm one of those who are quickly forgotten and more apt to kindle emotion than to keep it alive. The love I arouse is always that felt for something a little strange. Love, after all, is only a superior kind of curiosity, an appetite for the unknown that makes you bare your breast and plunge headlong into the storm.

As I said, I have been loved before, but *never the way you love me*; nor has there ever been between a woman and myself the bond that exists between us two. I have never felt for any woman so deep a devotion, so irresistible an attraction; never has there been such complete communion. Why do you keep saying that I love the tinselly, the showy, the flashy? "Poet of form!" That is the favourite term of abuse hurled by utilitarians at true artists. For my part, until someone comes along and separates for me the form and the substance of a given sentence, I shall continue to maintain that that distinction is meaningless. Every beautiful thought has a beautiful form, and vice versa. In the world of Art, beauty is a by-product of form, just as in our world temptation is a by-product of love. Just as you cannot remove from a physical body the qualities that constitute it – colour, extension, solidity – without reducing it to a hollow abstraction, without destroying it, so you cannot remove the form from the Idea, because the Idea exists only by virtue of its form. Imagine an idea that has no form – such a thing is as impossible as a form that expresses no idea. Such are the stupidities on which criticism feeds. Good stylists are reproached for neglecting the Idea, the moral goal; as though the goal of the doctor were not to heal, the goal of the painter to paint, the goal of the nightingale to sing, as though the goal of Art were not, first and foremost, Beauty!

JOHN RUSKIN
1819–1900

The parents of John Ruskin agreed to his marrying Euphemia Grey because the last time his passion had been thwarted he had burst a blood vessel and left Oxford with a fourth class degree. This was in 1859, when he had heard that Adele Domecq, daughter of his father's business partner in Spain, was to be married to someone else. On his wedding night, 10 April 1848, however, he took one look at Effie's mature beauty and found he had no appetite for the business. The excuses he offered never carried much conviction, from his concern on the honeymoon that she should preserve her strength for climbing the Swiss mountains, to his later judgement that she was mentally unfit to bring up children.

The explanation he produced at the time of the divorce six years later that the marriage had been arranged for him and that he had not really loved her, thus making consumation wrong from the highest romantic principles, cannot be sustained from the evidence of his love-letters, though the terror of female sexuality in his letter of 15 December 1847 is unmistakeable. Perhaps the most curious aspect of the divorce however, was the universal moral outrage from Victorian society at the wickedness of a man who refused to have sexual relations with his wife.

Nowadays, too, Ruskin is condemned, but as a Humbert Humbert figure, forever looking for his Lolita. In 1859 he fell in love with a ten year old girl, Rose la Touche, and asked for her hand as soon as she came of age, with, unsurprisingly, little approbation from her mother – who was, or had been, in love with him herself – but the girl contracted a form of religious mania and died in 1875. The whole episode is treated as a sublime romantic tragedy in Ruskin's autobiography.

However, it would beg a few questions to label as inadequate and destructive one of the greatest aesthetic and social reformers of the nineteenth century. In 1892 Gladstone put him up for poet laureate, until it was pointed out that Ruskin was, by then, out of his mind.

RUSKIN TO GRAY

Folkestone
30 November 1847

My Beloved Effie

I never thought to have felt time pass slowly any more – but – foolish that I am, I cannot help congratulating myself on this being the last day of November – Foolish, I say – for what pleasure so ever may be in store for us, we ought not to wish to lose the treasure of time – nor to squander away the heap of gold even though its height should keep us from seeing each other for a little while. But your letter of last night shook all the philosopher out of me. That little undress bit! Ah – my sweet Lady – What naughty thoughts had I. – Dare I say? – I was thinking – thinking, naughty – happy thought, that you would soon have – some one's arms to keep you from being cold! Pray don't be angry with me. How could I help it? – how can I? I'm thinking so just now, even. Oh – my dearest – I am not so "scornful" neither, of all that I hope for – Alas – I know not what I would not give for one glance of your fair eyes – your saucy eyes. You cruel, cruel girl – now that was just like you – to poor William* at the Ball. I can see you at this moment – hear you. "If you wanted

William was Effie's suitor, till usurped by Ruskin

154

to dance with me, William!" If! You saucy – wicked – witching – malicious – merciless – mischief loving – torturing – martyrizing – unspeakably to be feared and fled – mountain nymph that you are . . . .

RUSKIN TO GRAY

December 1847

I begged mama to thank you for your last letter – it is all just as I thought it would be – and – for your comfort – you may think yourself happy if you get out of Perth without doing any more mischief – and really, now it is not fair. So long as a young lady has her hand free, if people like to run the risk of coming near her – she cannot help it – they have their chance, – and have no right to complain if they lose it. But you know, now, my sweet, you are neither more nor less – stay – I don't mean that – for more you are – and a great deal more – but still you are a very sufficient and entire man-trap – you are a pitfall – a snare – an *ignis fatuus* – a beautiful destruction – a Medusa – I am sorry to think of anything so dreadful in association with such a dear creature – but indeed – people ought to approach Bowers Well now as Dante did the Tower at the gate of the city of Dis.

I don't know anything dreadful enough to liken you to – You are like a sweet forest of pleasant glades and whispering branches – where people wander on and on in its playing shadows they know not how far – and when they come near the centre of it, it is all cold and impenetrable – and when they would fain turn, lo – they are hedged with briars and thorns and cannot escape, but all torn and bleeding – You are like a wrecker on a rocky coast – luring vessels to their fate – Every flower that you set in your hair – every smile that you bestow – nay – every gentle frown even – is a false light lighted on the misty coast of a merciless gulph – Once let the ships get fairly embayed and they are all to pieces in no time – You are like a fair mirage in the desert – which people follow with weary feet and longing eyes – until they faint on the burning sands – or come to some dark salt lake of tears – You are like the bright – soft – swelling – lovely fields of a high glacier covered with fresh morning snow – which is heavenly to the eye – and soft and winning on the foot – but beneath, there are winding clefts and dark places in its cold – cold ice – where men fall, and rise not again – And then you say you "don't know how it is" – No – there's the dreadfulness of it, – there's the danger – Ah, Effie – you have such sad, wicked ways without knowing it – Such sweet silver under-tones of innocent voice – that when one hears, one is lost – such slight – short – inevitable – arrowy glances from under the bent eyelashes – such gentle changes of sunny and shadowy expression about the lovely lips – such desperate ways of doing the most innocent things – Mercy on us – to hear you ask anybody "whether they take sugar with their peaches"? – don't you recollect my being "temporarily insane" for all the day afterwards – after hearing you ask such a thing – and then all that is the least of it – but you are such a good girl, too – and so sorry for all the harm you do – and so ready to like everybody, in reason – and so surprised when you find they don't understand reason – and so ready to promise after you've half-killed them or driven them mad, that if they won't mind that once, you "won't do it again", and so everything that you ought to be, and can be , that I think you ought to be shut up in an iron cage – or in one of those things which you have got in the Perth Tolbooth – and not allowed to speak to or see anybody – until you are married. A strict convent might do – bye-the-bye – if there are any near Perth.

GRAY TO RUSKIN

Bowerswell
10 February 1848

My dearest John

. . . . You will indeed be a kind husband to me. Many trials we shall probably have but not from want of love on either part – that must be the greatest trial I think in married life finding that the only being perhaps in the world whose affection is necessary to you as a part of your being not loving and assisting you in all your joys and cares, leaving you with the utmost indifference when you are in trouble to get out of it the best way you can, and in Joy not partaking the feeling but perhaps trying to subdue it if not in a similar mood, this would be I think the summit of wretchedness and misery. You who are so kind as a son will be a perfect lover as a husband. What I meant by saying that we had much to find out in each other was not that I expected to find great faults in you, I think I know all that I have to expect, and I shall see your coat brushed and mend your gloves and especially keep you from wearing white hats and in order to compromise the matter with you I shall promise never to wear an excessively Pink Bonnet which can be seen all over the Exhibition although I suppose you have not particular objection to one of a

paler hue. Pink is a very favourite colour of mine but I will subdue the shade
out of respect to your superior discernment in these matters . . . .
Goodbye my dearest love. Ever Yours in all sincerity
Euphemia C. Gray

12 months after the wedding. Ruskin was still promising a
consummation:

Paris
24 April 1849

I expect a line from my dearest love tomorrow at Sens; Do you know, pet,
it seems almost a dream to me that we have been married: I look forward to
meeting you; and to your next bridal night; and to the time when I shall again
draw your dress from your snowy shoulders: and lean my cheek upon them, as
if you were still my betrothed only; and I had never held you in my arms.
God bless you, my dearest.

RICHARD WAGNER
1813-1883

A hasty glance at Richard Wagner the man reveals what would appear
to be a megalomaniac, racist, philandering composer of unbelievably
long operas. However, in view of the lasting stature of his work, he
cannot be dismissed so glibly. "Pity us" he wrote to one of his lovers,
"we are the raw material of the world spirit". As an artist, Wagner was
striking out alone in pursuit of an unprecedented aesthetic synthesis,
drawing together music, drama, art, Teutonic myth and philosophy into
profound and massive operatic structures that still require devotion and
dedication from their initiates even today. From this perspective his
amorous connections, and even his more unpleasant theorising in prose,
were necessary elements in the creative process.
Wagner married disastrously in 1836. His wife, Minna, never quite
got to grips with his occasional need, on behalf of the 'world spirit' for
the emotionally heightening experience of a love-affair; and of all his
attachments, the most passionate was undoubtedly Mathilde
Wesendonck. In 1857, a rich industrialist, Otto Wesendonck, gave the
Wagners the use of 'Asyl', the house next to his in the country. He also
gallantly acquiesced in Wagner's appropriation of his wife, Mathilde, as

the muse that would bring forth Wagner's ecstatic paean to love and death, 'Tristan und Isolde'. Up to a point, at least. Wagner's serenading of Mathilde on her birthday with an arrangement of his setting of her poem, 'Traume' while Otto was away on business, seemed altogether a bit much. The situation broke down completely when Minna intercepted the letter quoted below, and confronted each of the lovers with it.

WAGNER TO WESENDONCK

Zurich
7 April 1858

Just out of bed

Morning confession

Oh no! no! it is not De Sanctis* that I hate but myself for repeatedly finding my poor heart guilty of such weakness! – Shall I offer as an excuse my ill-health and the sensitivity and irritability that it fosters in me? Let us see what happens. Two days ago at noon an angel came to me, blessed and refreshed me; this made me feel so much better, and cheered me so much that in the evening I felt a sincere need to be among friends, in order that they might be allowed to share my inner happiness: I know I would have been most amiable and friendly. I then heard that no one in your house had dared hand you my letter, since De Sanctis was with you. Your husband was of the same opinion. I waited in vain, and finally had the pleasure of receiving Herr v. Marschall, who settled down here for the evening and, with every word he spoke, filled me with a terrible hatred of all the De Sanctises in the world. *The lucky many hours he kept her away from me!* And by means of what gift? Simply by dint of her patience. I could not hold it against him for being so much in earnest; for everyone who has dealings with you is almost certainly in earnest. I too, am in earnest! to the point of tormenting you! But why does she encourage this burdensome pedant? What does she care about Italian? Well, I soon found the answer to that. But the better I understood the reason why, the more annoyed I became with that tiresome man; in my dreams I confused him with Marshall, and from this confusion there emerged a figure in whom I recognised all the misery that the world has in store for me. – And so it went on throughout the night. In the morning I regained my senses, and was able to

De Sanctis is Matthilde's insufferably glamorous teacher of Italian.

158

pray to my angel from the very depths of my heart; and this prayer is love! Love! My soul rejoices in this love which is the well-spring of my redemption. When the day came with its miserable weather the pleasures of your garden were denied me; nor could I get on with my work. And so the whole of my day was a struggle between ill-humour and my longing to be with you and whenever I yearned with all my heart to be with you our tedious pedant kept on coming between us and stealing you from me and I could not help admitting to myself that I hated him. Oh what a wretch I am! I had to tell you; there was no alternative. But it was very petty of me, and I deserve to be properly punished. What is my punishment to be? – I shall spend the entire evening being utterly charming to De Sanctis, and shall speak French in a manner that will be a joy to hear. –

What nonsense I'm talking! Is it the pleasure of talking to myself or the joy of talking to you? – Yes to you! But when I look into your eyes I am lost for words; everything that I might say then becomes meaningless! You see, everything then becomes so indisputably true. I am then so sure of myself whenever these wonderful hallowed eyes rest upon me and I grow lost in contemplation of them! Then there is no longer any object nor any subject; everything then becomes a single entity of deep immeasurable harmony! There I find peace and in that peace the highest and most perfect life! He is a fool who would seek to win the world and a feeling of peace from outside himself! A blind man who would not have recognized your glance nor found his soul within it! Only inside, within us, only deep down does salvation dwell! Only when I do not see you – or may not see you – can I speak to you and explain myself. –

Be good to me, and forgive me and forgive my childishness yesterday: you were quite right to call it that!

The weather seems quite mild. I shall come into the garden today; as soon as I see you I hope I may find you alone for a moment! –

Take my whole soul as a morning salutation! –

When the conductor, Hans von Bulow, arrived at Asyl for a few quiet weeks with his new wife Cosima, he found the place gripped in a seething emotional turmoil, while his wife found the love of her life – Wagner. Five years later, on the 28 November, 1863 she and Wagner

declared their undying and holy passion for one another. On 6
December Wagner wrote this note to his housekeeper:

WAGNER TO MARIE VÖLK

Breslau
6 December 1863

Dear little Marie,
 I shall be returning home again next Wednesday, arriving at Vienna
North station at 7.30 in the evening. Tell Franz to bring the carriage and to be
there on time, and he should also prepare whatever is necessary for the trunk.
Now, my darling, prepare the house for my return, so that I can relax there in
comfort, as I long very much to do. Everything must be clean and tidy, and
well-heated. See that the best room is really welcoming for me: when you have
heated the stove, open the door, so that the temperature in the room warms
up. And plenty of perfume: buy the best bottles, so that it smells really sweet.
Heavens! how I'm looking forward to relaxing with you again at last. (I hope
the pink drawers are ready, too??)? – Yes, indeed! Just be nice and gentle, I
deserve to be well looked after for a change . . . .
 . . . . Love and kisses to my darling! Until we meet again.

 Cosima, daughter of Franz Liszt, was, however, already Wagner's wife in
 all but name, and produced three children by him before she was
 divorced from von Bulow in 1870. Minna had finally succumbed to
 heart disease in 1866, while von Bulow surrendered his wife without a
 murmur. It was simply not his place, as an unworthy acolyte, to offer
 any reproach to the master himself. With the following letter to his
 wife, von Bulow bequeathed her a lifetime of guilt. She lived until 1930.

HANS VON BULOW TO COSIMA VON BULOW

Munich
17 June 1869

 I am grateful to you, dear Cosima, for having taken the initiative and shall
give you no reason to regret it. I am indeed too unhappy myself – through my
own fault – not to wish to avoid wounding you by any unjust reproach whatsoever. As regards this most painful separation, which you have felt to be necessary, I recognize all the wrongs on my side and shall continue to lay stress on
them in the inevitable discussion on the matter with my mother and your
father. I have made you a poor, a sorry return for all the great kindness you

have lavished upon me in our past life. Your own existence was poisoned by me and I can only thank providence for having offered you some compensation, however inadequate, at almost the last moment, when courage to go on shouldering your burden must have been failing you. But, alas, since you left me, I have lost my sole support in life and in my struggle. It was your mind, your heart, your patience, indulgence, sympathy, encouragement, and advice – last and most especially, your presence, your face, and your speech – which, taken all together, constituted that support. The loss of this supreme good, whose full value I recognise only after its loss, has brought about moral and artistic collapse – I am a bankrupt. Do not think that this pitiful cry implies any irony or bitterness towards you. My suffering is so great that I may permit myself to express it since I abstain from accusing anyone of being the author of it but myself.

You have preferred to devote your life and the treasures of your mind and affection to one who is my superior, and, far from blaming you, I approve your action from every point of view and admit you are perfectly right. I swear that the only consoling thought that has from time to time lightened the darkness of my mind and mitigated my external sufferings has been this: at all events Cosima is happy over there . . . .

May God protect and bless the mother of the fortunate children to whom she continues to devote herself.

> While Cosima was able to offer her new husband the proper veneration and self-abnegation due to a great artist from his wife, and while he sort of worshipped her in return, there remained the problem of Wagner's libido, which refused to lie down and die, as hers had. In her diary she noted dispiritedly "R's craving for silk materials". For the creation of 'Parsifal', though Cosima was his official muse, he needed the physical charms of the novelist Judith Gautier to get his creative juices flowing:

WAGNER TO GAUTIER

Sept 1876

O how incredible it all is: you are the cornucopia, the overfulfilment of my life which has been so peaceful and protected since Cosima came to me. You are my largesse, my intoxicating superfluity! (Neatly put, don't you think?) But what does it matter – you understand me. Adieu, Judith!

FERDINAND LASSALLE
1825–1864

Ferdinand Lassalle was a German socialist agitator and demagogue who made use of Karl Marx's ideas while cultivating amicable relations with Bismarck. In calling for 'lebensraum' for 'civilised peoples' at the expense of peoples like the Turks he was in many ways a proto-Nazi, though he himself was from a wealthy Jewish background. With his electrifying effect upon women he gathered a reputation for 'unlawful gallantry'. But at his first sight of Helene von Doenniges, (who bore a striking resemblance to himself) he recognised his soul-mate and realised his destiny. Before they had been introduced he laid his hand on her arm: 'What is the use? We know each other already. You know who I am; and you are Brunnhilde.'

Her parents refused to allow the marriage – she was already being wooed by a young Romanian nobleman, Yanko von Rakowitza – and she was prevented from sending or receiving letters. However, using his connections, Lassalle was able to raise a storm to force an uncoerced statement from her to a third party. She simply announced that she was sick and tired of the whole business and was no longer interested. Humiliated, Lassalle insisted on 'satisfaction' from her father, but instead was sent Rakowitza, who mortally wounded him. His aristocratic and romantic end effectively secured his influence over the German workers against that of Marx and Engels for a quarter of a century. Helene married Rakowitza who died within a year. She re-married twice and went on the stage before eventually committing suicide. No doubt Lassalle would have been well satisfied with the effectiveness of the curse he laid on her in the following letter.

LASSALLE TO DOENNIGES

Munich
20 August 1864

Helene! I write to you, death in my heart. Ruestow's telegram has given me a deadly stroke. You, you betray me! – it is impossible. Yet, yet I cannot believe in so much felony, such horrible betrayal. They have bent your will perhaps for the moment, they have estranged you from yourself; but it is not credible that this can be your true, your permanent will. You cannot have cast from you all shame, all love, all fidelity, all truth to this utmost degree! You would have made yourself discreditable and have dishonoured everything that bears a human face – every better feeling would be a lie; and if you have lied, if you are capable of having reached this lowest degree of depravity, to break such holy oaths and to destroy the truest heart – beneath the sun there would be nothing left in which a human being could believe!

You have imbued me with the determination to struggle for your possession. You have requested me to exhaust first of all every conventional method, instead of eloping with you from Wabern; you have sworn the holiest of oaths to me both verbally and in writing; you have declared, even in your last letter, that you are nothing, nothing but my loving wife, and no power on earth shall prevent you from carrying out this undertaking; and after you have irresistibly drawn to you this faithful heart, which, once it has surrendered, has surrendered for always, you thrust me, with the battle hardly begun, after a fortnight, with scornful laughter down into the abyss, you betray me and destroy me? Yes, you would have achieved that which fate has attempted in vain, to break, to destroy the hardest man, who has withstood all outward storms without flinching...

Helene! my fate lies in your hands! But if you break me through this villainous betrayal, which I cannot endure, may my lot recoil on you and my curse pursue you to the grave! It is the curse of the truest heart, treacherously broken by you, a heart with which you have trifled most disgracefully. It will strike home... Once more I will and must speak to you personally and alone. I will and must hear my death-sentence from your own lips. Only thus shall I believe that which appears otherwise impossible. I am now taking further steps, to gain you from here, and shall then come to Geneva!

May my fate be on your head, Helene!

F. Lassalle

SARAH BERNHARDT
1844–1923

D.H. Lawrence saw Sarah Bernhardt perform in Nottingham when the actress was sixty-three. Afterwards he wrote: 'Take care about going to see Bernhardt. Unless you are very sound, do not go. When I think of her now I can still feel the weight hanging in my chest as it hung there for days after I saw her.' She was the most successful stage actress in history. At 20 she fell in love with the Prince de Ligne and her patron, Alexandre Dumas packed her off to Brussels to recover. However, at a masked ball where she was dressed as Elizabeth I, she met a man in the guise of Hamlet who gave her a rose with a note round its stem which read:

'This flower, Mademoiselle Bernhardt, is like your character, bristling with cruel thorns. Since I have learned your name but do not know your face, carry this rose tomorrow on the promenade and I shall find you. You owe that much to your melancholy Prince of Denmark.'

It was of course the Prince de Ligne. He was equally slick in dropping her. When she called in at one of his parties to announce she was pregnant he showed her the door, murmuring, 'you must realise that if you sit on a pile of thorns, you can never know which one has pricked you'. There is no point in listing the affairs that followed this one. Suffice to say they included half the crowned heads of Europe. She even seduced the flamboyantly homosexual model for Proust's 'Baron de Charlus', Robert de Montesquiou, though he promptly threw up after this novel experience. In 1869, a letter she sent to an early lover, Charles Haas, the model for Proust's hero, Charles Swann, read simply – beneath a drawing of a four-poster bed:

'Come! Come!! Come!!!'

Later she learnt to be a little more sophisticated. During the 1870s her career was linked with that of the actor Jean Mounet-Sully in Burton-Taylor fashion and their professional 'chemistry' made it difficult for them to drift apart personally. Her second letter here, suggests that she was a bit of an actress in bed.

BERNHARDT TO MOUNET-SULLY

Sunday morning, 27 July 1873

Yes, Jean, you were brutal, unjust, and you have gone too far, I felt that your despotism destroyed my dreams of the future forever, for I, too, had dreams . . . . I felt you degraded my dignity as a woman when, as I had asked my friends to wait while I undressed, you imposed yourself, despite everything, and entered my dressing room while they waited at the door. It was as though you were saying: "But I know her, she's my mistress: I see her like this, naked, every day." . . . . I had to submit to your violence in order to avoid a scandal. In fact, you've tortured me with weapons that I myself put in your hands. You used my affection and my love like a flag carried into battle.

Ah! You have hurt me very much, Jean, but I forgive you since that seems to be your wish. Still, to forgive is not to forget. Give my heart some time to reflect, and we'll see what can be made of the scraps that remain of our love. Don't be unhappy. In a few days Art will bring us together once again. Let us not force our love. I give you my brow which you brutalized in such a cowardly way. Perhaps your kisses will revive my love. I doubt it.

MOUNET-SULLY TO BERNHARD – JULY 1873

I promised myself never to write you again. The haughty, glacial manner in which you recalled all the wrongs that my only too violent love may have inflicted upon you filled my heart with sadness . . . . for now I can have no doubt that you no longer love me, if in fact you ever did. So it is not to speak of us, my ever-beloved that I write, but confronted by the attitude of several newspapers in regard to your latest role. I cannot help crying out across the ocean of ice that separates us: "Fear nothing!" You are on the true path . . . . Don't be discouraged. You have achieved a veritable tour de force . . . . If it ever occurs to the critics to see you again in that small role which you transformed into the poetic epitome of womanhood (I am quite serious!) you will be avenged . . . . For they will be forced to eat their words, or else to live forever with an uneasy conscience, the worst thing that can happen – especially to a drama critic.

On that note, dear angel, I kiss – as platonically as possible – the tips of your pretty pink claws . . . .

BERNHARDT TO MOUNET-SULLY – JANUARY 1874

As far as I know, I have done nothing to justify such behaviour, I've told you distinctly that I do not love you any longer. I shook your hand and asked you to accept friendship in place of love. Why do you reproach me? Surely not for lack of frankness. I have been loyal: I have never deceived you; I have been yours completely. It is your fault that you have not known how to hold on to what is yours.

Besides, dear Jean, you must realize that I am not made for happiness. It is not my fault that I am constantly in search of new sensations, new emotions. That is how I shall be until my life is worn away. I am just as unsatisfied the morning after, as I am the night before. My heart demands more excitement than anyone can give it. My frail body is exhausted by the act of love. Never is it the love I dream of.

At this moment I am in a state of complete prostration. My life seems to have stopped. I feel neither joy nor sorrow. I wish you could forget me. What can I do? You must not be angry with me. I'm an incomplete person but a good one at heart. If I could prevent your suffering I would do so!!! But you demand my love, and it is you who have killed it!

I beg you, Jean, let us be friends.

In 1883 Bernhardt was besotted with Jean Richepin, poet, playwright, all-in wrestler and general wild-boy. Unfortunately he was not so wild that he could put up with her other affairs, and he disappeared. She became ill with grief.

My adored, my maddening master, I ask you to pardon me. Oh yes! A great pardon. What I said to you must have been unspeakably vile since you write me in such a howling rage. I am completely stunned. Your words pierce me to the heart, and echo in all my being. I read the eight pages of your letter, each more insulting than the last. I am exhausted by all your reproaches, and still I am yours more than ever. I need you. I cannot exist without you. Come back, I beg you, come back, for I was born to be yours. I swear to you, adored seigneur, that I am not capable of deceiving you. Yes, I know that I like to deceive, that I am made of evil thoughts and betrayals. I deserve every bad name you choose to call me. I am all those things, but I behaved badly only because I felt superior to all who surround me. That is over. You appeared. You blew your powerful breath on my lies, and my equivocal "maybes" and "becauses" were blown away. I drank the truth of love from your lips, and, quivering in your arms, I felt the real, the wild sensations of the body's ecstasy, and I saw in your eyes the absolute supremacy of your being. I gave myself to you completely – and completely new – for I brought you a being that belonged to you and you alone. I did not invent anything about myself. Indeed, I rediscovered myself in you.

Jean, you must forgive my foul temper. You left me without giving me time to think, while I was still moist from your arms, still perfumed by the intoxicating scent of your body. I looked at our bed, thought of our night together, our awakening, our embraces, our —. All right, all right, let us pass over that. I ask your pardon with my arms about your neck, suffering for having cried aloud. Ah! Jean, hold me close, very close. Carry me off into the blue skies of tender loves, roll me in dark clouds, trample me with your thunderstorms, break me in your angry rages. But love me, my adored lover.

However strong my claws, they cannot leave a very deep mark in your heart, since your heart is made of love. Destroy my stupid letter, and tell me that you know I do not deceive you, that I am incapable of deceiving you. It would be cowardly, stupid, foolish.

I uttered a cry of vengeance – and you believed it! It was nothing but rage and pain. What you do not realize, my idol, my master, is that you are always near me, looking at me with your golden glance. Calm yourself, take pity, from the heights where you dwell, on my sad folly. I was sick. I was in the wrong. I submit to your will, and swallow my pride. It would be an unbearable punishment, if you refused to let me kiss your lips. Write me a sweet letter; the last one hurt me so. You aren't scowling any longer, are you? Your sardonic smile has disappeared, hasn't it? I gently kiss your small, beautiful feet.

Let us resume our flight! Never again will I stop its mad course. If you make me suffer too much, I shall simply throw myself from the heights, my love, and – I swear – I shall kill myself in the fall.

I fondle your adored body, I kiss your every hair – and my lips demand that your lips forgive me a thousand times.

PIOTR TCHAIKOVSKY   ANTONINA MILYUKOVA
1840–1893   1849-1917

The life of Piotr Ilyich Tchaikovsky, the leading composer of the Russian nationalist school, was in many respects a miserable one. This can be put down partly to his homosexuality – or rather, to the fact that he wished himself otherwise. Some instinct for self-destruction drove him to marry, and to a woman he hardly knew. But what should have been clear from the letter quoted below, which he received before they became engaged, was that she was mentally unbalanced and passionately in love with him. These facts alone should have been enough to rule her out as a mate for a homosexual.

Antonina Milyukova had fallen in love with him while she had been a student at the Moscow Conservatoire. However, he did not know her from Eve when he received the first of her declarations in May, 1877. But as he was thinking seriously of the advantages of a stable marriage at this time, he was not entirely discouraging. She sent a second letter which he simply put on one side and forgot about.

Tchaikovsky had just started work on what was to be his greatest opera, *Eugene Onegin*, from Pushkin's novel, and he had begun by writing the music for the famous 'letter scene'. In fact, he composed like a man possessed – identifying totally with the character of Tatyana, the writer of the letter. He later admitted that he was in love with this character and despised Onegin's callous treatment of her. Therefore, when Tchaikovsky received a second letter from Antonina, some kind of emotional confusion set in. He met her for the first time on June 1. A day or two later he proposed and was accepted. The next month they were married. By September she had driven him to attempt a kind of indirect suicide by standing in the river as long as he could in the hope of catching pneumonia. They were separated shortly afterwards. She died in a lunatic asylum.

MILYUKOVA TO TCHAIKOVSKY – MAY 1877

I've been in the most agonising state for a whole week, Pyotr Ilich, not knowing whether to write to you or not. I see that my letters are already beginning to be wearisome to you. But will you really break off this correspondence with me, not having seen me even once? No, I am convinced you will not be so cruel. Do you, maybe, take me for a frivolous person or a gullible girl, and therefore place no trust in my letters? How can I prove to you that my words are genuine, and that ultimately I could not lie in such a matter? After your last letter I loved you twice as much again, and your shortcomings mean absolutely nothing to me.

Perhaps if you were a perfect being I would have remained completely cool towards you. I am dying of longing, and I burn with a desire to see you, to sit with you and talk with you, though I also fear that at first I shan't be in a state to utter a word. There is no failing that might cause me to fall out of love with you . . . .

Having today sent a man to deliver my letter to you, I was very surprised to learn that you had left Moscow, and longing descended upon me even more. I sit at home all day, pace the room from corner to corner like a crazy thing, thinking only of that moment when I shall see you. I shall be ready to throw myself on your neck, to smother you with kisses – but what right have I to do this? Maybe, indeed, you take this for effrontery on my part . . . .

I can assure you that I am a respectable and honourable woman in the full sense of the word, and I have nothing that I would wish to conceal from you. My first kiss will be given to you and to no one else in the world. Farewell, my dear one. Do not try to disillusion me further about yourself, because you are only wasting your time. I cannot live without you, and so maybe soon I shall kill myself. So let me see you and kiss you so that I may remember that kiss in the other world. Farewell. Yours eternally, A.M. . . . .

The day before yesterday my letter was already written, and only today am I sending it, for I assume that you have still not returned to Moscow. Again I implore you: come to me. If you knew how I suffer then probably out of pity alone you would grant my request.

CHARLES DODGSON
1832–1898

In a looking-glass way, it is quite appropriate that the Rev. Charles Dodgson (1832–1898), author of little-read treatises on logic and – as 'Lewis Carroll' – best-selling works of 'nonsense' should feature in a book of intimate letters, as he never wrote anything that might be construed as a love-letter in his life. In fact, he was a celibate bachelor don of unerring, even forbidding, rectitude.

However, 'Alice in Wonderland' and other fantasy books for children have been meat and drink to Freudians looking for unconscious sexual imagery, and his eccentric social life has come under similar scrutiny. He loved little girls because he derived spiritual nourishment from contact with their pure and unsullied minds – and there is no evidence from any of his hundreds of 'child-friends' that they derived anything but delightful entertainment and improving instruction from contact with him.

He was also a keen photographer of little girls, but he insisted that they be either completely clothed or completely naked in order to qualify the results – according to Victorian codes – as 'artistic' rather than improper. He was able to carry on in this blameless way with pre-pubescent girls because the Victorians divided 'love' into two distinct categories, one of which only began to be possible after a certain age, at which point chaperones were required. This is, of course, a view diametrically opposed to modern proprieties.

At the same time Dodgson was aware of a certain, say, 'gallantry' in his relations with little girls. He knew that he had a positive antipathy towards little boys. He knew that he liked to entertain his child-friends on their own, and that he tired of most of them after what he called a 'honeymoon' of about a month. Also, he preferred to make friends with middle-class little girls because in Victorian times a friendship with someone of a different social class tended to carry extra complications.

But the most important point is that he only allowed himself a consistent tone of roguish flirtation in his letters on account of the fact that any sexual implications to his relationships were out of the question. Indeed, as he became definitely elderly and old-maidish, he began 'courting' mature teenagers and students.

He encountered the Chataways and four of their fifteen children in 1875 and Gertrude Chataway (1866–1951) became perhaps the most enduring of all his girl-friends. He met the Hulls in August 1877, and again in October, when he noted in his diary 'the children were as delicious as ever', of whom his favourite was Agnes (1867–1936).

'May' Mileham slipped and soaked herself at Eastbourne on August 8 1884, and Dodgson, who was passing by on the Parade did not miss his opportunity to succour and soothe the child. On Sept. 14 he wrote to her '...only to think of it, my dear May! If we haven't forgotten the lock I was to carry off with me! Would you send it please? It should be about 3 inches long, and should have a piece of silk tied around the middle...' In January 1887 he became aware that her parents had broken off their association – a unique occurrence for him.

Christ Church, Oxford
28 October 1876

My dearest Gertrude, You will be sorry, and surprised, and puzzled, to hear what a queer illness I have had ever since you went. I sent for the Doctor, and said "Give me some medicine, for I am tired." He said "Nonsense and stuff! You don't want medicine: go to bed!" I said "No: it isn't the sort of tiredness that wants bed. I'm tired in the face ." He looked a little grave, and said "Oh, it's your nose that's tired: a person often talks too much when he thinks he nose a great deal." I said "No: it isn't the nose. Perhaps it's the hair." Then he looked rather graver and said "Now I understand: you've been playing too many hairs on the piano-forte." "No, indeed I haven't! I said, "and it isn't exactly the hair: it's more about the nose and chin." Then he looked a good deal graver and said "Have you been walking much on your chin lately?" I said "No." "Well!" he said, "it puzzles me very much. Do you think that it's in the lips?" "Of course!" I said, "that's exactly what it is!" Then he looked very grave indeed, and said "I think you must have been giving too many kisses." "Well," I said, "I did give one kiss to a baby-child, a little friend of mine." "Think again," he said, "are you sure it was only one?" I thought again, and said "Perhaps it was eleven times." Then the Doctor said "You must not give her any more till your lips are quite rested again." "But what am I to do?" I said, "because, you see, I owe her a hundred and eighty-two more." Then he looked so grave that the tears ran down his cheek, and he said "You may send them to her in a box." Then I remembered a little box that I once bought at Dover and thought I would some day give it to some little girl or other. So I have packed them all in it very carefully: tell me if they come safe, or if any are lost on the way.

If I had thought of it while you were here, I would have measured you against my door, where I have Xie's height marked, and other little friends. Please tell me your exact height (without your shoes), and I will mark it now.

I hope you're rested after the eight pictures I did of you.

Your most loving friend,
Lewis Carroll.

The Chestnuts, Guildford
30 December 1884

My dearest May,

Thank you very much indeed for your two letters: and extra thanks and kisses for the lock of hair. I have kissed it several times – for want of having you to kiss, you know, even hair is better than nothing . . . . Well, and I should like to see you act a Fairy, very much. If I happen to be going past the Village Hall, while it's going on, I shall rush in (on the pretence that perhaps the house is on fire, or that I thought perhaps there was a mad pig in the road, or any excuse of that kind) just to see how you are getting on . . . .

7 Lushington Road, Eastbourne
6 September 1885

Dearest May,

Thank you very much indeed for the peaches. They were delicious. Eating one was almost as nice as kissing you: of course not quite: I think, if I had to give the exact measurement, I should say "three-quarters as nice." We are having such a lovely time here; and the sands are beautiful. I only wish I could some day come across you, washing your pocket-handkerchief in a pool among the rocks! But I wander on the beach, and look for you, in vain: and then I say," Where is May?" And the stupid boatmen reply, "It isn't May, sir! It's September!" But it doesn't comfort me.

Always your loving
C.L.D

HANNAH CULLWICK
1833-1909

Hannah Cullwick, a working class housemaid, met A.J. Munby (1828-1910), a barrister from an old Yorkshire family, in 1854 in Grosvenor Street, and it was love at first sight. He was a minor poet (admired by Browning), a teacher of Latin in one of the new working men's colleges, and something of a sociologist. This last distinction arose out of his obsession with working women – Wigan was one of his favourite resorts – and the diary he kept recorded his observations of them, which he illustrated whenever he could with photographs. For all his eccentric interests, however, he retained a taste for conventional decorum, and there is something Pooterish in his accounts of his pre-Raphaelite friends – particularly the outrageous Swinburne. The really bizarre aspect of Munby's relationship with Cullwick is not that it crossed the class barriers. It is not even in the fact that they secretly married, in 1873. It is that after the marriage she continued to work as Munby's maid – indeed, she insisted on it. She remained his 'servant wife', and called him 'Massa'. He did not lift a finger to help with the gruelling work involved in running a genteel establishment in those days, and that was the way she liked it. After fifty years this is how he remembered his first vision of her: 'A robust hardworking peasant lass, with the marks of labour and servitude upon her everywhere: yet endowed with a grace and beauty, an obvious intelligence, that would have become a lady of the highest. Such a combination I had dreamt of and sought for; but I have never seen it, save in her.' Eventually they settled in the country in separate houses – his suitably grand, and hers suitably modest.

CULLWICK TO MUNBY

Bearley

1 June 1882

. . . . One thing dear, I feel happy, and that's what I haven't done for many a day, I was singing this morning quite again with a lighter heart nor I have had for a good while. You didn't say anything to make me permanently happy .
. . . but I enjoyed your visit – you was very nice and as sweetmouthed as ever, for kissing, and I enjoyed working for you and waiting on you – so perhaps you'll wonder what's made me happier – It's this darling – I see that you love me as much as ever your nature will let you, and I also see that you enjoy being alone as a bachelor, and having no inclination like other men for a wife it's

decidedly better that you shouldn't be bothered with one about you, and so my mind is more settled and it would be weak and foolish of me to fret for what we have as it were done on purpose, tho' I was quite innocent as to the consequences of such a long engagement, but I must say I used to wonder how ever it would end, and I used to feel every year that the rod was soaking the longer for my own back – so it has proved, tho' I didn't expect this sort of suffering – to be alone in the world – that is of all things the worst thing that a woman can have to endure I am sure, still dear, I do not complain, and indeed you will not let me – so I will not seem to – Time passes wonderfully quick with me so quick that I hardly reckon it, therefore don't you be anxious about me, nor trouble for me....I send you my love and best wishes darling, hoping nothing I've said will vex you, for I'm sure I don't want to do that – I wish you all good and may God bless you as well as myself –

Your loving Hannah

CULLWICK TO MUNBY

Bearley
9 June 1882

My own darling Moussiri

Your letter is a nice one, and I feel so glad as you feel so much the better and happier for your visit to me – I am decidedly better and happier, and when I want to indulge a bit in love, I think over again the few minutes we had a kissing, in the train to Warwick that last day – I enjoyed it so much, and shall never forget it I hope – It was a feeling I very seldom give way to all the years I have known you, but it's delightful and no sin either now we are married, but for all that it has always seemed to me an indulgence that women shan't give way to, but I felt it was my last minutes with you, and I don't think you'll mind me telling you no more nor I mind what you have told me in yourn, and it pleases me to think you can enjoy the sight of me, if it's ever so little. God made the woman for the man, and it's a good thing to care only for one, as I care only for you...but then, when I'm away from you, I don't feel at home with any one else – I would liefer be alone or in bed, still I hope something will turn up for the winter – I should like to be in a little kitchen, and do for some gentleman, or an old lady what can do her own housekeeping, but old lady's are sometimes very fidgety . . . .

. . . . I doubt I shall hardly do justice to your letter my darling – but I'll write and tell you all while I am here if all's well, but I don't wish you to write me so much again – I don't like burning your letters and I don't like to keep them either – short and sweet is what I like from you, but I know you like to hear all you can from me about the folks I meet with . . . .

In March 1886 Cullwick discovered that Munby had been operated on for piles without giving her prior warning.

Bearley

12 March 1886

. . . . I told you in my last that I thought nothing as ever may happen could make me unhappy, but I see I am not sure o'that, for directly I'm not sure how you are I can be as restless as ever I was. And it must be always so while we're apart I reckon . . . . And to think as you've been through all that in this last fortnight, and had me so much on your mind as you even shouted out how you had loved me! Over and over again, and the doctors might have heard you. I am too much knocked back, to say anything about all this my darling, but I am very glad to hear you're better again – There must have been much to be done with you and for you that's only fit for a wife to do, but then you didn't want the gentlemen to know – so I'll say no more – but you did know that it would have been nothing but a journey of love and satisfaction for me...be quiet at home till you're quite well – the walk to your work will be enough to begin with. Oh the miserable and false step you took when you separated me from you, the doctor's orders – And this shows it more and more, without saying a word of all my loneliness and humiliation, and grief of mind and spirit all these years...I must say that if men and women wait for perfection in each other to live together, they'll have to wait till nearly their dying day, for as soon as they're made perfect in God's sight He takes them to himself. It is in this life we want companionship – to bear one another's burden, in the next life we shall not require that help – I could wish that you and me was already at rest – I feel sad and down hearted just now but it'll wear off with time.

OSCAR WILDE
1854–1900

The Victorians worshipped all their heroes and martyrs except one, Oscar Wilde, and he was destroyed for that most Victorian vice and most modern virtue – being himself. To lecture on aesthetics to the trigger-happy miners of Leadville Colorado dressed in knee-breeches, as he did early on in his career, was for him a typical act of bravado. But when, in 1895, he sued the Marquess of Queensbury for calling him a sodomite, he courted his doom closely enough to be set down as a true martyr. Queensbury was acquitted and Wilde was arrested on charges of indecency and sodomy. Ignoring every opportunity of escaping to the continent he chose to face out his triumphant accusers and was given two years hard labour in Reading Gaol.

His fall from success and celebrity was precipitous and inevitable. He was as kind as he was witty but he had one tragic flaw. This was his passion for Lord Alfred Douglas (1870–1945), the spoilt and hated son of the equally unpleasant Queensbury: it was Douglas who insisted on Wilde's original disastrous prosecution of his father.

Wilde never minded that the son had sponged off him shamelessly in his prosperity. But it was the father's pursuit of him with bankruptcy proceedings after   conviction which precipitated what is probably the longest love-letter ever composed. Addressed to Douglas, it was later published as *De Profundis*. He outlived the Marquess by just long enough to be refused financial support by the now freshly-funded Douglas.

The letter to his wife, Constance (1858–1898) with whom he continued on very good terms even after he had deployed his passion in other directions, was written shortly after their marriage.

The first letter to Douglas (Bosie) was read out at the Queensbury trial. His explanation that it was a 'prose sonnet' was too subtle to blunt its impact as a very flowery statement of very straightforward criminal carnality. The last letter to Bosie, which preceded the anagnorisis of the 'De Profundis' letter is taken from an article Douglas was having published in a French journal – until Wilde stopped it. It has been translated back from the French by Stuart Mason, with alterations by Rupert Hart-Davis.

OSCAR TO CONSTANCE WILDE

The Balmoral, Edinburgh
Tuesday
16 December 1884

Dear and Beloved,

Here am I, and you at the Antipodes. O execrable facts, that keep our lips from kissing, though our souls are one.

What can I tell you by letter? Alas! nothing that I would tell you. The messages of the gods to each other travel not by pen and ink and indeed your bodily presence here would not make you more real: for I feel your fingers in my hair, and your cheek brushing mine. The air is full of the music of your voice, my soul and body seem no longer mine, but mingled in some exquisite ecstasy with yours. I feel incomplete without you.

Ever and ever yours
Oscar

Here I stay till Sunday.

WILDE TO LORD ALFRED DOUGLAS

Babbacombe Cliff
January 1893

My Own Boy,

Your sonnet is quite lovely, and it is a marvel that those red rose-leaf lips of yours should have been made no less for music of song than for madness of kisses. Your slim gilt soul walks between passion and poetry. I know Hyacinthus, whom Apollo loved so madly, was you in Greek days.

Why are you alone in London, and when do you go to Salisbury? Do go there to cool your hands in the grey twilight of Gothic things, and come here whenever you like. It is a lovely place – only it lacks you; but go to Salisbury first. Always, with undying love, yours

Oscar

Savoy Hotel

London

Dearest of all Boys, Your letter was delightful, red and yellow wine to me; but I am sad and out of sorts. Bosie, you must not make scenes with me. They kill me, they wreck the loveliness of life. I cannot see you, so Greek and gracious, distorted with passion. I cannot listen to your curved lips saying hideous things to me. I would sooner (be blackmailed by every renter in London) than have you bitter, unjust, hating. I must see you soon. You are the divine thing I want, the thing of grace and beauty; but I don't know how to do it. Shall I come to Salisbury? My bill here is £49 for a week. I have also got a new sitting-room over the Thames. Why are you not here, my dear, my wonderful boy? I fear I must leave; no money, no credit, and a heart of lead.

Your own Oscar

Courtfield Gardens

20 May 1895

My child, Today it was asked to have the verdicts rendered separately. Taylor is probably being judged at this moment, so that I have been able to come back here. My sweet rose, my delicate flower, my lily of lilies, it is perhaps in prison that I am going to test the power of love. I am going to see if I cannot make the bitter warders sweet by the intensity of the love I bear you. I have had moments when I thought it would be wiser to separate. Ah! moments of weakness and madness! Now I see that that would have mutilated my life, ruined my art, broken the musical chords which make a perfect soul. Even covered with mud I shall praise you, from the deepest abysses I shall cry to you. In my solitude you will be with me. I am determined not to revolt but to accept every outrage through devotion to love, to let my body be dishonoured so long as my soul may always keep the image of you. From your silken hair to your delicate feet you are perfection to me. Pleasure hides love from us, but pain reveals it in its essence. O dearest of created things, if someone wounded by silence and solitude comes to you, dishonoured, a laughing-stock, Oh! you can close his wounds by touching them and restore his soul which unhappiness had for a moment smothered. Nothing will be difficult for you then, and remember, it is that hope which makes me live, and that hope alone. What wisdom is to the philosopher, what God is to his saint, you are to me. To keep you in my soul, such is the goal of this pain which men call life. O my love, you whom I cherish above all things, white narcissus in an unmown field, think of the burden which falls to you, a burden which love alone can make light. But be not saddened by that, rather be happy to have filled with an immortal love the soul of a man who now weeps in hell, and yet carries heaven in his heart. I love you, I love you, my heart is a rose which your love has brought to bloom , my life is a desert fanned by the delicious breeze of your breath, and whose cool spring are your eyes; the imprint of your little feet makes valleys of shade for me, the odour of your hair is like myrrh, and wherever you go you exhale the perfumes of the cassia tree.

Love me always, love me always. You have been the supreme, the perfect love of my life; there can be no other.

I decided that it was nobler and more beautiful to stay. We could not have been together. I did not want to be called a coward or a deserter. A false name, a disguise, a hunted life, all that is not for me, to whom you have been revealed on that high hill where beautiful things are transfigured.

O sweetest of all boys, most loved of all loves, my soul clings to your soul, my life is your life, and in all the world of pain and pleasure you are my ideal of admiration and joy.

Oscar

RAMSAY MACDONALD
1866-1937

Ramsay Macdonald was born in Scotland, illegitimate and desperately poor. His future wife, Margaret Gladstone, was well-to-do, from Kensington. She proposed to the up-and-coming Labour politician in 1896 on the steps of the British Museum. He resisted feebly – far too busy striving to do his Duty – too poor – 'still...you have been a Spring shower to me'. She persisted. He succumbed. The marriage was an enormous success. However, despite Macdonald's dour intimations of an early death for himself from overwork, it was Margaret who died young, in 1911. In 1924 he became the Labour Party's first Prime Minister. This love-letter from her is a model of clarity, awe and humility. In fact, it was she who was the pragmatist, he the romantic. He was even guilty of a novel, unhappily extant but happily unpublished. In the letter he writes to his wife on her birthday the stern, Scotch thistly manner blossoms into a surprisingly light romantic touch.

MARGARET GLADSTONE TO RAMSAY MACDONALD – JUNE 1896

My dear Sir

It is only just beginning to dawn on me a very little bit, since your last Sunday's letter, what a gift I have in your love. I can hardly write the word – it seems too big and good to belong to me. I shall not take it in much till I see you. I shall not take it in much then in its fulness – it will just come gradually to us through our lives.

You told me to enquire into my own heart, but I haven't done it. My heart is much too reserved to let me do it. It just gets cross if I ask it what it feels about you. But I am glad that I haven't any feelings of passionate worship because I think I have something deeper still which will wear through all time and all circumstance, and through eter.ity too, for even if, as you said, perhaps we don't have any personal existence after this life, we each have eternity within us here.

If you could have looked at my life the last few days – it is only 2½ now – you would have thought your letter made no difference to me – I eat and sleep and joke and talk just as normal. I don't even have a little underlying feeling of happiness all the time as I should have expected. As I said it is too big and great for me to take in.

But when I think how lonely you have been I want with all my heart to make up to you one little tiny bit for that I have been lonely too. I have envied the veriest drunken tramps I have seen dragging about the streets if they were man and woman because they had each other.

Perhaps after this I shall be cross and disagreeable to you sometimes. I can't bear to think about it, but I know that I may be. With people I don't care about I don't think I ever am, but I do ask your forgiveness for all my imperfections.

This is truly a love letter: I don't know when I shall show it to you: it may still be that I never shall. But I shall never forget that I have had the blessing of writing one.

M.E.G.

20 July 1896

My Dearest Lassie

A kiss to greet you on your birthday morning. May this new mile be crammed of everything that profiteth the soul for you. Not even in Lossiemouth with the bridesmaid photo by me did I think you so sweet as you were last night and as I am sure you are going to be today. I did try to show you how dearly I loved you but I laugh at my performance. I have been so long accustomed to consume my own feelings, that I am a frightfully bad subject for an angel confessor. But you know that, and I'll come out of it in time. You'll teach me to be spry. Everything is so changed to me that I sometimes wonder if I had died and left my body at home and am now in a new state of existence. But that can hardly be as I seem to have known you for some time. Only they say such delusions happen in heaven. Now you see I ramble all over existence to tell you that I greet you on your *dies natalis*. My dearest sweetheart you have made a fool of me. I am so happy. Under this you will find the tiniest wafer of a kiss – so tiny that only your heart will know it is there. Take it as my offering this morning at your shrine. The little book may remind us both in years to come of these early exquisite moments of true love.

> Ever thine, my dearest sweetheart,
> Ramsay

The Dook
X
His kiss

THE AGE OF
PARTNERSHIP

The particular charm of marriage is the duologue, the permanent conversation between two people who talk over everything and everyone till death breaks the record. It is this back-chat which, in the long run, makes a reciprocal equality more intoxicating than any form of servitude or domination.

Cyril Connolly: The Unquiet Grave. 1944

The early feminists of the nineteenth century gave short shrift to the romantic ideal, with all its purity and madness. Sexuality came out from under the covers of passion and romance. The mysterious inclinations of the heart were analysed by psychoanalysts. Birth control became widely available. It was even suggested in many quarters that homosexuality was not an inherently criminal act. Blushes and lingering looks were replaced by flirting and petting. Lovers discussed their relationships rationally.

It might seem that all this ought to have taken the romance out of the relations between the sexes, but quite the opposite is the case. The composer Gustav Mahler, for example, treated his young wife, Alma, in the usual self-centred way of the great nineteenth century artist. But in 1910, the last year of his life, he woke up to the fact that she was a separate individual when he found out that she was being courted by the architect, Walter Gropius. As he lay dying, the letters he wrote to her were those of an enraptured lover: "Oh, how lovely it is to love! And only now do I know what it is! Pain has lost its power and death its thorn. Tristan speaks truth: I am immortal, for how could Tristan's love die?"

The possibilities of amorous discourse were being extended as the barriers to human sexual expression fell. Greater awareness in no way dissolved the mystery. Joyce, for example, combined a frank, pornographic appreciation of his wife with a tender enchantment towards the same woman as the inspiration of his art and the love of his life. As for Janacek's letters to Kamila Stosslava – which are published here for the first time in English – they provide an incomparable record of the extraordinary alchemical workings of love. By their light it becomes clear that his love for her – his perception in her of the very mystery of life – was the essential agent that activated his creativity.

GILBERT CANNAN
1884–1955

Gilbert Cannan was one of the most brilliant stars in the Bloomsbury constellation, but despite a prodigious output of fiction and plays, failed to realise his potential before he went mad in 1923. In 1908 he was vying with Captain Robert Scott for the affections of Kathleen Bruce, the sculptor. Already a well-known explorer, Scott wrote letters befitting an Edwardian leader of men. Cannan wrote as befitting a member of the Bloomsbury group. Bruce must have enjoyed the contrast.

Cannan's sentimental obsession with babies and children seems to have been a feature of the age. (The Scotts' son, when he arrived, was named after Peter Pan)

CANNAN TO KATHLEEN BRUCE

14 April 1908

My dear K,

Quite quite impossible to sleep, after I left you I wandered miles and miles – and miles, exactly where I don't know; through mean streets and prosperous streets, vulgar streets and streets gentle, ... streets where the people were not asleep but all dead, and streets where there was God. N.B. all these beautiful reflections are of subsequent date. The cause of the wanderings was the wonderful you, the maker of beautiful things, the creator sole and without male assistance of enough lovely babies to stock the whole world civilised and uncivilised – though I imagine that in the babies' kingdom there is no knowledge of civilisation or they would surely refuse to visit civilised men and women...What about you? Oh! yes. That you should have – have – have – I don't know – given me so many hours of yourself, liked my works, liked me. Ye Gods. It seems incredible. – Do I sleep, do I dream, is babies about? There must be babies about and one of them has closed a little pink dimpled hand round my crooked and rather dimpled forefinger and let me clean out of myself, and everything that I have ever known before, into a dream. No. Everything before is the dream, drunken grandfather, political economist and all, and all the reality of all the world is concentrated in you! . . . .

Perhaps I have only dreamed it – never mind, I'll hug the dream and that won't be any nuisance to you as the reality might be, most precious of persons. I feel better. By the next time I see you I shall hope to have discovered whether I am standing on my head or my heels. Goodnight. G.C.

SCOTT TO BRUCE

H.M.S. Essex
April 19

Here is a little note to meet and greet you in London. If you've not done so on the instant, take pen and paper and write to your devoted man. Here is our programme with more definition . . . .

I am very depressed to think that I shall see so little of you, but when I can come I must be always with you. Do you understand, these are clear orders. Goodbye, take care of yourself, and you are not to go without lunch again.

CANNAN TO BRUCE

April 22, 1908

. . . . Suppose you give yourself to a good man who loves you and I myself to a good woman who loves me, there will be a want for the you in me and the me in you, which will never die however much we reason and reason and argue and argue. I see the bitter difficulty of it for you and I know that I should not try to influence you but there's a cold bread and butter for me too, and I think it cannot altogether be extreme youth that refuses to have any real misgivings about the future...

It is the child which has called to us, our child; we may make other children, but that child, if we shut our eyes to that cry, will be lost and left crying in the void, for ever wandering until in another state we come together again, and finally and for ever together. What is it that you lose by taking?

On 26 April, all three met up to talk things over. As a social engagement it cannot have been entirely to Scott's taste, but to Kathleen, the forty-year-old Captain Scott must have rung as true as any Englishman alive, while Cannan had only the puppy charm of the half-formed. When Scott went back to his ship he took one of Kathleen's sculptures with him, apparently not realising it was the head of his vanquished rival. In 1923 a pair of visitors to Cannan were told he was expecting an Admiral to arrive shortly. In his broken mind Cannan had become Scott of the Antarctic.

MAX BEERBOHM
1872–1956

Max Beerbohm, whose caricatures have influenced cartoonists down to the present day, was one of the most brilliant figures of the 'naughty nineties' without being in the slightest degree naughty himself. Though he enjoyed his greatest success with a novel about a girl on a visit to Oxford who drives all its undergraduates to drown themselves in despair over her unattainable beauty (*Zuleika Dobson*), he was essentially a non-combatant on the field of passion. In the following cautious declaration he discloses this 'defect in my nature' to his future wife, Florence Kahn. The next letter he wrote to her, presumably after she had admitted to sharing this so-called 'defect', reveals that it was no bar to the composition of genuine love-letters.

BEERBOHM TO KAHN – NOVEMBER 1908

48 Upper Berkley Street, W.
Friday

Very dear little friend,
 Your letter of this morning, saying that you expect to sail on the 30th, makes me very sad. I had so hoped you were going to act. Perhaps the chance which you say is too remote to wait for will yet come off. If you *do* sail, they might yet in due time want you to sail back. I hate the probability, meanwhile, of not seeing you when I come back. I had so thought you would still be there. However, I mustn't be selfish. And indeed in our great friendship I do think more of you than of myself. And I constantly reproach myself with what has so often seemed evident: that I tend to make you unhappy. It rather seems that making people unhappy is my metier. I like you better than any person in the world. But the other sort of caring is beyond me. I realise quite surely now that I shall never be able to care in that way for any one. It is a defect in my nature. It can't be remedied. Dear, you have brought *so much* happiness to me. I can't bear to think of being the cause of unhappiness to you. It is difficult to express myself. Whether or not you will have sailed on the thirtieth, nothing can alter our friendship, dear, can it?

Max

48 Upper Berkley Street, W.

Monday

Darling love,

Goodnight again, sweet. And I love you, and wish I could say it in heaps of different ways. If only you were a hat-box or a rocking-horse or something of that sort, I could evolve a lot about you. But literary talent flies out of the window when real feeling comes in at the door – my door, at least. However, you don't need me to tell you in words how much I love you darling.

I forgot I promised to lunch tomorrow at Herbert Vivian's. I will get away as early as I can, in a taxi.

Kisses

Your own loving

Max

ALBAN BERG

1885–1935

Alban Berg, whose masterpiece 'Wozzeck' is today firmly established in the twentieth century operatic repertoire, was a pupil of Arnold Schoenberg, the revolutionary inventor of the twelve note technique. Berg's life was dogged by illness, and later by Nazi aesthetics, but he was supported throughout it by his wife, Helene Nahowski. Of their relationship she wrote: 'For twenty-eight years I lived in the Paradise of his love. His death was a catastrophe I only had the strength to survive because our souls were long ago joined together in a union beyond space and time, a union through all eternity.' These letters, representing love as mystical experience, all date from before their marriage.

BERG TO NAHOWSKI – 1907

Vienna

Today, my darling, I have been unfaithful to you for the first time. You know, of course, that my idea of fidelity is different from most people's. For me it means a state of mind which never leaves the lover, follows him like a shadow and grows into part of his personality: the feeling that he is never alone, always dependent on another, that without the beloved he is no longer a whole person capable of sustaining life.

It was in this sense I was unfaithful to you tonight. It happened in the finale of the Mahler symphony [No.3], when I gradually felt a sensation of complete solitude, as if in all the world there were nothing left but this music – and me listening to it. But when it came to its uplifting and overwhelming climax, and then was over, I felt a sudden pang, and a voice within me said: what of Helene? It was only then I realized I had been unfaithful, so now I implore your forgiveness. Tell me, darling, that you understand and forgive!

BERG TO NAHOWSKI

Berghof

18 July 1908

'When someone writes a letter to a very good friend, or even more, to his beloved, he puts on his best attire, as well he may. For in the quiet of his letter, on the tranquil blue paper, he can express his truest feelings. The tongue and the spoken word have become so soiled by their every-day use, they cannot speak out loud the beauty which the pen can quietly write.'

I couldn't help thinking of that passage from Strindberg when I got your letter this morning . . . .

My longing for the mountains is roused again by the lovely little flowers you sent. How lucky you are! Only in my dreams can I gaze on the mountain meadows, with their mauve forget-me-nots and black bugles and fiery red rhododendrons, and the precipices with their scattered tree-stumps and branches, and the black salamanders in the white boulders, and flocks of grouse under stunted dwarf-pines. All that is your realm, in which you are queen. And we who live in the plains can only look fondly up at those heights in envy or admiration.

Yet I know the paths which lead up there, the less frequented paths too. And somewhere far above, amidst the clouds and winds, I shall be waiting for you, my hand outstretched in greeting – cold as ice yet warm with life in its love.

And woe betide anyone else who crosses my path whistling Wagner! I'll soon strike his top note off his shoulders!

But now out of my best attire (which looks a bit like tourist dress) and into every-day clothes, for the postman waits! More from Strindberg, though, to end up with: 'It is no pose or deceit if lovers' souls should show up better in their letters to each other than in real life. Nor is the lover false in his love letters. He is not making himself out better than he is: he is *becoming* better, and in these moments *is* better. He is truly himself in such moments, the greatest moments life can bestow on us.'

All yours
Alban

BERG TO NAHOWSKI – SPRING 1909

Thursday

There is a delicate scent in my room. I have before me the second of your lovely veils, and when I press it to my face, I can almost feel the sweet warm breath from your mouth. The violets you picked for me yesterday, which nearly withered in my buttonhole, are now blooming anew, and smell soft and fresh. The cushion on the divan and the chair by the window belong to you, Helene, they have become appendages to your presence. Indeed everything in my room is the same: the mirror in front of which you arranged your hair; the window I have seen you looking through so seriously (even in our gayest moments); the last pale rays of sunlight which make your hair gleam with gold; the glowing fire in the stove; and then the laurel wreath, and the dear little cover on the bedside table – everything, everything is yours.

And that's no wonder seeing that I myself have become so entirely your 'creation'. All my possessions and even thought are somehow a loan or gift from *you*. Dressing in the morning, for instance, when I get an idea for a theme, a mood, or sometimes even a single chord, at best a whole extended melody – then I always feel it has come flying in from you. It's the same with everything: if I read something out of the ordinary, with difficult parts in it, I imagine myself understanding those parts and penetrating its mysteries only through you, Helene. I mean this reading in the widest sense. If I look at nature with the eyes of a sensitive reader, when I hear music or see paintings or – but why go on with a list of all the things which have come to life in me only through you?

Oh, Helene, how can I live without you!

I am completely yours

6 p.m. Sunday, 25th July, 1909

My love has become so enormous and all-absorbing I can hardly credit others besides you with the right to exist! And I feel as if it's a different person performing all the external actions like breathing, eating, moving, thinking, reading, composing, drawing, etc; all these things only take place *through you*. I begin to doubt if I really exist at all, or whether I am not a mere creature of your imagination! Am I sitting here alone in my room, while the others are amusing themselves at the Annenheim? Perhaps I am lying dead in my bed, and they stand round in mourning, little guessing that my spirit imagines it is writing letters! Or perhaps when I was sitting by the lake a little while ago, I fell head-first into the water; or was that only what I wanted to do? But no, I can see in front of me the poster of the regatta, which I have just taken down from the wall. And next to it a time-table I have been studying, to find out how best to get to you . . . .

Mama and the Baroness have now come back from the Annenheim. With their 'too too solid flesh' they recall me to reality. I touch my forehead, which is full of cold sweat, and smile to myself in bewilderment, wondering if I am mad. Has my mind been clouded by the long absence from you and the pain of these last days? How can I tell? All I know is, I must come to you quickly, there is my salvation, life, eternity. Here at the Berhof, away from *you*, I am threatened from all sides, and would like to withdraw from everybody, until the time, beloved, when I can at last embrace you once more . . . .

. . . . But although I recognize how fully you love me, I can't solve the riddle, that your soul sometimes seems closed to me. This makes me start hating the other things to which it is open, like Nature, people going on their ways, the Sunday concerts, yes, even Wagner's operas. Whereas even when I'm absorbed in difficult scores by Mahler, Wagner and Strauss, I'm sure you must feel my soul should still eagerly open to yours. Do you understand now why at times I have been afraid of your soul's excessive reserve. But for Heaven's sake don't think that I want to reduce your wonderful capacity for *feeling*, as you unfortunately assumed, or that because I found a word to say in defence of prostitutes I was putting you on their level!

In fact the most painful and unfair thing is a suggestion of yours that I am depressed at the idea of seeing you now only 'on the street'. The complete falseness of the implication is one great proof of my *soul's* longing. Otherwise how is it that during the three summers I have been parted from you, I have not thought of physical satisfaction, and always declined opportunities of this sort with others; that I wrote hundreds of pages in letters thirsting for the union of our souls, and was as happy with your letters, even the less loving ones, as if I were celebrating my wedding night, not reading a few lines of handwriting?

Oh, Helene, my mind has stopped working. The evening has come, and I cannot write any more. My broken heart can scarcely dare ask for forgiveness; only a small spark of pity and understanding for all my faults and failings . . . .

NAHOWSKI TO BERG – MARCH 1910

Dear Alban,

I am so hurt at your reproaches on 'closing my soul' that I can hardly answer without agitation. Another girl might have deceived you, but I can't pretend or alter, you must take me as I am. My love for other things besides you is part of my spiritual life, just as my heart belongs to my body, without which I couldn't exist. Is it really a sin against you if I do not think solely of you but give myself, for instance, to the miracle of creation, so grand and yet mysterious, where every small flower or leaf has its own secret, which is perhaps its link with divinity? I cannot fathom all this, but I can feel it, so that I become quite devout.

Oh, leave me this sense of 'belonging' to my trees, flowers and stars! You are not losing anything of my love for you, since 'to him that hath, to him shall be given'. Just because of that my love is still growing, deeper and deeper, bigger and bigger, the more it includes. The same with my love for you, as I come nearer to the miracle of creation in you. For you are much favoured of God, or He would not have given you so bright and sensitive a soul. Your love makes me happy and binds me to you for ever. But it would be a lie if I told you: I give my whole soul to you alone.

Please understand that I am really not robbing you of anything if I some-times 'lose myself' to Music (which is after all God's best understood lan-guage), or to the forest or the starry sky. You should not be at once in despair at this, but should try to understand me and *trust me*.

Do I really have to tell you that you are enthroned in my heart over and before everything else? Don't you know this – can't you feel it?

If you come tomorrow, everything will be all right between us. It will, my dearest darling – you'll see.

Your own

Helene

BERG TO NAHOWSKI

Berghof, 20th August 1910

. . . . Some people are so overwhelmed by music that they almost faint when they hear an E minor chord on the piano. I am like that with Nature. Even as a small boy, when I was out in the country and the surroundings were too beautiful – I just couldn't bear it. I wouldn't join all the others on their excursions every Sunday, and so acquired a reputation for 'not liking the coun-tryside'.

This fear of Nature still clings to me, the knowledge that great beauty in the natural scene drives me into restlessness and dissatisfaction instead of joy. I shun these frightening ecstasies, as I shun sexual or drunken orgies or morphia dreams. I escape into my room, to my books and scores. I feel here that I am in my own element, my own realm; anywhere else I might fall ill, and in Nature I should disintegrate and be submerged.

Yet I know that whereas other pleasures, like alcohol, are bad for the health and bad too for the soul, those who can enjoy fully the beauties of Nature are benefiting their health and their soul. So there is one hope I cherish, and that is this: a man, intoxicated by delicious wine, leaning in rapture on the breast of his beloved, with vine-leaves in his hair, is trans-formed from a drunken beast to a sublime singer. A man shattered by Mahler's Third Symphony recovers his strength sobbing in the lap of his beloved. A rake obsessed with his need for sexual indulgence looks into the eyes of his beloved and sinks back in holy adoration. The morphia addict tormented by wildest dreams fall into a deep and dreamless sleep when the beloved lays her hand on his brow, and from then on experiences only the good effects of the drug. And I shall one day feel the same, have felt it already, when with Helene, my beloved, at my side, I saw the sunset in the Wachau, unharmed by Nature the drug, yielding at last to Nature as bringer of peace and wonder and joy . . . .

NAHOWSKI TO BERG

2nd May, 1911

My dearest and nearest!

Tomorrow is our wedding day. I am setting out with you into 'the land of marriage' full of confidence and high purpose. I will always be a prop and support to you, a faithful and loving companion, both here and over there 'in the other world'. Gladly and of my own free will I give up everything that made my girlhood so full of beauty, hope and happiness – my modest 'art'. I quench my own flame, and shall only exist for and through you. Now we shall be together for ever.

Amen

PERCY GRAINGER
1882–1961

Percy Grainger, born in Australia, was a composer, both populist, and in later years, avant garde. He was also a lionised piano virtuoso in the years leading up to the First World War – dubbed 'the Siegfried of the piano' – and an important collector of English folk-songs. To say that he was wildly eccentric, that his major passions were flaggelation, his mother, his own personality, race and physical fitness, and his lover, Karen Holten, more or less in that order, does not really do justice to him. The power of his love letters comes from the sense one has of a man with an urgent need to express everything – including things he could not tell his mother – and with an intense awareness of standing on the edge of some overwhelming gnosis. His letters to Holten, written, as he often admitted, with an eye to future publication, are translated from the Danish.

GRAINGER TO HOLTEN

7 June 1908

. . . . How amusing fleshly-love is. Your and my ways of thinking are indeed so entirely different. That is the good thing about it. I wish that I could hunger after you 20 times hotter than I do, and I should like to go off into a perfect fit when together with you. Curse all the soberness, reactionariness, control that is in me. I would with all my heart like to be saved and set free from everything clever good practical and brain-like . . . .

GRAINGER TO HOLTEN

22 March 1909

. . . . I love to sit in the train or lie on the ship with closed eyes and dream about you and the future. I wish that I had claws, like tigers have, to tear scratches in you, to really cut deeply into you. Never will I achieve that which I chase after in my cruelties. When I whip it should lie just under the skin. Even if I had claws and could cut inches deep into you, you soft tender Karen, that which I seek would move further in; for it is really something related to endlessness, unlimitedness, immortality one wants to grab and hold fast in such moments. In the fruitlessness of the chase our happiness grows. Do you know Keats "Ode to a Grecian Urn"? (Oh so lovely, soullit) The bliss of the beings on the urn are ours because the fleshly hunter never reaches his prey; yes, physically he does gain it, but spiritually – never. Our love is not driven out by sexuality. It is not that sexuality in us makes us feel love. Longings after depth, splendour, total absorption, extremeness, God, (what folk mean by God) Art, they work years long, and we strive the whole time after more or less attractive expressions for these deepest instincts. When we once reach the possibilities of love, these instincts immediately find their most complete solution there. Not quite complete, never that. Soulfulness chooses love from among the many deep things it knows because therein it finds its (so far) most extreme expression. If soulfulness could discover something deeper, sharper, more extreme, more divine than love it would push love aside and advance itself more splendidly with something else. (When I find something that does my soul better good than you, off you pack tomorrow) It is not the presence of sexuality in the body that causes love's soulfulness, it is rather the presence of soulfulness that necessitates the utilisation of sexuality's possibilites. Can I treasure art, science, religion, highest as expression of the soul when I have known Valhalla of the flesh with such a one as you? Impossible. (In Valhalla every hero is killed every day and gets up fresh the next morning. It is like sexuality's resurrection from daily death).

It is therefore that great soulful men give up kingdoms and art and God for love's sake. The best is good enough for them. They use judgement in choosing.

I wish I was dead and didn't have to go without you a second longer.

(All that doesn't prevent my acting practically in actual life.)

GRAINGER TO HOLTEN

22 September 1909

. . . . I long to lie restingly in your flesh with your strong protecting limbs around me, drinking in your breath, tickled by your small hands of love and by your hair, made crazy by your flaming mouth.

I long to lie with my body heavy on top of your breasts and face, to grasp your legs with my hands, to discover the way there between your legs through all the hair with my mouth and suck there lovingly in the soft barbaric flesh, there where thousands of years of civilisation end, where the power of nationality disappears, and where blended God, Brute, and Savage writhe in ecstasy and agony. The flesh there cannot be covered, the smell of sex cannot be entirely washed away, uncontrolled movements there twitch and quiver, spasms lurk, blind devil-gods lash wild-willing horses there within; in lowness, selfishness, and greediness there slumber lazily the highest gods.

I, also, need to demonstrate my lowness to you; sweat-dampened smelling arm-pits shall be laid over your wet mouth, heavy and thoughtless shall my body sprawl over your smothered woman-strong body, my proud swollen sex-organ (so ugly, animal, low, ignoble) seeks, mad with longing, your trembling forgiving misused mouth. I long for you to see me in all my beastly lowness. Nothing is more laughable, more repulsive, than a naked swollen man. I know it. Do you think I will be ashamed?

Unashamed regardless shall I stand before you or lie lazy in bed on you. You can gladly despise me, gladly laugh at me (I want passion, not respect). For you I entertain the most complete trust and confidence. Like a 2-hour old child I long to lie defenceless before you, spiritually and bodily . . . .

GRAINGER TO HOLTEN

2 October 1910

. . . . You, little comrade, will so well suit the sea and rain and primitive pleasures. You have the Scandinavian woman's toughness and singleness and contentment with unpleasant extremes.

Someone like you wakens naturalness in someone like me. I don't only love you with my English sharp singular sensuality and my personal cruelty (although I do that as well) but I love you with international impersonal naturalness, I long not only to love you as my sensuality demands, I also long to love you as your sensuality demands, I want to throw all separateness to hell, and glide gently with my thick strong phallus into your inner fjords, your smooth oily greasy slimy interior roads, that fog-up and bewitch away all mental consciousness, my phallus smelling sharp and animal-like of rotten fish, your sex passages smelling sharp and animal-like of something bitter and sour, and feel the thick rich cream stride forth from my body's interior dark earth and grow fruitfully forward against your womanliness's warmth and intoxicating sun, and stride up and forward with maddening thudding pumping pulse, enormous and threatening, till all personality is intoxicated away, till all nationality is sensualised away, till the difference between you and me is only thought and not felt, till I become woman and you become man in our crowning moment, and my life-infecting marrow-milk spits forward in your hidden mouth, where my stiff belly-tongue and your love-throat kiss with slimy wet greasy convulsive muscular kisses, tearing and revolutionary, beastly and joyous, and my tight boy's body, solemn, with singing ears and flayed will, pays its full tax of white blood into your Queen's treasure chest, and your soft pliable deluding seducing girl-entrails suck and draw out and consume and digest the stolen contagious world-enrichments, while our 2 forms lie enveloped in a steam of passion, sweaty-smelling under our arms and around our anus, our muscles relax, and grateful tiredness and joyful relief spread over us and our love-wet animal-smelling sexual parts.

Oh, if only you could spit your love-spit into my eyes, if only my mouth could suck your inner woman's penis, if only I could drink your sex-fjord's bitter juice, if only I could bear that you were sea-sick in my mouth, if only I might bear to see you eat my 2 testicles like boiled eggs, if only my 2 eyes were 2 small hairy caves (like your anus) and your 2 nipples were 2 stiff pointed finger-thick phalli which you could bore into my brain, so my life could be extinguished in ecstasy like an electric lamp.

GRAINGER TO HOLTEN

10 October 1910

When I close my eyes I think that you stand in front of me, just as when we are first quite alone after a long separation, and have not yet kissed one-another, but stand and feel both our breaths, and both bodies quietly touch each other, and feel beforehand the kiss coming, and the whole world seems full of cream, jam, and dizziness. Be merciful to me!

GRAINGER TO HOLTEN

January 1911

. . . . Some weeks ago in Brussum I began to brand a K (Karen) in my flesh right in the middle of my primeval forest, after 1st having shaved the trees away. But last night I was mad-sensual and burnt deeper in so that one heard the flesh melt . . . . and after that I whipped myself and was naughty the 1st time, then I read on for a long time, and then I bit my breasts with my tie-clip and was blissfully naughty again. I really believe that I feel relieved and healthier after such a night, and I believe that the frightful feelings I go through before important concerts stem partly from me zealously keeping good for possibly too many days in a row beforehand. I am not convinced of some-thing of that kind, but I must say I feel splendidly happy today, but then I have no concert, and that helps a lot.

One thing you can please foresee, and that is, that next time in Svinklov you shall be whipped so that your life only consists of blows and screams.

More and more my selfish animal unfettered hunger grows for you and for the heaven with you, and I will 'spare' neither you nor myself in the coming time in Svinklov in the realisation of my longings. Be certain that it will be different from last time in Svinklov. That time I was afraid of your screams. Not any more, for I know the remedy for them = just beat still more. Our divine service of love will be such that you will become downright eaten up and exhausted by its harshness; in your sufferings and agonies you will writhe painfully against me and our bodies will drink gladdening love-spit from each other. I won't take the slightest notice of what your mouth begs for or refuses, and you will know how keenly I love you, and your flesh day after day will burn helplessly under my boy's criminal deeds but our souls shall boil together in a celestial kettle of bliss, so friendly and each-other-tender.

Holten returned Grainger's whips in November 1911 and their affair petered out. In 1928, six years after his mother committed suicide, Grainger married a Swedish woman in the Hollywood Bowl in front of an audience of 23,000.

RUPERT BROOKE
1887-1915

One day in 1908, in the chapel at Rugby school, the poet Rupert Brooke pointed to a patch of wall beside the memorial to the poet A.H. Clough, and said, 'They are keeping that for me.' Within ten years he was indeed memorialised there. A Fabian, a free-thinker, a 'neo-pagan', bathing naked in Byron's pool at Grantchester and forever wondering if there would be 'honey still for tea', he became the prime icon of England's sacrifice in the First World War. He died in 1915, on the way to the horror of Gallipoli.

He was buried, Byronically, on the island of Skyros in Greece, his clean-limbed body unmarked except for the mosquito bite that took him off, and crowned with a wreath of olives. The same failure to connect the ideal to the real marked his love-affairs, of which the most passionate were unconsummated. Three months in Tahiti at the end of 1913 with a girl called Taatamata gave him at the last a taste of heaven without guilt. The following exchange of letters concerns one of his earlier, more complicated relationships. He fell in love with the fifteen-year old Noel Oliver in 1908, when she was still at Bedales, and he at Cambridge.

BROOKE TO OLIVIER

Jan.23-4. 1911
Munich

. . . . The Germans – oh, it turns out to be very simple about the Germans. They're Soft. That is all. Very nice, but . . . . Soft. It comes out in their books, and everywhere. All their views, of everything, just blur a little. Their grasp is of a fat hand. Pictures, books, ideas, faces – it is all the same. It's rather amusing, though, to find out what Soft Ideas *are*. I talk to Germans about scenery & the country. I explain laboriously why towns are often better. They are *always* shocked. Every German I have met has said to me. *"Ich habe gern die Natur"* They all – just vaguely – "love Nature". Nature has a captial N. Thoughts of English Nature lovers creep into my mind. Oh, it is so easy and so troublesome to love Nature – *that* way. The sentimentality and Fudge come out better with Germans, than with some English nature-lovers, more shapely. You hear and see a so fat, so greasy, so complacent and civilized German roll up his eyes and wheeze *"Ich habe gern die Natur"* – and the whole thing flies to pieces before you. You have a picture of that coated belly in the woodlands, waddling helter skelter from Pan, or Diana's hounds – But I talk of things I know not. Oh goddess, all the world lies about "Nature" (a soiled word) except you & me. For you are of Earth, and (if not in words) say so: and I am not, & say I'm not. On the peaks no one but you shall live, you alone. And I, below, shall wait in a town, and meet you every month half way down the mountains, where the woods end.

. . . . And that vision also fades, as less true than the other that puts us alone, above everything & everyone. Noel, we're equal and immortal and alone, and give and take as equals, & freely. I *can't* write. I wish I could tell you what we are. Oh we love & will love finelier than it has ever been done. Go out and take the splendid things of life, and clothe yourself in them, & crown yourself with them and we'll meet with all the world for a gift to each other. Damn you, read the truth that is under all this fustian I'm writing. You are more glorious than God: and I – Because you have taken me & kissed me the good outweighs all the evil there could possibly be and because we have kissed & you have, wonderfully, loved me (I don't only say with lips "Noel", but with every inch of me thrills & strains to you when I think the word) the world's an ecstasy, and there's no time to learn German or eat or do anything but sing. Read, and forgive, and glory. Noel, stranger, I, Rupert, am writing to you, I am afraid at the sound of your name, & of my own. Throw out arms across sea & lands to you. I love you.

Rupert

OLIVIER TO BROOKE

Feb. 10 1911.
Bedales, Petersfield, Hants.

Creature!

Last night I thought . . . . There is Rupert in Germany, very wise and clever (he is probably learning more German in one month than you have ever learnt with all your years of study); he seems to know about all the most important things, except music, & that he is trying to appreciate (I wonder if he ever will properly, why not? I've learnt to be excited by some pictures just through trying); and he is very beautiful, everyone who sees him loves him; when I first saw him cracking nuts in Ben Keeling's rooms with Margery, I fell in love with him, as I had fallen in love with other people before, only this time it seemed final – as it had, indeed, every time – I got excited when people talked of him & spent every day waiting and expecting to see him & felt wondrous proud when he talked to me or took any notice. When he talked for a long time on the river I got more & more in love and said so to myself when he was there. After Cambridge I placed him so: there are people (family, friends) & there is Rupert; with them I live generally and it is their influence which forms my ways & ideas; when Rupert is there, none of these ways will do, I must work up to his, I must talk about the important things, the only ones which he considers – I am ashamed at many parts of my mind, the way I think, but it is because they are bad & when he's there I realise it. At camp at Penshurst I was driven silly with love & it was perhaps at that time that I felt it most strongly.

Since then I have gradually begun to know him better, & would I think, have looked on him as a friend, a person whom I loved better than anyone else but from whom I neither needed nor expected more than to see him at times & talk to him; I wanted him to prefer me to others but not to everything. There is probably a good deal of sympathy in me. With many people I have known, I have sympathised so well that I could help them in no way by giving fresh suggestions (here, you see, my thought became obscure). And it was like that with Rupert, when he bowed his head & said the truth about what he felt; I understood & was sorry & I loved his head so I kissed it & then he & history made me believe that I was a lover as well as he.

I'm not, Rupert, I'm affectionate, reverent, anything you like but not that . . . .

I shall always love you

Noel

15 March 1911
Ohmstrasse 3, Gartenhaus 1, Munchen

Noel, whom I love!

. . . . How could you describe the feelings of a despicable and desperate worm who amazingly found himself in Heaven, but also discovered that he hadn't been selected Archangel? Even that is totally misleading. It suggests that he wasn't satisfied! God! As if I wasn't utterly utterly utterly satisfied! To use the word is a profane filthy and unspeakable imbecility. But I dare, now, be even imbecile to you. Only, I mean, let it be completely obvious and understood that I'm not wanting anything more. My state of mind is practically at no moment that of wanting anything more. I don't mean it is the same as yours; it has it always in reserve, so to speak. But I'm not crying for the moon. I haven't time. I have infinite riches given me – oh, that wouldn't stop me wanting more, I know! I could cry for the moon, if I liked. I could cry for anything if I liked. But I don't. You see, Noel, it's rather, I think, this way. It takes two to make a quarrel; and it takes two to make bodily love – which, with your kind permission, I will proceed to refer to as lust. (Understand, most clear eyed of women, two things: one, that lust has *not* a bad connotation, it can be very fine: two, that it means not the actual act of copulation, but the desires and feelings, the passionate state of mind, connected more or less with the idea of copulation). The situation's thus. To begin with, I am in love and lust and everything else with Noel. I centre round her radiate towards her. 'Lust' not overwhelming, but there, and on a level with the rest. But all this (when you are still unknown and unapproachable) is incomplete; the whole range of emotions is one-sided, hypothetical, not on the highest level of reality. (They're amazing & fine, oh God! they're fine enough!) For example, at that period, Love means at moments, perhaps "I want to kiss Noel." (You'll understand that this is scientifically and absurdly bald: it'd take too long to put in all the glory and heaven swimming round the words in 1909). But that really implies "I want to Kiss a Noel-who-wants-to-kiss-me" (with a codicil "which is unthinkable") Noel = not Noel-dead or Noel-unwilling or Noel-impassive or Noel-thinking-I'm-some-one-else but (profanity!) Noel-wanting-to-kiss-me. And so on all through. *Nicht wahr?*

Well! Then consider the next stage, when the unimaginable dream of August had changed all. Love meant something different thereafter. The hypothesis was fulfilled. Each emotion that didn't wing away into the void, but met its fellow and complement took on reality, became a million times more glorious. Love then meant "I love Noel who *does* love me", "I kiss" implied "am kissed" (I daren't comment in brackets. I should lose the last semblance of coherence!) Only poor little "I lust" is left in the old condition. All his brothers have gone up to heaven, fulfilled and deified. He stays, a shadow, an hypothesis...When the rest were so, he could take his part among them. Now, he is shunted down, eclipsed, negligeable, forgotten. If ever he joins them, the chorus might be fuller . . . . So *he* says. But, look you, in Heaven one does not make plans. If he never joins them – there's an excellent mathematical rule, my Noel, that if you take a finite number from an infinite number, you don't make it less. Is that clear? I feel that you understood it all before. But I thought I'd prevent any possible discomforts. It's nicer to have it said, accurately. It's part of our glory, Noel, that we say all things – or can say all things – you and I . . . .

I've got such a queer, deep happiness on me, because you're somewhere in the world, and we're lovers. I wish I could tell you, what it is. Sometimes – for instance when I was writing my last letter – I love you so much that I feel frightened at our very names. To think of them, of us, seems to reveal the strangeness of everything as by a flash of lightening, and I'm frightened. Tonight I'm different, so secure and content. The universe stands so fast and fine, and full of such glories for you and me . . . .

My dearest dearest – I love you

Rupert

LEOS JANACEK   KAMILA STOSSLOVA
1854–1928   1892–1935

In some ways it seems curious that Leoš Janáček once went on a walking holiday in southern Bohemia with Antonín Dvořák. Today, Dvořák is known as a nineteenth century composer, whereas nearly all of Janáček's major compositions date from the modernist era, after the First World War. This was a surprise to Janáček himself as much as anyone. Shortly before Dvořák died in 1904, Janáček had a premonition of his own death – or what he thought would be his own death – in 1917. If this premonition had been fulfilled, Janáček would be known today as the composer of one substantial work, his opera *Jenůfa*.

Something did indeed happen to him in 1917, but it was more like a rebirth. In the spa town of Luhačovice, where he used to go for his rheumatism, he fell in love with Kamila Stösslová, the wife of an antique dealer. The extraordinary Indian summer of creativity that he sustained from this point up to his death in August 1928 was fuelled by the passion that this vital young woman aroused in his heart.

Living far apart, she in Písek in South Bohemia, he in Brno, the Moravian capital, virtually the only way the old man could express the intensity of his feelings towards her was in words. He wrote to her almost every day, warmly passionately and above all, intimately, in words – and finally music.

His wife since 1881, Zdenka, did not enjoy these years much herself. No wife likes to see her husband rejuvenated by another woman. She could not have been expected to appreciate his song-cycle *The Diary of One Who Disappeared* which details the thoughts and feelings of a rich farmer's son who decides to desert his family and run off with a gypsy (Kamila was rather obviously gypsy-looking).

Under the spell of Kamila, Janáček also produced three great operas, which like his earlier masterpiece, *Jenůfa*, were all centred around female characters. But the work which carries the impress of his passion most emphatically is a purely instrumental one.

In fact, nearly everything he wrote was of programmatic or autobiographical origin – carrying some sort of extra-musical meaning – including his instrumental works. Sometimes this inspiration might be childhood, say, or his fierce pride in his homeland, Czechoslovakia. But his strongest inspiration was always erotic, and never more so than in his second string quartet, written in a couple of weeks just a few months before he died. He called it Love Letters though he later modified the title to'*Intimate Letters*. In Czech, the words are *Listy důvěrné* which can also mean 'confidential letters'. Nevertheless, it is an unambiguous tribute to Kamila.

For him, the Quartet was a final daring experiment. He wrote to her: "It's my first composition to spring from directly-experienced emotion. 'Intimate Letters' has been composed in a fire, the previous compositions only in hot ashes".

It is not known for certain whether the relationship was consummated. But nearly 700 letters emerged from this intense relationship – mostly from him. Both he and Kamila suspected that the letters might be published eventually, and in the originals some of his words are scratched out.

Janáček burned most of Kamila's letters, yet, there still exists the occasional response from her. Kamila's letters are more formal in tone – in many, she addresses him as 'Maestro' despite his frequent invitations and even remonstrations to adopt a more familiar style (though as a married woman with children, her caution was understandable).

Nevertheless, their exchange remains one of the most striking of all epistolary relationships.

JANACEK TO STOSSLOVA

Luhačovice
16th July 1917

Madam,

Please accept these few roses as proof of how greatly I hold you in esteem. Your personality and appearance are so pleasing that one feels light-hearted in your company; you breathe such sincerity and regard the world with such kindness, that one wants also to repay you only by goodness and kindness. You have no idea how pleased I am to have met you.

You lucky one! The more painfully do I feel my own loneliness and harsh fate.

Think of me always with kindness - that's how you will remain in my thoughts for ever.

Your sincerely devoted,
Leoš Janáček

Brno
3rd April 1924

Dear Mrs Kamila,

I have just delighted in reading your letter several times over.

Yes, in Písek I would say: "It's a second Luhačovice and I don't need to look for anything elsewhere!" There my mind would be cured; I would know neither grief nor sadness. My eyes would open wide so as to absorb that apparition which is to me a sweet fragrance, which is to me the essential air needed for me to live; as though surrounded in a sweet mist, which I could drink, which I would like to capture, could feel on me, could breathe; I cannot have enough of that bliss. I would stretch out my arms in order to embrace it; it is escaping and yet it is always around me.

That's how it is, Mrs Kamila.

And that dear apparition is deeply in my mind. Warmth fills my entire body when I talk with this precious apparition through these lines.

I believe that fate will unite me with this long-desired image . . . .

And who can help it that you, dear Mrs Kamila, are everything in the world to me, my single silent joy, and that I know no other desire than to think about you, to be intoxicated by your joyful, sweet appearance. You so faraway – and I here with my feelings and it's as though you were beside me.

So, keep well. Perhaps the sun will be good enough to look down on us one day, when you won't know whether its rays shine on you or on me.

I hate to stop – ardently thinking of you
Leoš Janáček

Prague
25th April 1927

Darling soul,

Believe me, I cannot get over those two walks of ours. As in a profoundly beautiful dream, a spell has been cast over me.

I know that in that fire, which cannot burst into flames, I would burn to death. Along those paths,I would plant oak trees which last for centuries and into their trunks I would carve the words that I shouted into the wind. I would like them to become public knowledge and not go astray.

Never before have I spoken to anyone with such urgency and desperation:

"You, you Kamila! Turn round! Stop!" And I read in your eyes also that something was binding us together, despite the wind and the heat of the sun. Perhaps in this indescribable delight there was something for both of us? Never in my life have I experienced such union between you and me. We were not even walking very close together and yet there was no gap between us. I, just your shadow; you, the necessity for my existence. I would have liked the path never to end; feeling no fatigue, I waited for the words that you whispered to me asking what I would do if you were my wife. Well, I already think of you as my wife. Alas, it's too little just to think it and yet even that feels as though the rays of a hundred suns were flooding me. I think it now and I shall not cease to think it.

Do what you will with this letter, with this declaration of mine. Whether you burn it or not, thinking all this revives me. Even thoughts can come true.

Keep well!

Yours

Brno

1st February 1928

At night

My dear Kamila!

I came to my post box, saw your letter lying there - and gasped with joy! I am now writing before opening your letter. I know that without you my life would be a parched meadow. At each step I would say, there a flower once blossomed, here another - and there would be sadness to choking point. Now I shall read your letter! I think that it will give me pleasure - if only because you have written! I have read both letters – and I am immensely pleased to recognise my Kamila again! No, Kamilka, do write. Even if you only write, I am fine, I think about with happiness – it will revive me as well as you.

I am glad that you have forgiven me. My letters, I know, have turned bitter. Now it will be different.

I have now begun to write something nice. Our life will be in it. It'll be called "Love letters".

I think it's going to sound delightful. After all, those pleasant experiences of ours have already been plentiful enough! Like little fires in my soul, they will light up into the most beautiful melodies.

Just imagine! I finished the first movement in Hukvaldy. That impression on seeing you for the first time!

Now I am working on the second movement; I think it will dawn on that hot <*> in Luhačovice. In particular, the whole work will be held together by a special instrument. It's called the *viola d'amour* – the viola of love. Oh, how I am looking forward to it! In this work I shall always be alone with you! No third person beside us. Full of longings as if with you there in that heaven of ours. How I shall enjoy working on it. After all, you must know that, apart from you, I know no other world! You are everything to me, I want nothing else but your love.

And how bitter I was when I read in your letter how you would like to forget everything beautiful that has passed between us! I was thinking, is it possible that my Kamila can forget it all? Could it be possible? Now I know that it couldn't! In our heaven we have reached that point where it's no longer possible to go back, only upwards! Draw strength from this; you are certain to find peace. If I am somebody and my works count, then it follows that you are also somebody – and higher and more important than that ordinary niece of mine, who will never be allowed to stand in my presence again. That's how it is, my dear Kamilka! Don't blame your nerves for everything; that bronchitis has put you into a terrible mood. It'll also pass.

And don't be ashamed of your nature. It's so dear, so very dear to me. You are laughter "mixed" from tears. It is that nature – I understand it quite a lot already – which is almost chroniclly sensitive. You are difficult to understand. What surrounds you is hard – and, Kamilka, heartless. It's better to avoid hard stones than to fall among them.

So, my precious Kamilka, keep writing; if it's only two or three words it'll satisfy me.

And were you to write "I am forever yours", you would open heaven for me!. . . .

Forever yours

L.

---

*A word was scratched out on the original letter.

Brno

8th February, 1928

At night

My dear Kamila,

You have no idea what impression yesterday's letter from you made on me! To wake up at night and not sleep till morning! In my head, a whirl of thoughts! How will you answer me tomorrow? Will you again avoid speaking directly? After all, you do know how to speak from the heart! . . . .

Today I wrote down in music that sweetest longing of mine. I wrestle with it, it's winning through. You are giving birth. What deal in life would that little son of ours have? What would be your lot? Just like you sinking from tears into laughter, that's how it sounds . . . .

Now I am just waiting for your reply. What will you do, so that it can never be gone back on?!

Be it as it may. I have never known what it is to look back. What's done is done! Come the new day, a new sun! That's you! For some it always comes out; for others it remains behind the clouds. I am not forcing you to anything. I shall be waiting devotedly, with complete trust. I shall fight my way through those clouds and – perhaps you shall be mine! It would be a strange fate – to fight for my one and only happiness and not achieve it! I need to have you close to me; that means Spring. Otherwise I become gloomy. Today I feel like that. Until you answer me how it'll be so there's is no going back! I shall grasp that letter as if it were fate.

Forever yours,

L.

P. S. Your letter led me into seventh heaven. May I remain there and you with me!

FROM JANACEK TO STOSSLOVA

Brno

18th February 1928

At night

My dear Kamilka!

Today I succeeded with that movement "when the earth trembled". It'll be the best. After all, it was amazingly beautiful! And it was truthful. Only the best melodies could be attached to it. Now there is the final movement to be accomplished. It will be like anxiety for you. You know, such anxiety, that I would tie you up as I would the little legs of a lambkin, so it wouldn't wander.

Today I am so depressed after work – and no refreshment! Sadness in my soul.

I know that you are as sensitive as I am. I think that if I now have some silent pain, you also will feel it. And it would be good if we were only to laugh. We can cover up a lot with laughter. And don't burn this letter. It will be just as well for people to know one day that our lives, just like anyone else's, have a rough and a smooth side. I have only that rough side. I need you to stroke it! . . . .

Forever yours,

L.

FROM STOSSLOVA TO JANACEK

Písek

14th March 1928

Dear Maestro,

I have been reading your letters many times over, they are nice and make me think of you even if I didn't want to. I am so glad about being alone here that I can't describe it to you. I go to bed at 7 o'clock every day. And the peace is the same as you have. While reading today's letter from you, I am thinking about all that has happened and about all our experiences, and I am happy. You make me think like this when you describe how your life used to be and how it is now. As for mine, I didn't know anything and didn't long for anything. And so it went by without any love and happiness. I went along thinking that that was how it was meant to be.

I now think that God has been testing you and me and when he saw that we were good and that we deserve it, he has granted us this joy in life. If I were to tell anyone that for the whole of my life I could find no one who would offer me his love and that perhaps I had been waiting for you, they would not believe me. All this I have tried to avoid and I have not sought any-thing – you alone, who have known me all these years, know this to be indeed true. Some people may doubt if it is possible; yes, it is possible for you to be dearer to me than if you were a young man.

I assure you that my life is an enjoyable one and that I wouldn't wish for any-thing better. And you alone are guilty of that; I must also thank you for it . . . .

FROM JANACEK TO STOSSLOVA

Brno
18th May, 1928
At night

My dear Kamila,

. . . . Today, at 3 o'clock, the Moravian Quartet are coming to my house to play my / your composition! I am keen to hear it . . . .

So they played me the first and the third movements! And, Kamila, it's going to be a beautiful, special, exuberant and inspired, composition, beyond all convention! Together we shall win through! It is my first composition to spring from directly experienced emotion. Previously, my compositions have been based only on memories; this work, Intimate letters, has been composed in a fire. The previous compositions only in hot ashes.

This work will be dedicated to you; you are the cause of it and composing it has been my greatest joy.

I am asking Prof. Vymetal to invite the Moravian Quartet to perform it in Písek in the Autumn . . . . When it goes all round the world, we shall rejoice together . . . .

Forever yours,
L.

KATHARINE MANSFIELD
1888–1922

Katherine Mansfield, born in New Zealand in 1888, wrote some of the best short stories in the English language, before dying of T.B. at the age of 34. Small, dark, passionate and experienced, she met and seduced John Middleton Murry (1989–1957) in 1912. He was very nearly as pretty as she was, and was to become, for a while after the First World war, the leading literary critic in England. Their life was peripatetic and their movements rarely synchronised, perhaps partly because their love could thereby be the more exalted in their literary imagination. The following extracts from their correspondence start in 1915, when she went off to the Western Front for a fling with the novelist and poet, Francis Carco, and end in 1918, when she first started coughing blood.

For much of this time she was in the south of France, while Murry was working in the War Office and writing a verse play about fairies called 'Cinnamon and Angelica' (and their friend D.H. Lawrence was writing 'Women in Love' in which they would appear as 'Gerald' and 'Gudrun'). Theirs was one of the great love-affairs of their time, but it has to be said that their correspondence, for all its beauty, can sometimes read like that of a couple of fey wee elfin folk.

MANSFIELD TO MURRY

20 March 1915

. . . . Very strange is my love for you tonight – don't have it psychoanalysed – I saw you suddenly lying in a hot bath, blinking up at me – your charming beautiful body half under the water. I sat on the edge of the bath in my vest waiting to come in. Everything in the room was wet with steam and it was night time and you were rather languid. "Tig chuck over that sponge." No, I'll *not* think of you like that – I'll shut my teeth and not listen to my heart. It begins to cry as if it were a child in an empty room & to beat on the door and say Jack – Jack – Jack and Tig – I'll be better when I've had a letter. Ah my God, how can I love him like this. Do I love you so much more than you love me or do you too – feel like this?

Tig.

MANSFIELD TO MURRY – MARCH 1915

Today it is very warm (so far) and sunny – The trams roll up and down, & clatters & squeaks fly up. Now I have had a scrupulous cat like bath & washed my ears beyond words. I feel we are about 15 today – just children. You and I don't live like grown up people, you know. Look at the way we soap each others backs & hop about in the tops of our pyjamas and scrabble into bed winking our toes – & I keep seeing in my minds eye, your back view as you go down to the cave for wood – & then your front view as you come up with your arms full. Life isn't half long enough to love all the different things about you in. I shall die in the middle of a little laugh at some new funny thing that I adore you for. Now I must go out and stop writing love letters – Perhaps I

didn't quite know until I came away what these months have brought or how
they have changed everything . . . .
Always your girl
Tig.

16 December 1915
Wig darling,
This morning I had two letters. When you wrote them, you had not yet
got one of mine – the other arrived as you were writing. Both your letters
made me sad; for in both you were ill. Oh, my dear darling, can you understand – of course you can, better than I – how small and infinitely precious,
infinitely fragile you appear to me? I am afraid for you, and our letters take so
long. You say that perhaps when I get your letters, you are no longer ill. I feel
that you may be worse. I feel, too, all the love that your letters bring, and I
wonder are mine strong enough to carry something back to you. Because of my
love for you and yours for me – Tig, precious, it is for *Toujours* – it has *Toujours*
written upon it – because of our love, I feel a stranger in my own land. This
England is my own land, I know, but yet the persons in it, even those who are
in some way dear to me, seem to be blunt of understanding. They seem to
laugh when they should not, and to talk when they should be silent, and not
to know how precious is the thing of ours I carry in my heart. To me it is something that I must bear in my cupped hands ever so lightly, like a flame – (not
that it may be blown out, but that it burns so brightly that they could not see
it at all,) or rather like that little bird you carried in the room at Cholesbury,
or even like O'Hara San* herself who is to me so delicate that I dare hardly
breathe when I smooth her hair. I wonder now, sitting here, whether you and I
in our common love are not too fine for those, even those, whom we call our
friends. Wouldn't they be somehow different, Wig, somehow more sensitive if
they really knew. Or do we suffer just because we have been chosen out of all
others to keep the one flame alive until we too have given it over to others? I
feel myself somehow aloof, terribly apart, though I would be of them. I try to
conquer myself to work with them. But I am not I any more, I am you, and our
common spirit will not submit. All our friends hurt me; Knot very deeply –

*A *doll*

213

Campbell insufferably; Lawrence least of all – but all of them hurt. I wonder are we, am I, as selfish and hard as they are? Perhaps, but I do not believe it; and now I seem to discover that even those silences and gruffnesses you do not like in me – they are going away, dearest, I am sure, so that I may be a new Jag to take you into my arms at meeting – were a God-given protection against the unmeant brutalities of people.

And now I am afraid you will think I am sad on my own account as well as on yours. It is not true, at all. I am sad for your illness, my nut brown goblin (and this morning I called to you in the dark, whistled my empty windy whistle to you, as you swung so sadly on that gate, and I think you must have heard) but in what I have told you before I am not sad. I am just laying my head upon your cool and wonderful breast, and telling you what I have found in the world to which I was sent. For you and I are not of the world, darling; we belong to our own kingdom, which truly is when we stand hand in hand, even when we are cross together like two little boys. Somehow we were born again in each other, tiny children, pure and shining, with large sad eyes and shocked hair, each to be the other's doll. I cannot speak save to you – and to you I have no need of words.

Oh, my dearest – I must not write any more like this; I do not believe it will make you happier, but rather sadder, for something in real love is sad – that knowledge of apartness, of an enemy world in which we dare not stay too long for the peril of our souls. And that is the sadness that has hold of me tonight. It is not sadness at all, but the final triumph of our love. Darling it is *toujours*. If you would not say the word now that I have opened all my heart, I feel that I should lie. But I hear you saying it, I even see your lips shaped to the word . . . .

Jag.

MANSFIELD TO MURRY

24 Redcliffe Road, Fulham
Saturday Night. May 18th. 1917

My darling

Do not imagine, because you find these lines in your private book that I have been trespassing. You know I have not – and where else shall I leave a love letter? For I long to write you a love letter tonight. You are all about me – I seem to breathe you – hear you – feel you in me and of me – What am I doing here? You are away – I have seen you in the train, at the station, driving up, sitting in the lamplight talking, greeting people – washing your hands – And I am here – in your tent – sitting at your table. There are some wallflower petals on the table and a dead match, a blue pencil and a Magdeburgische Zeitung. I am just as much at home as they.

When dusk came – flowing up the silent garden – lapping against the blind windows – my first & last terror started up – I was making some coffee in the kitchen. It was so violent so dreadful I put down the coffee-pot – and simply ran away – ran out of the studio and up the street with my bag under one arm and a block of writing paper and a pen under the other. I felt that if I could get here & find Mrs [illegible] I should be 'safe' – I found her and I lighted your gas, wound up your clock – drew your curtains – & embraced your black overcoat before I sat down – frightened no longer. Do not be angry with me, Bogey – ca a ete plus fort que moi . . . . That is why I am here.

When you came to tea this afternoon you took a brioche broke it in half & padded the inside doughy bit with two fingers. You always do that with a bun or a roll or a piece of bread – It is your way – your head a little on one side the while . . . .

– When you opened your suitcase I saw your old feltie and a French book and a comb all higgledy piggledy – 'Tig. I've only got 3 handkerchiefs' – Why should that memory be so sweet to me? . . . .

Last night, there was a moment before you got into bed. You stood, quite naked, bending forward a little – talking. It was only for an instant. I saw you – I loved you so – loved your body with such tenderness – Ah my dear – And I am not thinking now of 'passion'. No, of that other thing that makes me feel that every inch of you is so precious to me. Your soft shoulders – your creamy warm skin, your ears, cold like shells are cold – your long legs and your feet that I love to clasp with my feet – the feeling of your belly – & your thin young back – Just below that bone that sticks out at the back of your neck you have a little mole. It is partly because we are young that I feel this tenderness – I love your youth – I could not bear that it should be touched even by a cold wind if I were the Lord.

We two, you know have everything before us, and we shall do very great things – I have perfect faith in us – and so perfect is my love for you that I am, as it were, still, silent to my very soul. I want nobody but you for my lover and my friend and to nobody but you shall I be *faithful*.

I am yours for ever.
Tig.

Bandol [South of France]
24 January 1918

. . . . This is the news which comes from your country which I am visiting on your behalf just as much as mine. For the present, my love, you are the King in his counting house counting out his money and I am the Queen in her parlour eating bread and honey – Ah God, that there *wasn't* a door between us. All my joy here is half yours. It is my love for you which puts all the sweet breath into this. As I write, as I think of you I feel that I am love. Nothing else – Oh, I could weep like a child because there are so many flowers and my lap is so small and all must be carried home to you.

Farewell, my heart.

Your
Wig.

26 January 1918

. . . . Ah Love Love when I come back – we shall be so happy – the very cups and saucers will have wings & you will cut me the only piece of bread and jam in the world and I will pour you out a cup of my tea. Why aren't you here *now* NOW. But I am coming Bogey – and I am all yours, amen.

Tig.

27 January 1918

. . . . My love for you tonight is so deep and tender that it seems to be outside myself as well. I am fast shut up like a little lake in the embrace of some big mountains. If you were to climb up the mountains you would see me down below, deep and shining – and quite fathomless, my dear. You might drop your heart into me and youd never hear it touch bottom. I love you – I love you – Goodnight.

Oh Bogey – what it is to love like this!

MANSFIELD TO MURRY

20 February 1918

Since this little attack I've had a queer thing has happened. I feel that my love and longing for the external world – I mean the world of nature has suddenly increased a million times – When I think of the little flowers that grow in grass, and little streams and places where we can lie and look up at the clouds – Oh I simply ache for them – for them with you – Take you away and the answer to the sum is o. I feel so awfully like a tiny girl whom someone has locked up in the dark cupboard – even though its daytime – I don't want to bang at the door or make a noise but I want you to come with a key you've made yourself and let me out and then we should tiptoe away together into a kinder place where everybody was more of our heart and size. You mustn't think as I write this that I am dreadfully sad. Yes, I am but you know at the back of it is absolute faith and hope and love. Ive only, to be frank (like we *are*) had a bit of a fright – See? And I'm still 'trembley'. That just describes it.

MANSFIELD TO MURRY

5 April 1918
Select Hotel,
1 Place de la Sorbonne,
Paris
Friday night

To Ribni*
My Tiny

When I came in tonight a Miracle waited for me in the pigeon hole where key 30 hangs. Your little father had managed to send me another paper boat – and only launched on Tuesday night and for a sail oh! such a lovely poem by you both...Such a lovely poem that I don't know how to live another moment without you both. There is the poem you see rocking in my bosom but its not an awfully calm sea, my little man –

Ah, my Ribni, our small doorkeeper. Watch him when he goes out in the morning – and wait for him when he comes home at night. Be ready to wave to him. Walk all over him and kiss him for me. Tell him every way you know that I am coming as fast as the Uglies will let me come. When he sleeps walk

*A *doll*.

217

up and down by his pillow and keep guard. And see that the Lions and Tigers do not tear up our letters but that the doves carry them swiftly – guarded by eagles . . . . I languish – I languish away from you both. I have no little laughs, no one calls me a worm – no one is my size. You are both my size. But Rib, old fellow, I trust you. I can trust you utterly, cant I? To look after him? You know – don't you know that he's all I want. He's mine – and I am his and I shall never be happy again until all of us are sitting together looking at each other – holding each other tight. Don't give me up. Please keep on sweeping the doorstep with a feather and putting out the tiny lantern at night. For I am tired, my little tiny doll and I want to be home with him and with you. Its dreadful – being here. But all you've got to do is to keep him for me – see? Oh, Ribni, curl up in his heart & kiss him for every beat. My hearts nearly broken with longing.

MURRY TO MANSFIELD

Fulham

6 June 1918

Oh, love, love, – the influence which melts all stubbornness out of the soul, and makes it supple and tender and strong like a flower again. It seems to me at this moment that Art is only the despairing cry of Love forsaken by the world, or the song of Love Triumphant over the world.

I feel that Love has definitely been forsaken by the world now, and that the flame is kept alive by you and me alone. It is our secret and our secret strength. We shall keep the seed & cherish it during the bitter years, and one day it [will] spring up and flower again and the birds of the air nest in the branches there-of. You see, I can't bear the thought of final severance from the world. At the bottom of my heart something keeps crying 'Forgive them, for they know not what they do'.

I want our child, to live after us & carry the secret which we won after so long a struggle back into the world. I want the child born of my passion for you; into whose being the ecstasy & wonder, the childish utter surrender that is me when I kiss your breasts and we lie naked together, shall have passed. The extreme pinnacle of our love shall be the beginning of his life. If upon a mountain so high as ours, another mountain were to rise, it would touch the stars. The conception and birth of a child seem so marvellous to me. A miracle

– so simple & so mysterious – when we are absolutely one, and I have given up my last breath in the longing to be one flesh for ever with you, to be part of your beauty and living perfection, then – a new life begins to be. As though all time should have stopped and in that still moment, and of the very void & calmness of love – a child is born.

Boge.

EUGENE O'NEILL
1888–1953

Eugene O'Neill, America's greatest playwright, began his career while recovering from T.B. in 1912. He was married early and often, but in his brief affair with Beatrice Ashe in 1914 he was as seriously uxorious as he would ever be. There is a boyish willingness in his letters to her to go right over the top, that would give way to a more guarded and rational enthusiasm over his later, more significant, relationships. It seems that Ashe found his centre-stage style irresistible rather than hammy. However, a constant theme of his letters to her that failed to strike a responsive chord in her girlish heart was his repeated request for her to mail him 'that something' – by which he meant something choice from her laundry-basket.

O'NEILL TO BEATRICE ASHE

1105 Massachusetts Ave.,
Cambridge, Mass.
Thursday morning, February 18, 1915

My Own

Your last letter in answer to my special was a revelation, and yet not so much a revelation, for I had guessed intuitively what was taking place in your mind. However, it is well that the matter is at last clearly stated, for the situation, as it stood, was impossible for both of us.

It is up to you to choose for once and for all time!!! It is up to you to make a decision for once and for all time!! In justice to me, I ask it. If you love me, as you say, then bury your dead!! How often have I implored you to do that! You must! You must! I will have none of these spectres of your past arising to mock my love and make me miserable!! I cannot and I will not bear it! I have work to do, work which must be done, and these phantoms come between me and my work, fill my heart with agony and my soul with misgiving, stifle inspiration and all creative joy. I will not bear it!

My past is dead. There is not a single thread that binds me to it. I stand before you, I am yours free and unfettered! There is no room for doubt. I am yours. Not a single emotion remains. I have buried my dead because I thought, I felt, it would be unworthy of you not to do so. No ghosts can arise at my feast. My cosmos contains nothing, or rather no one, but you.

I demand the same of you. I am worth, my love is worth, all of you or nothing at all! Though to the world at large my value may be small, yet to myself I am all I have. I will not give myself for a part of you! All or nothing! If I were content with less I would be unworthy of myself, and of my love for you.

I have no former loves, under the guise of friends, to steal my thought away from you. All my former loves are now my enemies as it is natural they should be. However I have accomplished my purpose. The slate is clean. Never again could they love me or I love them. We are dead to each other, and our lives have definitely separated.

All this trouble, all this agony in your own mind and mine, is caused by the fact that you have not thrown away the past. You have not seen the utter impossibility of transforming someone who has really loved you into a friend. The history of a thousand broken lives proves my contention: it cannot be done! Their supposed friendship is, at best, only a subterfuge behind which the old love hides and looks out with envious eyes.

You love me, you cry? Very well, then. Write to whatever-his-name-is and tell him in such a way that he cannot doubt, that he is out of your life forever. Be cruel! It will be the greatest kindness you can do him. It will be but simple justice to me who loves you and am living and building for you. It will ease your own mind and free it from uncertainty. It is the one solution.

If you love him and do not love me, why marry him in May, as he suggests. And I – well, I promise you neither you nor anyone else will realize the extent of my pain, or see the wounds on my soul.

If you love me, and still are lured by the manifold attractions of Canadian lodges and ridiculous mahogany groves in Liberia – If you are so fascinated by these things that, in spite of your love for me, you allow him to write you letters proposing to "forgive" your "affair" with me, and urging you to forget me, and then you consider his proposition seriously, and think of selling your love for me and mine for you, for a "miserable ease," a platter of bread and butter glorified in a Canadian lodge, a house on Montauk Ave. masquerading as a castle in Liberia, – why then, I release you, I don't want you, I urge you as my greatest revenge to marry him in May! I shall take great delight in watching life punish you for being untrue to your own soul. It will fill my life with bitterness, it will convince me that my judgment of women in the past was justified, but it will not hurt me! If you, confessing that you love me, were to marry him, you would be in my eyes such a mean and pitiful caricature of my ideal of you, that only hate and disgust would remain of my love!!

I have nothing but my love for you, my need of you, my life, to offer you! Put in the balance against his Canadian lodge et al., I confess it makes a poor showing. If I add my brains, my power of creation, my dream children whose future no one knoweth, will it balance? Then choose! All or nothing for either one of us! As far as your love is concerned, one of us must die! There is not room there for him and me!

I am enclosing a picture of myself. It is a good picture. Look at it and then at his. Which of us will win the most in the end? Which of us belongs to the future? Which of us can give you a home and servants, etc.? Which of us expects you to do your share, to work and win with him, to fight and endure with him? Which of us contains the most "man"? Which of us loves you the most? Look into our eyes! Who will be your lover and who your husband down the long trail which leads from the green certificate? Who has the most poetry, – and therefore, the greatest capacity for emotion, in him? Then choose! For all time! All or nothing for either one of us!

O'NEILL TO BEATRICE ASHE

2 March 1915

I know that now there is nothing in the world I would not do for you, no sacrifice I would not make to render your happiness complete and flawless. You are beyond and above everything, a Dream of All Dreams, a Desire of All Desires. You are the craving of my soul for the joy of living, the Ideal, the uttermost star beyond which is nothing. My world looks out at me from your eyes. To be your lover and husband combined in one – why, I search my mind for its every emotion, but I find all combined and consumed in that. The Meaning of My Life – that's what you are.

The happiness that comes to me when you are in my arms! Can you guess it? No, for I can't even explain it to you. It's just a feeling of being at harmony with Life itself, of having found the Thing-In-Itself, of having reached the ultimate goal of all my striving. I become a part of God and He of me. For are you not – my God?

And also, even better, my Mother whose loving pity reaches out in her letters and draws her own tired Child back to the haven of her arms where there is ease for bruised heads and anodyne for sorrow.

I love you, yes; but you are above me, Lovely One, and so I lay at your feet, "one hand clasped round your ankle," and adore you! Eugene

Write to me! Write to me!

Dear God, please make Bee O'Neill send me that "something" soon. I'm going to take it to bed with me, God, and kiss it, and hug it close, and sleep with it in under my head, and even say my prayers to it; but You won't be jealous, will you, God? for You know I never believed in You till I loved Bee and she loved me.

DUFF COOPER   LADY DIANA MANNERS
1890-1954   1892-1986

Duff Cooper and Lady Diana Manners were terribly bright – not to say brilliant – young things, before and after the Great War. After their marriage in 1919 Diana pursued a short but glittering stage career and Duff, after a short but dashing spell at the front, where he collected a D.S.O., subsequently enjoyed a distinguished career as statesman, diplomat, and man of letters.

COOPER TO MANNERS

23 June 1914
Foreign Office

Suicide wears in my eyes an ever increasingly alluring aspect. A life spent in going from one place to another in order to see you, and seldom having a moment's conversation when I get there, is driving me to despair without in any way reducing my weight. Ceasing upon the midnight – with no, or practically no pain, is perhaps my best chance. But perhaps I shall feel happier after lunch. I generally do.

Do you ever feel good, Dotty? I must confess I occasionally do. Don't be alarmed. Nothing happens. The feeling passes off in a few hours and leaves me unaltered. I have it usually after having stayed up too late and drunk too much. Then I think I should like to live a simple life in the country and be a saint, a real saint with a halo and a day of my own and taking precedence over half the people in heaven: I see myself getting good at prayer and fasting and becoming holy and beautiful and very thin. The feeling sometimes goes on till half way through lunch.

Goodbye, my darling – I hope that everyone whom you like better than me will die very soon.

Duff

COOPER TO MANNERS

9 Berkeley House
July 1915

My little silver fish with broken fins, my wine, my perfect Pommery, my pure pale Perrier Jouet, my snowy coon, my pampas grass, my bed of asphodel, my crazy little outrigger, my submarine, my dangerous marsh mallow, my button on the coloured cap of life, my duck, how are you.

Last night we dined with Montagu and were once more faced with those little gobbets of lost moist lamb on tepid plates and Bongy bald and unashamed. I drank like some great stag that comes down to a pool in the evening after having been hunted all day long. My face grew fiery red like the sun sinking in a fog, and then after more brandy it grew white and distorted and terrible like a waning moon looked at through twisted glass.

Her Grace says no visitors for seven days, but I know that she lies in her teeth, as sure as Iris lies with a Jew, and as I, alas, alas, lie alone.

Duff

COOPER TO MANNERS

9 Berkeley House
30 August 1915

My darling heart, though you may doubt it I adored seeing you this evening, for I have now reached the stage when Grace or no Grace I am happy to be with you.

This is the third time that I have fallen into love with you. Oh see to it, my lily, that I do not fall out.

I wish I was more beautiful so as to be worthier of you. I should like to marry you and then go round the world to look for lovers lovely enough to deserve you. I should like to find a nearly perfect one, and bring him back and wash him and prepare him and tell him all about Aristotle and Alexandria and coach him in every engaging artifice of love, and then I would serve him up to you – a morsel for a goddess – and you would kill him in a fortnight and love me better than you did before.

Duff

Cooper is now on the Western Front. Manners does her bit to raise morale.

MANNERS TO COOPER

Breccles Hall

11 August 1918

My light, I have been lying on a wide sofa since dinner while Edwin read aloud a story by Galsworthy (the first one: I have sent it you today) that I had read before. I made him read it, because I wanted the others to be engrossed that I might be free to enjoy your complete empire over me. I was so happy – half a bottle of champagne had put you nearly out of harm's way. These rooms are lit by a few spare candles and my limbs in this demi-light seemed to flow with peculiar grace, and my green film cloak to foam and curl round them like Aphrodite's birth-waves.

I ordered my waking dream and it was obedient, so that my greatest imaginings of joy seemed realisable in a fairy way. I wanted you to see me, almost as greatly as my eyes wanted you; and I wanted your love to transcend its own clear maximum immeasurably. I wanted you to take me up in your arms to a prepared bed, and above all I wanted to yield you there all my treasure at a price of pain, and that that price should be high that you might know the zeal of the giving.

If I could have written then, I could have made your soul aflame as you read: but Edwin's voice would up and there has been an hour's good nights and Bradshaw talk, and Alan's asthma has claimed my attention as a hypodermic expert . . . .

MANNERS TO COOPER

16 Arlington Street

28 September 1918

My soul. I write for the second time today. I feel nearer you when I write and as if I was holding you to me with greater hope and force. I scarcely know myself anymore – all old egoisms have been dissolved away by this heat of passionate concentration for your safety and content and glory.

I cannot any longer be free from the terror of any pain physical or mental, for you. I would bear twice the desperate dread that bows me, to ensure your not knowing a moments apprehension. If God were only more of a Jew I would be blinded and maimed – a loathed toad even by dint of many bargains – to save you my love in life – my darling Duff.

I read a letter from you tonight – a veiled adieu, and cried a drenching patch on Alan's shoulder. He shall not have my letters. No one must know me as you have and shall. It is I that must edit them, and if I must be old it is I that shall read them to the envious young – flauntingly, exultantly – and when they hear yours they'll dream well that night, and waking crave for such a mythical supreme lover and regret that they are born in the wrong age – as once I did before I saw your light, crying for Gods and wooers.

The war will not have been all calamity if it protects you, for it will have shown me my own heart and emotions undreamt of.

MANNERS TO COOPER

16 Arlington Street

2 October 1918

My divine Duff. I'm on the crest of my spirits. Ask me how many letters I have from my love today, and I will say five with a famished voice. One before the battle and four since. One warns me of Paris leave, and shows indecision of how or whether you shall tell me all of it. You never have full faith in me, my darling – or you would know that my desire is your inclination. Tell me as much or little as you enjoy to confess. You know that I want your happiness above my own and that I delight in your shadow love (keep it shadow) but that from your arrival in Paris I absolve you from all letters, sincerity, superficial thoughts – 'rush into the folly', baby darling. Tell me nothing or all. I shall love you the same. I only warn you against getting drunk because Paris is a sink of English scandal and its a rumour, though not a habit, that I want killed, and it bids fair to be so, since you 'made good'. If I was forced to voice a whim it would be that a) you absented yourself from felicity with my own 'caste' – Rose, Diana, Laura etc. b) that with help of every known device you keep your body clean for me. c) That you do not gamble – but where these scruples count as a ha'pth of tar, your boat must not be spoilt.

This letter will read like Polonius's to Laertes so let it break, and I'll write at the same time to the Battalion in case you miss a post.

My dearest – good night. Diana

COOPER TO MANNERS

Hotel Ritz, Paris
13 October 1918

My darling – just after I had written yesterday – a lovely letter came from you and two more this morning forwarded from the Battalion.

Last night we dined at the Café de Paris where I fell into temptation and was not delivered from evil. We went on the Zig Zag in increased numbers and then to a rather pleasant illegal dancing place where there was music, wine and sandwiches, then to a very pretty flat from which I returned this morning with the proverbial milkman from whom I was able to buy butter for breakfast. As I was lying in my bath Carroll came in and said "The War is over." And really it would appear to be so, and now we can be married and live happy ever after.

VIRGINIA WOOLF (née Stephen)
1882–1941

Virginia Woolf was the author of some of the most important and experimental novels of the twentieth century. Leonard Woolf (1880-1969), Fabian socialist, political commentator and a founder of the League of Nations, had embarked on a career in the colonial service when he fell in love with Virginia Stephen in 1911, while on a year's leave from Ceylon. He turned out to be the ideal husband for her, though as her extraordinarily ambivalent letter accepting his proposal of marriage makes clear, she felt nothing for him physically. On their honeymoon he found that when he tried to make love to her she began to go mad, and he soon realised too that were he to have an affair with another woman this would also drive her mad. However, he was happy to deny himself any sort of sex-life whatsoever in order to provide her with the stability she needed, simply because, as he said, 'she was a genius'. Virginia Woolf drowned herself in 1941.

LEONARD WOOLF TO VIRGINIA STEPHEN

12 Jan 1912
Frome

I find the post doesn't go out until evening, so I can try & write about what, with you sitting there, it was so difficult to discuss calmly & dispassionately. I dont think I'm selfish enough not to be able to see it from your side as well. From mine, I'm sure now that apart from being in love, I should be right to say – & I would – that if I were in love, it would be worth the risk of everything to marry you. That of course – from your side – was the question you were continually putting yesterday & which probably you ought to. Being outside the ring of fire, you should be able to decide it far better than I inside it. God, I see the risk in marrying anyone & certainly me. I am selfish, jealous, cruel, lustful, a liar & probably worse still. I had said over & over again to myself that I would never marry anyone because of this, mostly because, I think, I felt I could never control these things with a woman who was inferior & would gradually infuriate me by her inferiority & submission. (I have had to be motored to Bath & back & it is now evening again.) It is because you aren't that that the risk is so infinitely less. You may be vain, an egoist, untruthful as you say, but they are nothing compared to your other qualities: magnificence, intelligence, wit, beauty, directness. After all too we like one another, we like the same kinds of things & people, we are both intelligent & above all it is realities which we understand & which are important for us. You wanted me to give you reasons for my state of mind: here they are & damnably truthful at any rate. I feel like knocking nails – with Walter & Sydney – into my coffin. I would even go so far – in the cause of truth – as to admit the possibility of my desire for you blinding me to the knowledge that no woman ought to marry me – but I don't believe it in your case – if you ever did love me.

As you dont, you ought to be able to know now exactly what the risk would be if you were & married me.

The people have come for the post so I must stop.

Yr. L.

May 1st 1912
Asheham

Dearest Leonard,

To deal with the facts first (my fingers are so cold I can hardly write) I shall be back about 7 tomorrow, so there will be time to discuss – but what does it mean? You can't take the leave, I suppose if you are going to resign certainly at the end of it. Anyhow, it shows what a career you're ruining!

Well then, as to all the rest. It seems to me that I am giving you a great deal of pain – some in the most casual way – and therefore I ought to be as plain with you as I can, because half the time I suspect, you're in a fog which I don't see at all. Of course I can't explain what I feel – these are some of the things that strike me. The obvious advantages of marriage stand in my way. I say to myself, Anyhow, you'll be quite happy with him; and he will give you companionship, children, and a busy life – then I say By God, I will not look upon marriage as a profession. The only people who know of it, all think it suitable; and that makes me scutinise my own motives all the more. Then, of course, I feel angry sometimes at the strength of your desire. Possibly, your being a Jew comes in also at this point. You seem so foreign. And then I am fearfully unstable. I pass from hot to cold in an instant, without any reason; except that I believe sheer physical effort and exhaustion influence me. All I can say is that in spite of these feelings which go chasing each other all day long when I am with you, there is some feeling which is permanent, and growing. You want to know of course whether it will ever make me marry you. How can I say? I think it will, because there seems no reason why it shouldn't – But I don't know what the future will bring. I'm half afraid of myself. I sometimes feel that no one ever has or ever can share something – Its the thing that makes you call me like a hill, or a rock. Again, I want everything – love, children, adventure, intimacy, work. (Can you make any sense out of this ramble? I am putting down one thing after another). So I go from being half in love with you, and wanting you to be with me always, and know everything about me, to the extreme of wildness and aloofness. I sometimes think that if I married you, I could have everything – and then – is it the sexual side of it that comes between us? As I told you brutally the other day, I feel no physical attraction in you. There are moments – when you kissed me the other day was one – when I feel no more than a rock. And yet your caring for me as you do almost overwhelms me. It is so real, and so strange. Why should you? What am I really except a pleasant attractive creature? But its just because you care so much that I feel I've got to care before I marry you. I feel I must give you everything; and if I can't, well marriage would only be second-best for you as well as for me. If you can still go on, as before, letting me find my own way, as that is what would please me best; and then we must both take the risks. But you have made me very happy too. We both of us want a marriage that is a tremendous living thing, always alive, always hot, not dead and easy in parts as most marriages are. We ask a great deal of life, don't we? Perhaps we shall get it; then, how splendid! . . . .

Yrs VS

VIRGINIA TO LEONARD WOOLF

Asheham House, Rodmell,
Lewes, Sussex
Sunday 7 December 1913

Immundus Mongoosius Felicissimus, I could write this letter in beautiful silver Latin, but then the scurvy little heap of dusty fur could not read it. Would it make you very conceited if I told you that I love you more than I have ever done since I took you into service, and find you beautiful, and indispensable? I am afraid that is the truth.

Goodbye Mongoose, and be a devoted animal, and never leave the great variegated creature. She wishes me to inform you delicately that her flanks and rump are now in finest plumage, and invites you to an exhibition. Kisses on your dear little pate. Darling Mongoose.

Mandril

VIRGINIA TO LEONARD WOOLF

Monk's House, Rodmell, Sussex
28 March 1941

Dearest,

I want to tell you that you have given me complete happiness. No one could have done more than you have done. Please believe that.

But I know that I shall never get over this: and I am wasting your life. It is this madness. Nothing anyone says can persuade me. You can work, and you will be much better without me. You see I cant write this even, which shows I am right. All I want to say is that until this disease came on we were perfectly happy. It was all due to you. No one could have been so good as you have been, from the very first day till now. Everyone knows that.

V.

You will find Roger's letters to the Maurons in the writing table drawer in the Lodge. Will you destroy all my papers.

VIOLET TREFUSIS
1894–1972

As the daughter of Mrs Keppel, Edward VII's mistress, Violet Keppel was authorised to call the King of England 'Kingy' and thus grew up with very little respect for convention. She and Vita Sackville-West fell in love in April 1918. Together they wrote a novel, 'Challenge', portraying themselves in the two protagonists, 'Julian' and 'Eve', and after the Armistice they eloped to Paris and then to Monte Carlo with Vita dressed as 'Julian'. After Violet's marriage to Denys Trefusis, their relationship descended into farce. Both ladies behaved rather badly, and their husbands and various relatives pursued one another across France attempting to sort out the emotional tangle. It was over by 1921, though Vita was still fending Violet off twenty years later. Between the wars Violet wrote novels and entertained a succession of lovers of both sexes. She was even on one occasion challenged to a duel. In 1950 she was awarded the Legion d'Honneur, in recognition, so it was said, of her work for French Letters. Vita's letters were destroyed by Denys Trefusis.

TREFUSIS TO SACKVILLE-WEST – 1919

Men tiliche,

I have been talking all the evening about Paris – Paris when we first arrived there – Knoblock's flat – O Mitya! It makes me drunk to remember it, and the hoard of days, weeks and months we had ahead of us.

I shall never forget the mad exhilaration of the nights I spent wandering about with Julian as long as I live! even Monte Carlo was not better. As good, but not better. It makes my brain reel to remember! The night we went to the Palais Royal and the night we went to *"La Femme et le Pantin"* were the happiest in my life. I was simply drunk with happiness. We were just bohemians, Julian and I, with barely enough to pay for our dinner, free, without a care or a relation in the world. O god! I was happy! I thought it would never come to an end. I was madly, insatiably in love with you.

Julian was a poet *sans sou ni maille*. I was Julian's mistress. One day Julian would write great poetry and make money – but, *en attendant*, we just had enough to live on. I worshipped Julian. The Paris of Francois Villon, *Louise, La Boheme*, Alfred de Musset, all jumbled up, lay at our feet: we were part of it, essentially.

As much part of it as the hairy concierge and the *camelots* who wear canvas shoes and race down the boulevards nasally screaming, "La Petue! La Pressue!" and "La Femme et la Pantin." I lay back in an abandonment of happiness and gave myself up to your scandalously indiscreet caresses, in full view of the whole theatre!

Not ladylike perhaps! But then I had never known what it was like to be a lady!

Then we drove back in the dark taxi, and the chauffeur smiled knowingly and sympathetically at you. I'm sure he thought: *"C'est pas souvent qu'ils doivent se payer ca, pauvres petits . . . .'* Then the flat, the deserted, unutterably romantic Palais Royal, Julian's impatience, Julian's roughness, Julian's clumsy, fumbling hands...My God! I can't bear to think of it!

Mitya . . . . Mitya . . . . How I adored you! Our life, our blessed bohemian life! It *can't* be at an end! It *can't*. It can't. I love you as feverishly, as passionately as I did then. I love you with a passion that only increases, never diminishes.

As Professor Ross said to me tonight, you are made for passion, your perfectly proportioned body, your heavy-lidded brooding eyes, your frankly sensual mouth and chin. You are made for it and so am I.

I said to Professor Ross that I thought you were one of the most moral people I knew. He spat with derision: "Pah! With that mouth, with that chin. With those antecedents! Tell me another!"

TREFUSIS TO SACKVILLE-WEST – APRIL 1920

Darling, yesterday there was something 'soft and clinging' about you. You were well dressed, and tiny – Yes, feminine and most flagrant, of all inconsistencies. I like you to be rough and uncouth and fierce and untidy.

But I've noticed it before. You get like that when you are with – [Harold]. All that is feminine in you mounts to the surface – All that isn't remains in abeyance. Most scandalously, I prefer *all that isn't!* To put it brutally, a masculine interior beneath a feminine exterior . . . . Your eyes were like a primeval forest, dark with some crouching, nameless menace . . . .

I love all the ambushed atavism...I love the latent fierceness in you, the guarded sensuality...It makes me feel terribly insecure. . . . . You build walls and walls around you, and the sentry passes up and down, day and night. But if it were ever to break loose – ! I would go by the board, and so would everything else! You wouldn't have a scruple in the world! Everybody who attracted you would become your prey. The earth would be strewn with the bloody corpses of the people you had loved – for one night!

I don't think you realize it yourself fully, do you, Mitya? . . . .

TREFUSIS TO SACKVILLE-WEST – MARCH 1921

What a pity you are such a fool, Mitya. I was overjoyed at hearing your voice, and all I get from you is flippancy and indifference. I *hated* you for it. *Beware*, Mitya, beware of laughing at my love. By Heaven, you will regret it if you do. Who are you that you should presume to do such a thing? If I can love, I can also hate, and I could hate you more than anyone in the world. You have had what dozens of people (and I am not exaggerating when I say dozens) have grovelled and gone down on their knees for. I have loved you. I have given you everything. I have withheld nothing and you seem to think I am here at your beck and call, to come if you raise a finger, or to stay away as long as it is your pleasure.

Damn you, I say. Curse your insolence. I am not your slave. How dare you trifle with my most sacred sentiments!

VITA SACKVILLE-WEST   VIRGINIA WOOLF
1892-1962   1882-1941

The aristocratic Vita Sackville-West, a minor poet and novelist, met the middle class Virginia Woolf, a major literary figure, in 1922, and a subtle mutual fascination with each other's eminence cemented their intimacy, which continued for several years and was succeeded by a firm friendship. Woolf's novel 'Orlando' (1928) is, in some way, Woolf's most passionate love letter to the grand and fantastic figure she saw in Sackville-West. To a friend she confided in 1924 that 'her real claim to distinction, is, if I may be so coarse, her legs. Oh they are exquisite – running like slender pillars up into her trunk, which is that of a breast-less cuirassier (yet she has 2 children) but all about her is virginal, savage, patrician'. For her part, Sackville-West's love letters date from her years of travel as a diplomat's wife. After her travels, Sackville-West settled down with her husband and tended her garden.

SACKVILLE-WEST TO WOOLF

Milan [posted in Trieste]
Thursday 21 January 1927

. . . . I am reduced to a thing that wants Virginia. I composed a beautiful letter to you in the sleepless nightmare hours of the night, and it has all gone: I just miss you, in a quite simple desperate human way. You, with all your un-dumb letters, would never write so elementary a phrase as that; perhaps you wouldn't even feel it. And yet I believe you'll be sensible of a little gap. But you'd clothe it in so exquisite a phrase that it would lose a little of its reality. Whereas with me it is quite stark: I miss you even more than I could have believed; and I was prepared to miss you a good deal. So this letter is just really a squeal of pain. It is incredible how essential to me you have become. I suppose you are accustomed to people saying these things. Damn you, spoilt creature; I shan't make you love me any the more by giving myself away like this – But oh my dear, I can't be clever and stand-offish with you: I love you too much for that. Too truly. You have no idea how stand-offish I can be with people I don't love. I have brought it to a fine art. But you have broken down my defences. And I don't really resent it.

WOOLF TO SACKVILLE WEST

Tavistock Square
31 January.
. . . . Yes, I miss you, I miss you. I dare not expatiate, because you will say I am not stark, and cannot feel the things dumb people feel. You know that is rather rotten rot, my dear Vita. After all, what is a lovely phrase? One that has mopped up as much Truth as it can hold.

Berg

SACKVILLE-WEST TO WOOLF

Moscow
31 January 1927
I went to see Lenin tonight. He lies embalmed in a scarlet tomb just below the red flag, and the crowd walks round his glass case two by two. A woman had hysterics just behind me; screamed like an animal; sobbed; screamed again; nobody took any notice – And oh my God, there's a dinner party of twenty-two people tonight – and I collided with Denys Trefusis in the hall – and is he coming to the dinner? – and shall I be put next to him? and then there's to be a concert – when the only thing I want is bed and sleep. I so nearly sent you a telegram, but thought you would think that silly; I had written it out, and then tore it up. Would you have thought it silly? or been pleased? and do you know where I am, I wonder, or have you lost count? It's seven o'clock here, but only five in London – so you're having Sibyl to tea at this moment, instead of me, and *she* won't sit on the floor or say my lovely Virginia, and you won't rumple *her* hair – and it won't be nearly so nice. I hope you miss me, though I could scarcely (even in the cause of vanity) wish you to miss me as much as I miss you, for that hurts too much, but what I do hope is that I've left some sort of a little blank which won't be filled til I come back. I bear you a grudge for spoiling me for everybody else's companionship, it is too bad . . . .
Oh heavens, I must dress for this thrice bloody dinner party, when I want to go on writing to you. And how angry it makes me that you shouldn't be here, and I do ache for you so all the time – damn it – it gets no better with time or distance. – and I foresee that it won't – Nor shall I have a word from you for ever so long – oh damn, damn, damn – You would be pleased if you knew how much I minded . . . .

Your V.

SACKVILLE-WEST TO WOOLF

Rostov-on-Don
2 February 1927

. . . . and then the extraordinary mixture of one's thoughts, half one's brain being concentrated on looking out of the window, and not losing the tickets or the passports or the money, and the other half living with a great intensity in the life one has left behind, – what does Leigh think of? what does Dottie? what does Miss Jebb? what does Miss Elgood? of the museum? Sherfield? Lower Sloane Street? Hurstmonceux? and what do I think of? Virginia in her blue overall, leaning against the doorpost of Tavistock Square, and waving, while the rapidly greying glass of milk stands in front of the gas-fire in a hopeless effort to get warm, and Gissing lies on the table – That's what I think of, here in the steppes, with a twisted heart and an ache of homesickness and a regret for the second night at Knole – which now cannot be made up for until Long Barn in May when the nightingales sing outside in the thorn bush and the irises come into flower in the night between sunset and sunrise – My darling, you will be in England, won't you, when I come back? and I can come and see you, the first person in London? You see, I'm already thinking of that – and I shall think of it for the next three months . . . .

WOOLF TO SACKVILLE-WEST

52 Tavistock Square
Wednesday, February 16th, 1927

. . . . But don't you see, donkey West, that you'll be tired of me one of these days (I'm so much older) and so I have to take my little precautions. That's why I put the emphasis on 'recording' rather than feeling. But donkey West knows she has broken down more ramparts than anyone. And isn't there something obscure in you? There's something that doesn't vibrate in you; It may be purposely – you don't let it; but I see it with other people, as well as with me; something reserved, muted – God knows what . . . . It's in your writing too, by the bye. The thing I call central transparency – sometimes fails you there too, I will lecture you on this at Long Barn . . . . Darling donkey West – will you come at 2.30 – to the Press, I think; and then how nice I shall lie on the sofa and be spoilt. But my (headache) pain is going already. Was Irene nicer than I am? Do you know this interesting fact, I found myself thinking with intense curiosity about death? Yet if I'm persuaded of anything, it is of mortality – Then why this sense that death is going to be a great excitement? – something positive; active?

Yr

V.W.

P.S.

The flowers have come, and are adorable, dusky, tortured, passionate like you – and I've had lunch and feel ever so much better, and have read my letter, and am ashamed of its egotism, and feel tempted to tear it up, but have no time to write another. And don't I lecture you nicely? That's what comes of attacking your poor Virginia and dog Grizzle. They bite instantly.

But at the same time they adore; and if you hadn't the eyes of a newt and the blood of a toad, you'd see it and not need telling –

HAROLD NICOLSON   VITA SACKVILLE-WEST
1886-1968   1892-1962

Vita Sackville-West married Harold Nicolson, a brilliant diplomat and less successful politician, in 1913. After producing two children, each pursued homosexual affairs and – as Nigel Nicolson puts it – 'encouraged in the other separate achievements, separate pleasures, separate holidays, separate lovers, without loss of trust or affection'. Indeed, they appreciated opportunities to miss one-another. The only relationships to cause any threat to the marriage were two of Sackville-West's: her infatuation with Violet Trefusis, and her deeper attachment to Virginia Woolf.

NICOLSON TO SACKVILLE-WEST

St. James' Club, Piccadilly, W.1
9 September 1918

My little Viti

.... Violet in her clever way had made you think I'm unromantic. And oh dear! Oh dear! how can an impoverished, middle-aged civil servant cope with so subtle an accusation? You see, if I was awfully rich I could have a valet, and an aeroplane and a gardenia tree, and it would all be very Byronic – but not being rich, or successful, it is just "poor little Hadji, he's such a darling and *so* patient..."

Little one – I wish Violet was dead: she has poisoned one of the most sunny things that ever happened. She is like some fierce orchid, glimmering and stinking in the recesses of life and throwing cadaverous sweetness on the morning breeze. Darling, she is evil and I am not evil. Oh my darling, what is it that makes you put her above me? . . . .

NICOLSON TO SACKVILLE-WEST

Paris
18 March 1919

I want you to think: "Well, whatever I do, there is one person whom I need never consider, who always will understand – and that is my fat, ugly, red-faced, bourgeois, sentimental but so loving Hadji." I want you to feel that I shall always take your point-of-view and that I realise it is all as if you had been run over by a bus and broken your leg, and however bloody, it is not your fault.

SACKVILLE-WEST TO NICOLSON

Long Barn
1 February 1920

There is so much in my heart, but I don't want to write it because *a quoi bon?* Only if I were you, and you were me, I would battle so hard to keep you – partly, I daresay, because I would have have the courage and the reserve to do like you and say nothing. O Hadji, the reason I sometimes try to get you to say things, to say that you would miss me and that sort of thing, is that I long for weapons to fortify myself with; and when you do say things, I treasure them up and in moments of temptation I say them over to myself and think, "There, he *does* mind, he *would* mind, you *are* essential to him . . . . It is worthwhile making yourself unhappy if it is to keep him happy," and so on, but then when you say things like that you don't miss me in Paris, and that scandal matters, I think, "Well, if it is only on account of scandal and convenience and above all *because I am his wife* and permanent and legitimate – if it isn't more personal

237

than that, is it worthwhile my breaking my heart to give him, not positive happiness, but mere negative contentment?"

So I fish, and fish, and fish, and sometimes I catch a lovely little silver trout, but never the great salmon that lashes and fights and *convinces* me that it is fighting for its life.

You see, I know you can do anything with me; you can touch my heart like no one, no one, no one (the nearest is Ben) and I try to *make* you fight for yourself, but you never will; you just say, "Darling Mar!" and leave me to invent my own conviction out of your silence.

And O Hadji, what you don't realise is that I am very weak, and that my life for the past year almost has been one resistance of bitter temptation; and that it is simply and solely love of you which has kept me. You are good and sweet and lovable, and you are the person I loved in the best and simplest way; but there is lots that is neither good or simple in me, and it is that part which is so tempted. And I *have* struggled, I *have* stayed; I tore myself away and came to Paris in June last year; you know I have. And it is only, only, only out of love for you, nothing else would have weighed with me the weight of a hair, so you see how strong a temptation it must be, to sweep everything aside, and you see also how strong my love for you must be.

My darling, my darling, I shall love you till I die, I *know* I shall.

NICOLSON TO SACKVILLE-WEST

Teheran
12 May 1926

Tray is writing his article about alternatives to chastity. It is very good – perfectly simple and closely reasoned. He concludes (having watched the Mars and knowing how much they love each other) that the best life is marriage plus liaisons. Or rather his argument is: –

(1) Passion, i.e. being 'in love', can only last a certain number of years.

(2) After that both sides instinctively search for variety.

(3) If the doctrine of fidelity is too rigid, then they both have a sense of confinement and frustration, and irritation results.

(4) But if there is mutual physical freedom, this sense of bondage does not arise: good relations are maintained – and from this emerges community of life, and *'love'* (with a big L) – which is something quite different from passion,

and far deeper than affection. He says that only really fine characters and determinedly intellectual people can attain to this. But that the confusion of 'love' and 'in love' – and the idea that "Love equals merely affection" leads to great confusion. There is something in all this, but I expect there is a snag somewhere. You see, our love is something which only two people in the world can understand. The first and dearest of these two people is Viti. The second, poor man,

is your own
Hadji

SACKVILLE-WEST TO NICOLSON

Sissinghurst
27 October 1959.

My own darling Hadji,

I was thinking this morning how awful it would be if you died. I do often think that; but it came over me all of a heap when I looked out of the bath-room window and saw you in your blue coat and black hat, peering into your scoop. It is the sort of sudden view of a person that twists one's heart, when they don't know you are observing them – they have an innocent look, almost as a child asleep – one feels one is spying on some secret life one should not know about. Taking advantage as it were, although it is only the most loving advantage that one takes.

Anyway, the scoop would be the most poignant coffee-cup [relic after death] ever made.

I often think I have never told you how much I love you – and if you died I should reproach myself, saying, "Why did I never tell him? Why did I never tell him enough?"

Your Mar

HENRY MILLER   ANAIS NIN

1891–1980   1903–1977

At first glance, the correspondence between Anais Nin and Henry Miller seems no more intimate than anything else they wrote. However, Miller's semi-autobiographical novels, banned until the sixties, made up for lack of imagination by being plentifully sauced with fantasy, while Nin's best work was addressed to herself - in the Diaries - though her pornography is also highly regarded. The virtue of the letters is that the unevasive style they both practised in their work is here put to the service of a totally honest communication. They fell in love in 1932, drawn together by a common passion for Miller's wife June, with whom Nin had had an affair. Nin's passionate appreciation is followed by a wolfish, alcohol-induced disclosure by Miller, the feminist's nightmare.

NIN TO MILLER

9 March 1932

I can't write to you, Henry, though I was awake last night telling you – all night – of that man I discovered yesterday...the man I sensed with my feelings the first moment – all the mountains of words, writings, quotations have sundered – I only know now the splendour, the blinding splendour of your room – and that unreal moment – how can a moment be at once unreal and so warm – so warm.

There is so much you want to know. I remember your phrase: "Only whores appreciate me". I wanted to say: you can only have blood-consciousness with whores, there is too much mind between us, too much literature, too much illusion – but then you denied there had been only mind...

My face makes you think that all my expectations go up, up . . . . but you know now that it is not only my mind which is aware of you.

Aware of you, chaotically. I love this strange, treacherous softness of you which always turns to hatred. How did I single you out? I saw you with that intense selective way – I saw a mouth that was at once intelligent, animal, and soft . . . . strange mixture – a human man, sensitively aware of everything – I love awareness – a man, I told you, whom life made drunk. Your laughter was not a laughter which could hurt, it was mellow and rich. I felt warm, dizzy, and I sang within myself. You always said the truest and deepest things – slowly – and you have a way of saying, like a southerner – hem, hem – trailingly, while

240

off on your own introspective journey – which touched me.

Just before that I had sought, as I told you, suicide. But I waited to meet you, as if that would solve something – and it did. When I saw you I thought, here is a man I could love. And I was no longer afraid of feelings. I couldn't go through with the suicide (idea of killing off romanticism), something held me back. I can only move wholly...

I don't know if it was love – there was a long moment of interruption – the love for June. Henry – the love for June is still there. I couldn't bear seeing her [photograph] yesterday. She possesses us both – everything else is only a temporary victory.

I thought I was in love with your mind and genius (I read you what I thought of your mind and writing) chaos only with June. I felt your mind watching me. I didn't want love because it is chaos, and it makes the mind vacillate like wind-blown lanterns. I wanted to be very strong before you, to be *against* you – you love so to be against things. I love to be *for* things. You make caricatures. It takes great hate to make caricatures. I elect, I love – the welling of love stifles me at night – as in that dream which you struggled to make *real* yesterday – to nail down, yes, with your engulfing kiss.

When you will feel me veiled, holding back, Henry, it is June. What power you had that first day, tearing from me pages from my journal about her. You do not know to what extent I guard myself, and my feelings. It is strange how you get truth from me.

MILLER TO NIN

Clichy
21 March 1932

Anais

All I can say is that I am mad about you. I tried to write a letter and couldn't. I am writing you constantly – in my head and the days pass and I wonder what you will think. I am waiting impatiently to see you. Tuesday is so far off. And not just Tuesday – I am wondering when you will come to stay overnight – when I can have you for a long spell – it torments me to see you for just a few hours and then surrender you. When I see you all that I wanted to say vanishes – the time is so precious and words are extraneous. But you make me so happy – because I can talk to you. I love your brightness, your preparations for flight, your legs like a vise, the warmth between your legs. Yes,

Anais, I want to demask you. I am too gallant with you. I want to look at you long and ardently, pick up your dress, fondle you, examine you. Do you know I have scarcely looked at you? There is still too much sacredness clinging to you.

This is a little drunken, Anais. I am saying to myself "here is the first woman with whom I can be absolutely sincere." I remember your saying – "you could fool me. I wouldn't know it." When I walk along the boulevards and think of that. I can't fool you – and yet I would like to. I mean that I can never be absolutely loyal – it's not in me. I love women, or life, too much – which it is, I don't know. But laugh, Anais, I love to hear you laugh. You are the only woman who has had a sense of gaiety, a wise tolerance – no more, you seem to urge me to betray you. I love you for that. And what makes you do that – love? Oh, it is beautiful to love and be free at the same time.

I don't know what I expect of you, but it is something in the way of a miracle. I am going to demand everything of you – even the impossible, because you encourage it. You are really strong. I like even your deceit, your treachery. It seems aristocratic to me. (Does "aristocratic" sound wrong in my mouth?)

Yes, Anais, I was thinking how I could betray you, but I can't. I want you. I want to undress you, vulgarise you a bit – ah, I don't know what I am saying. I am a little drunk because you are not here. I would like to clap my hands and, *voila* – Anais! I want to own you, use you. I want to fuck you, I want to teach you things. No, I don't appreciate you – God forbid! Perhaps I even want to humiliate you a little – why, why? Why don't I get down on my knees and just worship you? I can't. I love you laughingly.

Do you like that?

And, dear Anais, I am so many things. You see only the good things now – or at least you lead me to believe so. I want you for a whole day at least. I want to go places with you – possess you. You don't know how insatiable I am. Or how dastardly. And how selfish!

I have been on my good behaviour with you. But I warn you I am no angel. I think principally that I am a little drunk. I love you. I go to bed now – it is too painful to stay awake. I love you. I am insatiable. I will ask you to do the impossible. What it is I don't know. You will tell me probably. You are faster than I am. I love your cunt, Anais – it drives me crazy. And the way you say my name! God, it's unreal. Listen, I am very drunk. I am hurt to be here alone. I need you. Can I say anything to you? I can, can't I?

Come quickly then and screw me. Shoot with me. Wrap your legs around me. Warm me.

Achensee

6 August 1932

Oh Henry, I was so upset by your letter this morning. When it was given to me all the artificially pent-up feeling overwhelmed me. The very touch of the letter was as if you had taken me all into your arms. You know now what I felt when I read it. You said everything that would touch and win me and I was *moist*, and so impatient that I am doing *everything* to gain a day. This note I'm enclosing, which I wrote you last night two hours after mailing my letter, will help you to understand what is happening. Anyway you must have received the telegram almost at the same time. I belong to you! We're going to have a week such as we never dreamt yet. "The thermometer will burst." I want to feel again the violent thumping inside of me, the rushing, burning blood, the slow, caressing rhythm and the sudden violent pushing, the frenzy of pauses when I hear the raindrop sounds . . . . how it leaps in my mouth, Henry. Oh, Henry, I can't bear to be writing you – I want you desperately, I want to open my legs so wide, I'm melting and palpitating. I want to do things so wild with you that I don't know how to say them.

Anais

Clichy

14 August 1932

Anais

Don't expect me to be sane any more. Don't let's be sensible. It was a marriage at Louveciennes – you can't dispute it. I came away with pieces of you sticking to me; I am walking about, swimming, in an ocean of blood, your Andalusian blood, distilled and poisonous. Everything I do and say and think relates back to the marriage. I saw you as the mistress of your home, a Moor with heavy face, a negress with a white body, eyes all over your skin, woman, woman, woman. I can't see how I can go on living away from you – these intermissions are death. How did it seem to you when Hugo came back? Was I still there? I can't picture you moving about with him as you did with me. Legs closed. Frailty. Sweet, treacherous acquiescence. Bird docility. You became a woman with me. I was almost terrified by it. You are not just thirty years old – you are a thousand years old.

Here I am back and still smouldering with passion, like wine smoking. Not a passion any longer for flesh, but a complete hunger for you, a devouring hunger. I read the paper about suicides and murders and I understand it all thoroughly. I feel murderous, suicidal. I feel somehow that it is a disgrace to do nothing, to just bide one's time, to take it philosophically, to be sensible. Where has gone the time when men fought, killed, died for a glove, a glance, etc? (A victriola is playing that terrible aria from *Madam Butterfly* – "Some day he'll come!")

I still hear you singing in the kitchen – a light, niggerish quality to your voice, a sort of inharmonic, monotonous Cuban wail. I know you're happy in the kitchen and the meal you're cooking is the best meal we ever ate together. I know you would scald yourself and not complain. I feel the greatest peace and joy sitting in the dining room listening to you rustling about, your dress like the goddess Indra studded with a thousand eyes.

Anais, I only thought I loved you before; it was nothing like this certainty that's in me now. Was all this so wonderful only because it was brief and stolen? Were we acting for each other, to each other? Was I less I, or more I, and you less or more you? Is it madness to believe that this could go on? When and where would the drab moments begin? I study you so much to discover the possible flaws, the weak points, the danger zones. I don't find them – not any. That means I am in love, blind, blind. To be blind forever! (Now they're singing "Heaven and Ocean" from *La Gioconda*.)

I picture you playing the records over and over – Hugo's records. *"Parlez moi d'amour."* The double life, double taste, double joy and misery. How you must be furrowed and ploughed by it. I know all that, but I can't do anything to prevent it. I wish indeed it were me who had to endure it. I know now your eyes are wide open. Certain things you will never believe any more, certain gestures you will never repeat, certain sorrows, misgivings, you will never again experience. A kind of white, criminal fervour in your tenderness and cruelty. Neither remorse nor vengeance; neither sorrow nor guilt. A living it out, with nothing to save you from the abyss but a high hope, a faith, a joy that you tasted, that you can repeat when you will.

All morning I was at my notes, ferreting through my life records, wondering where to begin, how to make the start, seeing not just another book before me but a life of books. But I don't begin. The walls are completely bare – I had taken everything down before going to meet you. It is as though I had made ready to leave for good. The spots on the walls stand out – where our heads rested. While it thunders and lightens I lie on the bed and go through wild dreams. We're in Seville and then in Fez and then in Capri and then in Havana. We're journeying constantly, but there is always a machine and books, and your body is always close to me and the look in your eyes never changes. People are saying we will be miserable, we will regret, but we are happy, we are laughing always, we are singing. We are talking Spanish and French and Arabic and Turkish. We are admitted everywhere and they strew our path with flowers.

I say this is a wild dream – but it is this dream I want to realize. Life and literature combined, love the dynamo, you with your chameleon's soul giving me a thousand loves, being anchored always in no matter what storm, home wherever we are. In the mornings continuing where we left off; resurrection after resurrection. You asserting yourself, getting the rich, varied life you desire; and the more you assert yourself the more you want me, need me. Your voice getting hoarser, deeper, your eyes blacker, your blood thicker, your body fuller. A voluptuous servility and a tyrannical necessity. More cruel now than before – consciously, wilfully cruel. The insatiable delight of experience.

HVM

JEAN-PAUL SARTRE   SIMONE DE BEAUVOIR
1905–1980   1908–1986

If Jean-Paul Sartre, existentialist philosopher, novelist, playwright and political activist, ruled French literary and intellectual life from the Second World War until his death, his queen was Simone de Beauvoir, author of the seminal feminist document of the twentieth century: *The Second Sex*. To get a flavour of the lofty plane on which these two brilliant thinkers conducted their extraordinary lifelong passion for one-another, we have to catch, not the many tender endearments they exchanged – what Sartre termed 'Erlebnis' – but the sense of total trust in each other, their philosophy of authenticity, engagement, freedom and moral health put to the test in daily life. Sartre's letter describes a confrontation with another very influential philosopher, the neo-Marxist phenomenologist, Maurice Merleau-Ponty (1908–1961), over a girl (showing, by the way, that being a small ugly man is no excuse for not being devastatingly attractive to women).

SARTRE TO DE BEAUVOIR

14 July 1938

Le Dome is cool and dark, and I love you very much. More than once I've thought of your little trip. I've imagined you reading *Plume* in your cozy corner, and then this morning at 4, having dropped Martine Bourdin at her hotel, I was about to take a cab when it came to me that it was four, that the day was breaking, and you were at Culoz, awake and running the length of the dark train with your little bag. That set up a simultaneity so close and so real that I went home on foot, imagining all the way the dark and distant Alps under the same mauve sky, a little train in a station, and you, my love, so small beside that little train. I loved you very much, I was totally with you, separated merely by the fact that our heads weren't heavy with the same kind of drowsiness at all. I love you. I long for Morocco and you, I'd be very happy if I could simply finish my story.

Let's move on to the Bourdin affair. It's going too well: yesterday I kissed that fiery girl, who pumped my tongue with the force of a vacuum cleaner (it still hurts) as she coiled against me with her whole body. She seems very pleased with the turn of events. But no oath has been exchanged, rest assured. But let's take things in order. I met her at 9 at Le Mathieu because for no valid reason she'd gone to find me at Le Dome. Her aunt had left during the afternoon. Little Bourdin had seen Merleau-Ponty and Jean Wahl. Merleau-Ponty had reproached her: "Don't keep Sartre up to all hours – he doesn't like to go to bed too late." He also told her pensively, "In theory Sartre is a very good guy, morally speaking, but I wonder if he's as good in practice." She considered it a warning. She had been given another by her aunt, who had asked, "Why are you staying on?" "To see Sartre, a very fine man, a professor who is advising me on my thesis." The aunt cried out, "Sartre! Beware! He lives with Simone de Beauvoir as husband and wife, and the Barrys tell me that no woman can resist him . . . ."

We went to Le Dome; I took her hand and said, "I've got a taste for you. You've unleashed my rough side, which is rare, since I'm rather thin-blooded.

Unfortunately I don't know what to do with you, I'm no Boutang to make you false promises. You came into my life like a dog into a game of ninepins; I wanted to take you without having the least *need* for you, which is even more flattering. I have three days to give you – let's take them and try to make the most of them." Shameful little speech but delivered with all the artifice of Thucydides, which doesn't show to its best here, perhaps, but which worked wonders. The next minute she was in my arms, and we kissed all the way back, she silent and all mine, with an enchanted smile, and I from time to time trying, as usual, to say something. I suspect she wanted to ask me up to her place, but I didn't want to recognize it, because I don't want to sleep with her. I came back on foot, with the poetry that you know in my head (on rereading, I find that phrase disgusting). It was five when I got to bed.

Friday afternoon: Catastrophe. The Merly-Ponteau is in love with Martine Bourdin. And rather deeply, it turns out. Last night I was a bit heartsick about it, and this afternoon I'm somewhat uneasy because I'm going to have a meeting with Merloponte. Yet I have a clear conscience, and the Lady has granted me her absolution. But see what you think: I saw the strapping girl last night after writing to you. She was beside herself. France, the wolf-trap she lives with, had left her that afternoon in tears (jealous of me), and when she entertained the Ponteaumerle, Martine was all stirred up with stifled tears. Thereupon Merleau-Pont shows up and she tells him she has broken off with Boutang, which seems to leave him absolutely cold. Thereupon he suggests she go out with him that evening: "But I'm going out with Sartre." "Oh, Sartre doesn't bother me," he replies candidly. She she tells him she'd rather see me alone. Apparently, those simple words are enough to make him furious. There's a long silence, then he says to her, painfully, "If I'd asked you the day before yesterday to kiss me, what would you have done?" "Well, I don't know, since you didn't ask me it means you weren't eager enough or else you felt I didn't want to . . . . In a word I guess I'd have said no." At that point he stammers and seems on the verge of tears; she too. He takes off his jacket and goes out onto the balcony, and there he says, "Basically I don't love you – no, I don't love you. I don't think I love you." Tearfully, then, "I think I'll never love again . . . ." and then, "I have no easy explanation, but last week I slept with a woman I didn't love, it was awful." He comes back into the room, sits down, and with great pain in his voice says, clasping his hands and studying his thumbs, "You don't realize that you have extraordinary charm." After which he spoke of me: "What Sartre did is rotten, he's basically like all the rest; he said he was watching out for you because he's interested in you for your mind, and ultimately this is what he wanted." After that he turned anxious: "But what are you leading up to, you two? You haven't given it enough thought; where will you end up?" She said that the whole thing was coming to a crashing halt on Sunday. "But that's crazy – you're counting on a separation to settle the question, which isn't very brave of you." He also said, "You know, Sartre isn't the kind of guy who'll hold your hand and kiss you: he'll simply ask you to sleep with him. Is he in love with you?" He also said, "You should go a few days without seeing each other, so you can really understand what you mean to one another. At any rate I'll be spending the night at the Ecole, and if you need me, you can wake me up at any hour." And he left, worn out and pale. Whence it was evident, first of all, that he considered me a bastard (and I am not indifferent to the judgment of the Pontaumerle), secondly, that he had immediately thought there was passion between Bourdin and me. I was very uneasy, because I was afraid she too might have gotten that impression. A painful conversation followed in which I told her, dotting the i's and crossing the t's, that I was in love with her but that there was no place for her in my life, and in which I spoke not only about you but also about Tania. Of course she said with a heavy heart, "But I knew all that, you don't have to rub it in." But I went on to the end. I asked her if she thought I'd acted like a bastard. "No. We both knew that the other was touched. You'd have been a bastard if you hadn't kissed me." "For how long have you thought that you would let me kiss you if I asked?" "Since the first night, at Gabriel Marcel's place." Nonetheless, after that she began to sulk, on the pretext that I'd told her I loved her. "I can't get used to that, I can't help it. You'll be like everyone else if you're in love with me." You'll soon see the real reason for her sulking.

Saturday. My love, I won't have much time to put in the sweet things I'm thinking about you if I want to tell you the rest of this story. But do realize that I love you very much . . . .

So she sulked and griped. We went to the Falstaff and I gave her a good scolding. Whereupon she fell, like a tree uprooted, right into my arms and invited me to take her to my place, which I did. She spent the night there (and again the next night – and she'll spend the coming night; she's leaving the following morning, Sunday). We played around together on the bed in complete silence, which shortens the account of the night. Except for sleep with her, I did *everything*. As her figure rather suggests, she is what Boubou would call a "great lover", in addition, she is delightful in bed. It's the first time I've slept with a brunette, actually *black-haired*. Provencale as the devil, full of odours and curiously hairy, with a little black fur patch at the small of her back and a very white body, much whiter than mine. At first her slightly violent sensuality and her legs that prickle like a man's badly shaved chin surprised me a bit, and half disgusted me. But once you get used to it, it's rather powerful. She has teardrop buttocks, solid but heavier and more spread out at the bottom than the top, with a few small pimples on her chest (you well know that sort of thing: the little pimples of an ill-fed, not very well groomed student – rather endearing). Very lovely legs, a muscular and absolutely flat stomach, not the shadow of a breast, and, all in all, a supple, charming body. A tongue like a kazoo, which unreels endlessly and reaches in to caress your tonsils, a mouth as pleasant as Gégés. On the whole, I'm happy as an undertaker's assistant. However, read herein the expression of my satisfaction with *the night just passed*, which was perfection on the emotional side, unlike the previous night, which was more strained because something was bothering her. I didn't want to be too encouraging, and anyway my pronouncements had deprived me of the means, and she didn't want to say she loved me, particularly after the things I'd told her. All by itself the music of the open-air orchestras on the Avenue du Maine created a bond between us, I mean an auditory bond. At one point they were playing "Some of These Days" under my windows. It was just what she'd wanted to hear, and I said, "There's 'Some of These Days.'" We didn't have to say much else. She wanted to sleep in my arms, which meant I didn't sleep a wink all night. In the morning she said, "I'm not jealous of Tania, I would never accept what you offer her. I'm jealous of Simone de Beauvoir." A reasonable feeling, in my view . . . .

DE BEAUVOIR TO SARTRE

Sunday 29 October 1939

My love,

It's late and I ought to go to bed, but instead I'm going to write you a long letter. I have a frantic desire to speak to you, and such a strong and – alas! – vain desire to hear you answer me! I love you, o yourself! All day I've been beset by countless memories which wring my heart. I've seen again in my mind's eye a street in Pompeii, where we walked in bright sunlight; and a terrace in Tetouan, where you squeezed lemonade for me; and a dinner at the Louis XIV, where we talked about war; and a stopping place in the Pyrenees, on the way up to Quillan, on a wet road. My sweet little one, each time I felt such an impulse towards you that my heart was bursting; but then it was checked there, unable to reach you, and the pain was terrible. I'm also beginning to imagine a room: I'm there, it's 11 in the morning – or 9 at night – and my heart's thumping; suddenly there's a knock at the door and you come in. I feel my breath cut short when I imagine that really happening – and perhaps it's going to be true. My love, I'm so overwhelmed by waiting. I want so very, very much to see you.

Yesterday I had a note from Bost – a letter, even, and a very nice one. However, calling in after that on Kos., I was foolish enough to glance at a letter from Bost that was lying around: it gave me a jolt to see how tender it was. I accept the idea abstractly – indeed he told me expressly he was involved in the hilt – but when I really feel that he loves her, I can no longer believe he loves me too. Once again – albeit in a paler version, and against a strange background of unreality and absurdity – I had the same impression I told you about last year: something you have to swallow down quickly, without really identifying the taste on the way; something you'll keep and brood over, but that you don't have time to turn over right away to extract all the venom, so that you keep it as it is, with all its menace. For I had to go on talking to Kos., without being able to think. I left her pretty hastily and went off to the Coupole where, thanks also to the rain and a headache, I had a sticky moment – a moment of sheer absurdity, disgust and indifference. I ate, then updated my journal. I remembered the pine-wood at Juan-les-Pins, and how you'd reasoned with me so sensibly one day when I had the [same] blues, and then I felt a great, clear, violent pain – so passionate that it bordered on happiness. It's still there, and since the hour's so late it makes me weep. My sweet little one, I'll never tell you enough what you are for me. You're my strength, my ethics, and all I have that's good. I see your face again so clearly at present, so affectionate and tender – my love – I see it.

BENJAMIN BRITTEN
1913-1976

Britten's mother made the decision that he should be a great musician when he was born on the feast day of the patron saint of music, St. Cecilia. In the event he came up with sufficient talent to make him the greatest English composer since Purcell, producing, like his august predecessor, mainly operatic and vocal works.

In June, 1939, at Grand Rapids, Michigan, he established an intimate relationship with the tenor, Peter Pears, that lasted with unerring fidelity till his death. The dynamics of their partnership, which was professional as well as personal were complex. Pears was comfortable with his homosexuality, while Britten was ambivalent, even guilt-ridden, and was attracted throughout his life by the purity and innocence of adolescent boys.

Though Britten was the more 'masculine' of the two, Pears was the dominant partner, both sexually and psychologically, and Britten's attachment to him was evidently an extension of his intense attachment towards his mother, who died in 1937. In 1942, W.H.Auden warned Britten that the solid security of the relationship would stifle his creative life, and it seems that Britten even voiced the hope that Pears would get married one day – naming Kathleen Ferrier as a possible wife for him.

His feelings about his own sexuality inform much of his music, from his numerous works for children, and children's voices, to his operas, such as *Peter Grimes* (which can be heard as an extended reflection on Auden's warning) *Billy Budd* and *Death in Venice*. In 1937 he wrote in a letter to a friend: "It is cruel, you know, that music should be so beautiful. It has the beauty of loneliness & of pain: of strength and freedom. The beauty of disappointment & never satisfied love."

PETER PEARS TO BENJAMIN BRITTEN

Boosey Hawkes Belwill Incorporated
43-45-47, West 23rd Street New York, N.Y.
Tuesday [9 January 1940]
My darling Ben– It was marvellous to get your letter. The first from Champaigne and then from Chicago – I don't suppose you'll get my last letter for a bit, as I sent it care of Goldberg at Chicago. I only hope he doesn't open it, as my letter was compromising to say the least of it! You poor little Cat,

frozen to death in 12° below zero weather – I do hope it's not quite so cold now. It's 5° above here and that's summery compared to you. I got your night letter by post yesterday morning, and it was quite a bit different from the way I got it over the phone on Sunday. I was so sad that you were so depressed and cold – I wanted to hop into a plane and come and comfort you at once. I would have kissed you all over & then blown you all over there & then – & – & then you'd have been as warm as toast!

I'm writing this, sitting in a large chair in Mildred's office, balancing it on my knee – (not the chair). I came up with her & Bill this morning & gave old McNamee her lesson – and I rang Heinsheimer to see if he knew anything of Ralph. The Rex [steamship] isn't due according to the papers till Saturday, that may mean she won't come till Sunday, but H imagines he'll fly straight to you (grr!) you little much too attractive so-and-so – in order to hear the Concerto (so he says – Personally I don't think he gives a damn for the concerto). Mildred has been terribly low lately – not on edge but just sort of worn out, so while Bill goes to his bloody lectures tonight, I thought I'd give her dinner & take her to a movie somewhere. I'm finding it pretty difficult to face sitting with them in the evenings now, it's easier when you're there. Dr. Mayer misses you very much. Everyone does – except me, and of course I don't care a brass farthing how long you stay away, because if you stay away a day longer than Wednesday I'm going to come & fetch you, wherever you may be, & as long as I'm with you, you can stay away till the moon turns blue.

I'm reading *Of Human Bondage* of Somerset Maugham's & it's terribly good – some wonderful school stuff of course the whole thing, in his subtle way, is quite itching with queerness. Perhaps I'll send you a copy to Chicago to read in bed.

Please give Harold & Mary a whole lot of my love – I feel foul at not having written to them before, but I have every intention of writing to them in the next day or two. I shall never forget a certain night in Grand Rapids. Ich liebe dich, io t'amo, jeg elske dyg (?), je t'aime, in fact, my little white-thighed beauty, I'm terribly in love with you.

P

BRITTEN TO PEARS

Friston Field, Nr. Eastbourne, Sussex.
East Dean 316
December 1942

My darling man,

Eth is just going off to the post; I hadn't realised that it went so early, – so this can only be a scribble, to say how your letters have been life & breath to me. My darling – to think I have been so selfish as to make you unhappy, when you have so much strain, & such hard work to bear. But I too have come out of this week-end a better person. I seem to be getting things into order a bit. Again it seems to be a matter of 'O man, know thyself, – & of knowing what I really want – & living that knowledge. I promise, my darling . . . .

It is lovely being here. You must come soon & consummate it.

B

BRITTEN TO PEARS

Snape
February 1944

My darling –

This is only a scribble to say a few things that one can't say over the bloody telephone. I love you, I love you, I love you. I am hopelessly homesick without you, & I only live every day because it brings the day, when we shall be together, nearer. Take care of yourself – don't sing too soon, & rest as much as you can. I shall listen to you on Friday – I do hope it goes well, & Sunday too.

After a slow start P.G.* is now swimming ahead again – I've nearly finished the scene! Montagu & I have made some good improvements I think, & I'm writing some lovely things for you to sing – I write every note with your heavenly voice in my head. Darling – I love you more than you can imagine. I'm just incomplete because half of me is in Manchester!

All my everything,

B

Peter Grimes

JACK YEOMAN
DIED 1943

Flying Officer Jack Yeoman was killed on a raid over Germany in Sept. 1943, a few months after writing this letter to his sweetheart, Stella O'Hare.

R A F April 1943

Stella Darling,

This is a letter written despite our decision not to write again – it is a letter I hope you will never receive because it will only be sent to you if I am killed, posted as missing or something equally final.

This, especially put as such a bold statement, will probably be a most unpleasant shock to you. I am very sorry about that, but there are one or two things I want to tell you which will hardly be breaking our agreement as I shall have ceased to be the Jack you knew and loved.

I feel somehow that our decision not to marry is now justified. You have at least been spared a lot of anxiety you would otherwise have had, even though it has been at the cost of the happiness I know we would have enjoyed together.

Hundreds of times since we said goodbye I have felt I had been an idiot, that I was needlessly torturing myself and you too, my darling – that we should have married in March and hang the consequences, let the future take care of itself, leave the problems of family and education until the question arose, that we should treat ourselves to the happiness of each other's company and live only in the present.

Now that this has happened, maybe you will agree I was right in Reeces that first time we went out to lunch together. Now you are still free and have no family to hinder the future of a young girl alone in a world where everyone will be fighting for jobs and livelihoods. You may for all I know be married. If so, I hope your husband is worthy of you and that he appreciates what a real treasure he has for a wife. I envy him and I hope – I sincerely and genuinely hope – you will be happy.

On the other hand, you may not be married – perhaps it is more than likely you are not. I can't, of course, know now as I write when I shall meet the fate that will send this letter on to you . . . .

For myself, I have few regrets and have never regretted joining the RAF. I only hope I have got a few cracks at the Hun or Jap before meeting my own end and that I am killed while engaged on an operation and not just run down by a bus or crashing on a practice flight or something equally unexciting. But as far as the possibility of death is concerned, I am a complete fatalist: nor strangely enough, am I particularly worried or scared about the possibility. I can say honestly, while I like living with a fervour I perhaps never show very obviously, the prospect of an early finish to my life, which this job must of necessity entail, has never held any terrors for me.

You may find this strange in a barbarian such as I since I do not rely on any thoughts of peace or comfort in an hereafter. To my way of thinking, I cease to be at the moment of biological death – that little good I may have done may live in someone's memory, but for the time being I was, I can conceive of no future.

To you, my darling Stella, I am grateful for having loved me. You can have no idea what that has meant to me.

For as long as I can remember, I have been a quiet, unassuming nonentity, seeking refuge in work and on the whole being reasonably successful at it, whether at school or in the RAF. To some extent, that success has been its own reward, but I have never been the life of the party. The few people who knew me well have, I feel, been very fond of me – but you were more than just "fond"...you wanted to have me with you always, to share everything, including yourself, with me, and for that I cannot easily express my gratitude.

Whether or not we were wise at the time may be a debatable point. Deliberately to cause ourselves so much pain seems very foolish, yet I find myself glad to think we did agree to part now that this has happened.

However big a shock my death is to you now, it is nothing compared with what it would have been had we been married. I have wondered whether I ought to reopen old wounds by writing this letter at all, but I can't bear the idea of your hearing of this casually in a newspaper . . . .

Despite our decision not to write or see each other, to me you have always been the girl I love. I often re-live our all too short time together. If you knew how much your photo has meant to me, you would never have regretted the agony of having taken it.

Well, my sweetheart, there is so little and yet so much left for me to say.

Don't, above all, let our having loved one another interfere in any way with your own future – that would be breaking a solemn promise. It was only with the genuine hope that you would not suffer from our friendship that I believe we were right to call it off.

In a way, I wish I could have seen your point of view on religion, but that – and I think you understood fully – was quite impossible, even when it meant losing you. And knowing how much your religion meant to you, I would never have expected you to change it. I would have been a very poor substitute for your faith . . . .

I only hope you will find someone who will love and cherish you as I would have and who can also share your religion with you as a belief as sincere as yours should be shared. If so, everything will have been worthwhile and our decision more than justified. For myself, I have done what I know at least to be right, just in joining the war of my own free will and giving up a chance of supreme happiness with you. What more can anyone ask?

So this is my final goodbye. Thank you once more, my darling, for your love and may God bless you and grant you the success and peace in your life to come which you so richly deserve.

My love goes with you always.

Jack

ACKNOWLEDGEMENTS

The editors and publishers wish to thank the following for giving their permission to use extracts from the stated works.

John Murray for *The Last Attachment.*by Iris Origo, 1949.
Faber and The Britten Estate for *Letters from a Life. Selected Letters and Diaries of Benjamin Britten* edited by Donald Mitchell and Philip Reed, 1991.
Hutchinson for *The Letters of Vita Sackville-West to Virginia Woolf* edited by Louise de Salvo and Mitchell A. Leasle, 1984.
Radius for *Simone de Beauvoir: Letters to Sartre* translated by Quintin House, 1991.
Hogarth Press for *Congenial Spirits. The Letters of Virginia Woofl* edited by Joanne Trautmann Banks, 1989.

The editor and publishers acknowledge the following:
Frederick Muller for *Daily Life in Roman Egypt* by Jack Lindsay, 1963.
Penguin for *The Letters of Abelard and Heloise* translated by Betty Radice, 1974.
Collins Harvill for *The Prettiest Love Letters in the World* translated by Hugh Shankland, 1987.
Cassell for *The Love Letters of Henry VIII* edited by Jasper Ridley 1988.
Owen for *The Letters of Michelangelo.* Trans. E.H. Ramsden, 1963.
Longmans for *Selected Letters* and *Voltaire's Love Letters to his Niece* by Theodore Besterman, 1969.
Yale University Press for *Boswell In Holland*, 1952 and *Boswell in the Grand Tour*, 1955, edited by Frederick A Pottle.
Catherine the Great by John T. Alexander, 1989.
The Letters of Mozart and his family, edited by Emily Anderson, 1966.
John Murray for *To Lord Byron* by George Paston and Peter Quenell, 1939.
University of Pennsylvannia Press for *The Letters of Alexander Pushkin.* Trans. J. Thomas Shaw, 1963.
Pan Macmillan for *Contemplating Adultery*, by Lotte and Joseph Hamburger, 1991.
British Museum for unpublished letters by Charles Kingsley.
Hodder and Stoughton for *The Beast and the Monk* by Susan Chitty, 1974.
The Letters of Gustave Flaubert translated by Francis Steegmuller, 1980.
The Order of Release by Admiral Sir William James, 1947.
Macmillan for *The Letters of Lewis Carroll* edited by Morton N. Cohen, 1979.
John Murray for *Munby: Man of Two Worlds* by Derek Hudson, 1972.
The Letters of Oscar Wilde edited by Rupert Hart-Davis, London 1962.
Harrap for *Ramsay McDonald: A Singular Marriage* edited by Jane Cox, 1988.
The Divine Sarah: A Life of Sarah Bernhardt by Robert Fitzdale and Arthur Gold, 1992.
Chatto for *Gilbert Cannan. A Georgian Prodigy* by Diana Farr, 1978.

Letters of Max Beerbohm edited by Rupert Hart-Davies, 1988.

Faber for *Alban Berg: Letters to his Wife* translated by Bernard Grun, 1971.

Macmillan for *The Farthest North of Humanness: Letters of Pery Grainger, 1901-1914* edited by Kay Dreyfus. 1985.

Bloomsbury for *Song of Love. Letters of Rupert Brooke and Noel Olivier*, edited by Pippa Harris,1991.

Constable for *The Letters of John Middleton Murry to Katherine Mansfield*, edited by C.A. Hankin. 1983.

Clarendon for *Collected Letters of Katherine Mansfield* edited by Vincent O'Sullivan & Margaret Scott, 1984.

Yale University Press for *Selected Letters of Eugene O'Neill* edited by Travis Bogard and Jackson R. Bryer, 1988.

Collins for *A Durable Fire: the letters of Duff and Diana Cooper* edited by Artemis Cooper,1983.

Letters of Leonard Woolf edited by Frederic Spotts 1989.

Violet to Vita. The Letters of Violet Trefusis to Vita Sackville West edited by Mitchell A. Leaska and John Philips.

W.H.Allen and Co. for *A Literate Passion: Letters of Anais Nin and Henry Miller* edited by Gunther Stuhlmann, 1987.

Hamilton for *Witness to My Life: the letters of Jean-Paul Sartre to Simone de Beauvoir 1926–39*. Trans. Lee Fahnestock and Norman MacAfee, 1992.

Hamish Hamilton for *Despatches from the Heart* edited by Annette Tapert. Letter lent by Stella O'Hare, Liverpool.

Gollancz for *Tchaikovsky: To The Crisis*. David Brown, 1992.

Dent for *Selected Letters of Richard Wagner*, translated and edited by Stewart Spencer and Barry Millington, 1987.

The editor and the publishers apologize if any person or estate has been overlooked in these acknowledgements. They would be grateful to be informed if any copyright notice has been omitted, or if there have been any changes of ownership or location concerning letters quoted.

INDEX

A Final Bouquet

SIR CHRISTOPHER HATTON TO QUEEN ELIZABETH I – 1573

Would God I were with you but for one hour. My wits are overwrought with thoughts. I find myself amazed. Bear with me, my most dear sweet lady. Passion overcometh me.

WILLIAM CONGREVE TO MRS ARABELLA HUNT – 1695

Recall to mind what happened last night. That at least was a lover's kiss. Its eagerness, its fierceness, its warmth, expressed the god its parent. But oh! its sweetness and its melting softness expressed him more. With trembling in my limbs and fevers in my soul I ravish'd it.

J. J. ROUSSEAU TO COUNTESS SOPHIE D'HOUDETOT – 1757

What! your touching eyes will never droop again before my glances with that sweet shame, which so intoxicated me with sensuous desire? I am never more to feel that heavenly shudder, that maddening, devouring fire . . . .

NAPOLEON BUONAPARTE TO JOSEPHINE – 1796

I hope before long to press you in my arms and rain on you a million kisses burning with equatorial heat.

FRANZ LISZT TO MARIE D'AGOULT – 1834

I am not writing to you, no, I am close beside you. I see you, I hear you . . . . Eternity in your arms . . . . Heaven, Hell, everything, all is within you, redoubled . . . . Oh leave me free to rave in my delirium . . . . This is to be! to be!!

JAMES JOYCE TO NORA BARNACLE – 1909

Nora, my faithful darling, my sweet-eyed blackguard schoolgirl, be my whore, my mistress, as much as you like (my little frigging mistress! my little fucking whore!) you are always my beautiful wild flower of the hedges, my dark-blue rain-drenched flower.

TZARINA ALEXANDRA TO TZAR NICHOLAS II – DECEMBER 1916

How will the lonely nights be? I cannot imagine it. The consolation to hold you tightly clasped in my arms – it killed the pain of soul and heart and I tried to put all my endless love, prayers and faith and strength into my caresses. So inexpressibly dear you are to me, husband of my heart . . . . Sun of my life.